Speaking From The Heart
Daily Devotionals

Written By Members of the
Karns Church of Christ

Copyright © 2012 Karns Church of Christ
ISBN: 1-62080-986-9
ISBN-13: 978-1-62080-986-0
Library of Congress Control Number: 2012951041
Version 1.0

HOPKINS
publishing
PO Box 962
Manchaca, TX 78652
HopkinsPublishing. com

**Discover Other Titles
By Hopkins Publishing
HopkinsPublishing. com**

Dedication

This book is dedicated to the members of the Karns Church of Christ in Knoxville, TN.

Due to their unwavering commitment to the mission of Jesus, this congregation has been a beacon of light, not only in Knoxville, but throughout the world through their commitment to the training of preachers.

Acknowledgements

A project as large as this one could not be completed by any one person. There are several people who contributed greatly to the completion of this book.

First of all, I want to thank my daughter, Kelli Boitnott. Without Kelli's expertise in layout and Adobe InDesign, we would have never been able to get this book "print ready."

I also want to thank our proofreaders, Jennifer Alsup, Kelli Boitnott, Natalie Davis, Cindy Powell, and Ann Wagner for the hours that were required to critically read all the articles.

Also, I want to thank Cindy Powell for formatting all the pictures so that we could meet our deadline.

And finally, I would like to thank all the members of the Karns congregation who contributed articles to this devotional book. Thanks for sharing your insights, and for challenging us to walk more closely with Jesus. Some of your messages will make you laugh out loud, while others will cause your eyes to well up with tears.

It's my hope that through this book, we can "outlive ourselves" by our written words, and continue to encourage people to live for Jesus, even after we've gone home to be with Him.

Steve Higginbotham

Preface

The Karns congregation had its beginning in June, 1953 when nine people obeyed the gospel of Christ in a tent meeting conducted in Karns. From these humble beginnings, the Karns Church of Christ has faithfully served the Lord, their community, and has trained more than 400 men to go out and preach the gospel.

Those who know anything about the people who comprise the Karns Church of Christ know that they are a very special group of people. Not many congregations of God's people have been as blessed as the Karns church. The wealth of Bible knowledge, the spiritual maturity, and the varied talents within the congregation make this church a place where people can grow and thrive in their spiritual development.

Consequently, we have decided to publish this book as an avenue to tap into that wealth of knowledge, experience, and spirituality to share those thoughts in a devotional book.

When this project was presented to the congregation, I was hopeful that we would get 100 people to participate. My expectations were far surpassed. We had 160 members contribute articles for this book. Not only did such a large number of members participate, but there is also a wide age range among our contributors. In fact, our youngest contributor is 4 years-old and our oldest contributor is 93 years-old.

I commend this devotional book to you. Make reading it a daily habit. And as you read this book, it is my prayer that you will be blessed by listening to the hearts of these godly men, women, and children of the Karns Church of Christ.

– Steve Higginbotham

Keeping Spiritual Focus

As Christians, we know what we need to think about most in life: 1) God—His greatness, goodness, power, love, mercy, grace, care and protection; 2) Christ—His life, teaching, death for our sins, burial, resurrection, ascension, intercession, and second coming; 3) the church—the privilege of membership in it, our involvement, service, spiritual growth, and worship experienced therein. These are the things that we want to think about and give priority to in our lives.

But we live in a busy world. Life is fast, frenetic, and demanding. We all have to earn a living, make mortgage or rent payments, car payments, utility payments. We have to buy groceries, clothes, insurance, and take care of our physical health and that of our families. Our children (or grandchildren) are involved in a multiplicity of activities, each demanding a piece of our time and involvement. There are deadlines and expectation of all kinds to be met. In such a world how do we keep our spiritual focus?

Consider the words of 1 John 3:1-3. Summarized, John tells us that before we get too caught up in thinking about the things of this life we need to reflect on God's love that enabled us to become His children, to understand that the world does not know us (in the sense that it does not accept our standards), to remember that something better is waiting for us after this life, and to keep in mind that with Christ's second coming we shall be like Him. These exhilarating truths will enable us to keep our spiritual focus!

Hugh Fulford has been a gospel preacher for almost sixty years. He was the first full-time minister of the Karns church (1959-1962). He and his wife Jan make their home in Gallatin, TN. Hugh continues to preach, lecture, and write.

Can God Forgive Me. . . Again?

Have you ever felt like you have sunk to the absolute bottom of the barrel? That you can do no worse? In this situation you may think, "how can God possibly forgive me and take me back?" It is difficult to understand God's love for us because it is a perfect love and we are imperfect beings. The closest I can come to making the connection is to think of my reaction as a parent to my children when they disobey or make poor choices. No matter the offense, even if it happens repeatedly, if my child comes to me with a penitent heart and expresses how sorry they are, I, as a parent, will always forgive them and accept them back. If we, as imperfect beings, can forgive in those instances, how much more capable is God to forgive even more?

If you do not have children, then you can consider the question that Peter asked of Jesus in Matthew 18:21-22 about how many times to forgive a brother or sister who sins against you. Jesus replies that you should forgive seventy times seven, indicating that you should forgive as many times as you are offended. If God expects us, as imperfect beings, to forgive essentially an unlimited number of times, how much more capable is God, in His perfect love, to forgive us?

So, the next time you find yourself broken and in a position to ask God to forgive you for the one-millionth time that you have done something, and start wondering how He can possibly forgive you yet again, consider, REALLY consider, His perfect, unyielding love.

John Seibel serves as a deacon for the Karns Church of Christ. John is married to Christy and they have four children, Lindsey, Mary Beth, Emily, and Jeanne. John enjoys playing bass guitar, home theater, and being a dad!

Giving God Our Best

Giving is a hard subject to write or preach about. We tire of television preachers ending their lessons with pleas for money, which we're told will increase our blessings; but in reality, increases the bank accounts of the preachers.

God expects our best, off the top, not after taxes, IRA's, Social Security, or other monies our government thinks it needs. God does not want our leftovers. We have never had a problem with this way of giving and even at our poorest, our church contribution was never reduced.

Once we sold a house to an elderly man. We took back a note with a specified monthly payment. Monthly payments were not on his agenda, but when we were practically broke as we were starting our business, he would come by and pay a few months at a time. Coincidently, his name was Mr. Fortune. The Lord has blessed us abundantly and we are proof that He fulfills our needs (Luke 6:38). We always need to trust our God who says He will take care of us (Matt 19:26, Luke 12:22-31).

There is a poem written by an unknown author that says:
"Use your money while you're living,
Do not hoard it to be proud;
You can never take it with you,
There's no pocket in a shroud."
- Anonymous

June Agee was born and raised in the UK and came to the United States when she married Wendell and became a U. S. citizen in Santa Fe, NM. June and Wendell have four living children and five grandchildren. June is a member of the Karns Church of Christ.

More to Christianity Than a Pew

To a nonbeliever, a Christian's commitment to worship services and Bible classes might seem over the top. A friend once commented that going to church all the time (her impression of what we did) just "wasn't her." Apparently it seemed like too much of a commitment. Compared to someone who never attends, a Christian who goes to church three times a week must seem extremely religious. Oh, if she only knew: church attendance is only the beginning!

Even a newly-born Christian can understand what faithfulness actually means. It's pretty easy to define, isn't it? Faithfulness is "walking in the light" (1 John 1:7). It is loving and obeying Jesus (John 14:15). As we continue to feed our souls on the word of God, though, we develop a deeper understanding of how Christ's example informs our attitudes, our thoughts, our words, our decisions, and our treatment of others. We get better—or we should—at allowing His will to permeate every corner of our lives.

Being faithful becomes so much MUCH bigger than we could have grasped at the very moment we chose to follow the Lord. But isn't that what's supposed to happen?

"For everyone who partakes only of milk is unskilled in the word of righteousness, for he is a babe. But solid food belongs to those who are of full age, that is, those who by reason of use have their senses exercised to discern both good and evil" (Heb. 5:9-14).

Let us never be satisfied with defining faithfulness in terms of our earliest glimmer of understanding. Let's grow.

Evelyn Apple is married to Jody Apple, and they lived in Pennsylvania before moving to Knoxville in 2009. They have three grown children whom Evelyn home schooled. She enjoys yearly mission trips to Perú.

Do You Remember

The Summer of 1942 was a very dark time for the United States as we had just entered the war. I lived in a small town in northeast Texas; a farming town. In July and August, the church would choose to have gospel meetings. These meetings usually lasted ten days or two full weeks.

It was during this time that V. E. Howard was holding a meeting. He would preach in the morning and evening, and during the afternoons, he would visit. This was a time when all members were much energized.

It was during this meeting that I realized that I was in a lost condition. At this time, if someone wanted to be baptized, prior preparations had to be made. The church did not have any baptismal clothes and probably not any towels.

On the way home one evening, I finally got the courage to tell my mother that I desired to be baptized. When we got home, my statement brought forth many questions as mom wanted to know if I knew what I was doing. These questions were still being asked the next day. Mom knew that I knew what I was doing.

That night, I responded to the invitation. Meetings were held outside at this time because we had no air conditioning in the building. We went inside and V. E. Howard baptized me with Leige Glass looking on (one of our elders). That was the best decision of my life and it has had a profound impact on my life. Ever since that day I have lived with purpose and hope.

Bob Anderson was born in Farmersville, TX and was baptized by V. E. Howard. He attended East Texas State Teachers College, then entered and retired from the Navy. He also retired from Oak Ridge National Laboratory and attended ETSPM. After school he preached for Spring Creek Church of Christ. Bob serves Karns as a deacon and a Bible class teacher.

Commitment and Involvement

Most likely you had breakfast this morning and it may have included eggs and bacon. Obviously that breakfast needed the contributions from a chicken and a pig. The chicken was "involved" in providing the eggs but the pig was fully "committed" in providing the bacon. There is a big difference between being involved with something and being fully committed to something.

We often find ourselves with opportunities to be involved in good works, but we also have opportunities to become fully committed. Take today and look for something good that you can go beyond involvement and become fully committed to.

In 2 Corinthians 8:4-5, Paul urged participation in the support of needy saints, but the Macedonians did more than participate, they gave themselves.

Commit to draw nearer to God and Christ, to become closer to the brethren, and to get to know non-Christians better. Commit to become more active in your service to God. . .

1. Improve your attendance at church.
2. Volunteer for more things.
3. Say YES when asked for your help.
4. Don't wait to be asked to serve; serve!
5. Live every day fully for the Lord.
6. Give yourself to the Lord.

Ask yourself if you are just involved in good works or are you fully committed?

Gregg Woodall is an elder of the Karns Church of Christ. Gregg is married to Sherrye and they have four children, Stephanie, Tiffany, Benjamin, and Jonathan. They also have four grandchildren, Wrigley, Walton, Adalynn, and Brooklynn. Gregg enjoys golfing, dirt bike riding, spending time with family, and is a fan of the Tennessee Volunteers.

Encouragement

It was the biggest game our softball team faced all year. A win assured us of at least a share of the championship. A loss would send us to third place. Everyone was ready to play. When the game started, however, I had problems. My normally reliable glove seemed to have a hole in it and my batting was pathetic. Needless to say, I was very discouraged. Then I noticed how encouraging my teammates were. They told me to shake off my mistakes and keep my chin up so I would be ready to help the team on the next play. They let me know they had my back, even though my play was letting them down. Because the members of the team were willing to pick up the slack for one another, we staged a great comeback at the end of the game and won.

After the game, I thought of the similarities between the softball team picking up a discouraged teammate and the church encouraging every member to keep living for Jesus. We all make mistakes, and we all let the "team" down. It is our job as Christians to help each other when that happens (Galatians 6:1-2).

The team that picked me up during a bad game was more than a team—it was a group of my Christian brothers bearing my burden. Sure, that softball game is unimportant in the grand scheme of things, but the principal of helping out a brother still applies.... and the championship we will have a share in when we do so is far greater than winning a softball game.

Brad Alsup serves as a deacon at the Karns church of Christ. He is married to Jennifer, and they have two children, Evan and Allie. Brad is a hunter, a cyclist, and an avid reader.

Overcoming Worry

Recently, Steve Higginbotham's Sunday morning auditorium class studied the subject of worry. This brought to my mind a class which met in the lower recesses of the oldest building in this complex.

The small classroom was packed every Wednesday night with such people as Martha and Jerald Insell, Norma Myers, Alma Weaver, Gary Teague and Becky Allen (now Mr. and Mrs. Gary Teague), and myself. Millard Myers taught this class. He was the kind of teacher who searched the scriptures and found things we needed to dig into. He would come down the hall with a scribbled note about some subject he had been studying. He would say, "See what you think about this."

One of these subjects was "Worry." He came up with a three-point solution to the worry problem:

1. Worry about Nothing (Matthew 6:25–34)!

2. Pray about Everything (Matthew 7:7-8)!

3. Be Thankful for Anything (I Thessalonians 5:18)!

Not only is this good advice, it's biblical advice. And as you know, God would never steer us wrong. Put this advice into practice, and see if it won't help you overcome worry.

Margaret Cagle is 89 years old and has attended the Karns Church of Christ since 1955. She has six children, thirteen grandchildren, and five great-grandchildren. Margaret loves playing games. Just let me know when and I will bring my bat and glove!

You Can't Do It All

It was Thanksgiving night 2011 and I was in line like most of America waiting to get some good deals at a local department store when I saw a fellow church member. A conversation started up and there was something said I will always remember. We were talking about service in the church and I stated that I wanted to do as much as I could. The response I got was "How can you let anybody serve you if you are not willing to be served?"

That statement was very profound to me and a way I had never looked at service. Christians are deep in service but there comes a time when you realize your strengths and weaknesses. I want to do as much as possible for the church, but it was at that moment that I realized everybody has different talents within the church.

I believe God has put everybody where they are because they have a talent to help wherever they are. We have to find that talent and use it to the best of our ability but also not feel bad if there is something we are not good at and therefore can't help with a certain project within the church.

Yes...we as Christians should go out and try to serve as many as possible in the name of the Lord but also realize that there are times we need to know that if we serve all the time, we might miss out on something else because we are not willing to rest and receive something Jesus wants to give us.

Wayne Begarly has been a member of the Karns Church of Christ since 2011. Wayne graduated from UT in 2007 with a Bachelors in Communications. Wayne is involved with the local United Way and American Cancer Society. He enjoys sports and the outdoors in his free time.

Core Values

Each military service has established some golden rules that are often referred to as their "Core Values." These core values are made up of phrases, slogans, or influential words that are supposed to become intertwined in the moral fabric of each Sailor, Airman, Soldier, and Marine.

The Core Values for the Navy are Honor, Courage and Commitment. But, this was not always the case. When I enlisted in September of 1986, they were very different. In the early 90's, we adopted the current values from U. S. Marine Corps. This change made the Department of the Navy (which includes our Marines) uniform in a common belief system.

Jesus also had some core values he wanted Christians to live by. Unlike those that man institutes, our core values don't change and are the same for all Christians. Matthew 22:37-39 lays out our core values and they should be our belief system. These two commandments along with all the other teachings of the Bible must become intertwined in the fabric of our lives and guide us each and every day as Christian Soldiers.

"Jesus said to him, 'You shall love the Lord your God with all your heart, with all your soul, and with all your mind. ' This is the first and great commandment. And the second is like it: 'You shall love your neighbor as yourself'" (Matthew 22:37-39).

Adrian Marsh is a retired Navy veteran and is married to his high school sweetheart Lisa Marsh. He enjoys family time, traveling, cooking, sports and serving God.

Impact

Naomi says in Ruth 1:13, "the hand of the Lord has gone out against me."

At times of deep pain and grief we can be tempted to lash out and blame God. We can lose our vision for our future and life seems pointless. We die a little every day and can forget who we are. If we remain in this state we end up believing lies about God, ourselves, and life.

Naomi, like us, needed help to see that God was her future, and that she needed to run her life in a way which invested in her future with God. God worked through Ruth to restore Naomi, and remind her HE is and who she was. Ruth was God's instrument to lead Naomi back home to HIM where she found hope and healing.

I like to think that for years Naomi shared her faith with her daughters-in-law and as a result that faith in God was planted deep in Ruth. When Naomi had her faith struggle, her own faith was hard to find. It was Ruth's faith that restored Naomi's. In chapter 3 Naomi begins to remember who she is in God; begins to see her future in Him and her faith is being restored. She is still in grief yet her focus is renewed. She understands and accepts her reality. She has decided to go on because of her faith in God. She has been encouraged by the strength, loyalty and love of Ruth.

Let us not underestimate the impact our lives can have for causing others to believe!

Julieanne Anderson is married to Allen and they have two daughters, Caitlin and Rebecca. Julieanne enjoys reading, studying, and spending time with family and friends.

The First Step is the Hardest

The view atop Buzzard's Roost is simply amazing. There I found myself standing on the edge of a 150 foot cliff with a small group of friends. I spent the next half hour talking myself into doing something that my brain said shouldn't be done. While evaluating the repelling equipment, I figured the weakest link was the tree to which we attached our rope. I would much rather have tied my rope to a huge oak tree, not to some scrawny tree that somehow found a way to grow on top of a solid rock. It was an agonizing half hour.

They told me the first step is the hardest, but oh, was it worth it! By my fifth rappel, I no longer agonized over those things my brain had earlier warned me about. Now all I could think of was the thrill of the ride.

How many times have you found yourself standing on the side of a spiritual cliff, talking yourself into doing something that you knew shouldn't be done and that God wouldn't approve? We've all been there many times, haven't we? We understand the consequences, but we manage to suppress the voices in our head. We rationalize and we convince ourselves that no harm will be done, and so we take that first step. By the time we've been to the edge of the cliff a few times, we no longer give it a second thought. Before we know it, we have lost the ability to blush at that particular sin. (Jeremiah 6:15)

That first step is hardest for a reason. Listen to your conscience, while you can still hear it!

Chris Cox serves as a deacon at the Karns congregation. He is also a computer programmer and small business owner. Chris is married to Hannah, and they have two children, Samuel and Rachel. Chris enjoys gardening, reading non-fiction, learning new things, teaching others, and spending time with his family.

Forgiveness

When we put on Christ in baptism, we are born again as Christians. But even when we become Christians, we will still fall short of the glory of God. That's why He sent His Son to die for us. So we can be forgiven of our sins. Jesus' blood continually cleanses us so that when we sin, we can pray for forgiveness and He will forgive us.

Also, after you have asked for forgiveness, God forgets what you've done to begin with. Keep in mind though, that His forgiveness doesn't give you free reign to knowingly commit sin. We can't just sin knowingly and say, "No big deal. I'll just pray for forgiveness."

When you pray for forgiveness, you need to make a vow to yourself and God that you will try your best to not do it again.

We are not perfect, but don't use His forgiveness and the fact that you're not perfect to justify committing sin whenever you feel like it.

Forgiveness is the ultimate blessing we have in Christ Jesus.

Chloe Gill is the great niece of Kim Gill, daughter of Jamie Gill, granddaughter of James and Mae Gill. Chloe is 15 and is a freshman at Karns High School. She loves studying her Bible and talking to her friends about their eternal souls. Chloe also enjoys reading Anime and Manga as a hobby.

God's Plan

"Therefore, my beloved brethren, be steadfast, immovable, always abounding in the work of the Lord, knowing that your labor is not in vain in the Lord" (1 Corinthians 15:58).

I'll never understand why my mother is dead at the age of 52; in my opinion, decades cheated. What does a person do that they deserve such a horrible and painful death? Why her? We all sin. We all fall short. All the chemo and radiation seemed to be for nothing. All of our labor, and all of our prayers seemed in vain. What I didn't realize so much then as I do now is that it was allowing me more time to be with my mother, more time to say goodbye, more time to let go.

However, looking back at decades of my own life, things always took the path that God intended for them. This becomes more evident with time. I will never understand my mother's battle with cancer, but what I do know, and know well, is that God has a plan. He is in control, and that the plan is perfect by design. If He so desires, then it happens, we just need to trust and have faith that it will reveal itself in due time. Things happen for reasons that we may never understand or even see until we stand before God.

Heatherly Stiles was born and raised here in Knoxville. She is married to Jeremy Stiles and is the mother to baby Avery. She is also a fan of the Tennessee Volunteers.

For Such a Time as This

Esther 4:14 ". . . Yet who knows whether you have not come to the kingdom for such a time as this?"

This verse keeps me on my toes. Whenever I wonder why I have received a blessing or am being tested, I think of Esther. I ask myself what is it that God would have me to do with the blessing or what he wants me to learn from the test. I pray harder, read my Bible more intently and keep my eyes and ears open to discover God's plan for me.

Last year, after being laid off from work for a year and a half I got called back to my job. I was happy to go back to work, but I knew that being in my work environment was different than my homemaker life filled with mostly church friends and family. I prayed that I would find opportunities to maintain good Bible study habits, and that I would be stronger in standing up for Christian principles at work than I had been in the past. God provided clear answers to my prayers. A girl that works with my husband who I barely knew called me and asked me to join her and some girls for a six-week Bible study in her home. I did. Back at work, the desk next to me was filled by the guy in the office that is very spiritually minded and loves to have open conversations about religion.

Ultimately, the blessing was in being laid off and having an opportunity to grow in faith and learn to recognize God's work in my life. . . for such a time as this.

Pam McCoy and her husband Darren have worshipped at Karns since 1997. Pam was the church secretary from 1998-2001. She is now working part-time for an architecture and design firm doing interior design for commercial projects. She enjoys her full time job as a homemaker, traveling, and spending time with family and friends.

Daily Religion

" And he said to them, if any man will come after me, let him deny himself, and take up his cross daily, and follow me" (Luke 9:23).

Acts 17:11 says, "These were more noble than those in Thessalonica, in that they received the Word with all readiness of mind and searched the Scriptures daily, whether those things were so."

Where is the Bible knowledge of the church of Christ today? Many who have been members of the church for many years are unable to answer even fundamental questions concerning the Bible. Why does such a condition exist in the church? The answer is a lack of study.

If one has an appetite for food, he will eat. If one has no appetite for food, no encouragement will entice him to eat. Many in the church today have no appetite for God's Word. If we do not study, we will not know. If we do not know, we will not do. If we do not do, we will be lost. Jesus said, "Not everyone that says to me, Lord, Lord, will enter into the Kingdom of Heaven, but he that does the will of my Father which is in Heaven" (Matthew 7:21).

Some will say, "I don't have time." We take the time to do the things we want to do. If we want to go hunting, fishing, golfing, or anything else, we take the time for it.

Again, as we take a look as ourselves, let us take note if our daily efforts will lead lost humanity to the Lord.

Tony Williams is originally from Chattanooga and was baptized at the East Ridge congregation. He is married to Deanna, and they have three daughters, Claire, Maggie, and Ella. Tony has a Bachelor's and Master's Degree from UT. Tony and his family have been at Karns since 1999, and during that time he has served as a deacon, and currently as an elder.

If I Were the Preacher

If I were the preacher, these are some things that might cross my mind:

- Please don't be offended if after services I am a little flat. I've used a lot of emotional energy presenting the sermon.
- I know today's sermon might not have done much for you, but I was trying to help a struggling brother or sister.
- The decision of what to wear to church can be trying, but try to imagine what selecting the topics for two sermons and a Bible class is like every week.
- I enjoy general compliments, but specific statements really tell me you were listening and that I touched your heart.
- There will be those Sundays were things do not go as planned. Remember, I always have three sermons when I enter the pulpit: the one I prepared, the one I wish I delivered, and the one I delivered. Sometimes, they just aren't the same. Please forgive me!
- I've slept through a few sermons myself, but every Sunday?
- I hope Saturday's football game was at 1:00 p. m. , otherwise, only half will be awake enough to hear what I say.
- I hope they remember I have my faults and we are all on the same team.
- What if I preached like the congregation sings?

When the day is long, and the struggles wearisome, Lord help me to always remember Paul's words of encouragement to Timothy: "Preach the word! Be ready in season and out of season. Convince, rebuke, exhort, with all longsuffering and teaching" (2 Timothy 4:2).

Jeff Smith is married to Sherry and they have two children, Lauren and Hannah. Jeff and his family have been members at Karns since 2001. Jeff has served the congregation as an elder and is often referred to as "The Bible Bowl Man." He enjoys reading, writing, congregational singing, and passionate gospel preaching.

Cades Cove

If you have attended Karns for any length of time, you will remember that we once had, "Bicycle Around Cades Cove Day." To be honest, I really didn't want to go. I didn't have a bicycle, and I didn't want to spend my Saturday doing something I didn't want to do. However, a friend said it would be fun and there would be extra bicycles, so I relented.

I was not disappointed. The morning was so beautiful; the mist was rising off the ground; and the sun was coming up and reflecting off the dew on the leaves. I saw a deer in a distant field. The air was free in those mountains, the way it always is.

What else could a twenty-year-old want? To bask in God's beauty, to be with church family and friends. It was a good day to be alive! I peddled ahead of our group. The pedal of the bicycle I borrowed kept coming off. I stopped to fix it when a little girl passed by. She was 7 or 8, with blond hair. Her bike was new, with multi-colored tassels on her handle bar grips. She was beautiful, she was the future, but she was not with our group. Other people were bicycling around the Cove. As she passed, she wheeled back around to where I was working on my bike. I thought, here comes a knock-knock joke. She said, "Excuse me sir, but are you a 'N----word?'" I was so hurt. I almost said something very regrettable to that little girl because it caught me by such surprise! I said, "No, little girl, I'm just a man." She shrugged her shoulders, and disappeared. That was the last time I ever saw her. I think of my little baby sister, after all these years, who probably has kids of her own by now. How fate had brought us together on that beautiful Spring morning.

Bennie Williams has been a member at Karns since he was 13 years-old. He is employed at B&W at Y-12 for over 30 years. Bennie loves discussing the Bible, history, exercising, playing the guitar, and restoring old cars. He is married to Jacquie and has one son, Jerrell Williams and two grandchildren, Levi and Avani. My favorite Bible verse is: Psalm 139.

Peace, Perfect Peace

Luke 2:14 says, "Glory to God in the highest, And on earth peace, goodwill toward men!"

The shepherds who were seeking the Christ were told that they would find the baby in a manger. The angel and heavenly host praised God and made this statement. We are seeing peace come to earth. But allow me to raise this question: "Where is the peace of which the angels spoke?"

Every night, our evening news informs us that we still have wars, famines, earthquakes, and hurricanes. Sometimes these come with a huge loss of life and property. This is not very peaceable. Some of the disasters are natural and some are man-made, but one thing is for sure, all these events seem to rob us of peace.

However as Christians, our peace is not secured in having just the right circumstances in life. Rather it is secured in the fact that we know where we are going. As we look forward to our home going, what can we do to be a better Christian? Does it mean being a better neighbor? Does it mean being a more regular attendant at worship services? Does it mean being more charitable?

We each can strive to be a better Christian today because we have the peace of Jesus in our life. Our peace is in John 3:16, "For God so loved the world that He gave His only begotten Son, that whoever believes in Him should not perish but have everlasting life." God loves you. Live today with peace!

Ken Couch is a sales representative for Royal Brass and Hose, an industrial hose and fitting supplier in Knoxville Tn. He regularly travels in his job throughout East Tennessee, Eastern Kentucky and Southwestern Virginia. He enjoys High School football and following the Tennessee Volunteers.

A Sermon from the Hearth

I have a fireplace with an 8-inch raised hearth on which little children love to play. It has been the stage for many "concerts" orchestrated by our grandchildren. Most recently, our 8 month-old great grandchild discovered it and is auditioning for the next show.

We have had many laughs, but there was one incident I will always remember with sadness. A 5 year-old foster child, Lydia, had recently joined our family. She was unhappy and wanted little to do with us. One morning, after the older children had gone to school, I heard singing and talking. I quietly went to investigate and found Molly, another foster child, standing on the hearth "preaching." She and Lydia were "playing church." Molly was telling Lydia about Jesus and how some day we would all go to heaven and live with Him. This upset Lydia, and she said that she was not going. Molly jumped down from the hearth, started shaking Lydia and said, "Yes, you are going." I broke up the demonstration and told Molly that Lydia didn't have to go if she didn't want to. Lydia's problem was that she didn't know about heaven. She thought it was another foster home where love did not exist for her.

How sad that a child would fear heaven, but even sadder are Christians claiming to be heaven-bound, but the road they are traveling doesn't go there. Let's truly strive for that beautiful home in heaven and stop "playing church." That game belongs to the little children, and they play it well. Listen to them sometime. Their sermon from the hearth may pleasantly surprise you.

Jane Higdon is a widow of 28 years and a retired Administrative Secretary. She has a daughter and a son, three grandchildren and five great grandchildren. She enjoys cooking and eating; watching sports, especially Tennessee football and Braves baseball; eating; grading Bible Correspondence courses; and get-togethers with her church family.

The Broken Limb

Looking out my mother's door I can see a large limb that had broken off the pecan tree. The pecan tree is still green and full of pecans, but the limb that had broken off is brown and dead. It had left its source of life.

I began to think that the same thing happens to us spiritually when we break away from our source of spiritual life, God. God is like that pecan tree, He doesn't move. He is where He has always been. We have to choose each day to be a part of Him or to break away from Him.

I think about the words Jesus spoke about Jerusalem in Matthew 24:37 when Jesus was heartbroken because the Jews had chosen to reject him. . . "I would have gathered your children together as a hen gathers her chicks under her wings." What a beautiful, comforting picture.

It is so amazing to me that the great God wants to be my Father and love, protect and comfort me. It is also amazing and shameful to me that sometimes I break away from Him, and for what? The darkness and death that comes from leaving the source of life? Every day I make the choice to either serve God and have life or break away from Him and die like the limb from the pecan tree. God doesn't go anywhere. I must choose to accept His gift of life or refuse Him. "Choose you this day whom you will serve. . . ." (Joshua 24:15).

Linda Solley has been a member of the Karns family since 1974. She and Edward (her late husband, a deacon for 20+ years) had one daughter, Sherri who married Blake Graham. Linda, aka "Nana" has 2 grandsons, Nathan and Caleb, the joy of her life.

Many Rooms

When I was born, we were living in a small, three-room house. I was the 9th of 10 children. It was difficult for 9 children and our parents in such crowded conditions. When the last of our siblings was born, we were still living there, so it became even more crowded!

When I was 6 years old, a farm that was a mile or so from our house became available for renting. There was a big house on the farm. My daddy talked with the lady who owned it and plans were made for us to move. I remember the day we moved into that big house!! It was like being in a fairy tale! There were 4 big rooms upstairs, 4 big rooms downstairs, a front porch on both levels, a long side porch and a long back porch. There were two stairways: one from the front entrance hall and one going up from the kitchen. We weren't crowded any more, for sure! Just wonderful! Sadly, when I was 12 years old, the lady who owned the house accidentally caused a fire that destroyed it! Such a sad, sad day!

I'm now married and live in the house my husband designed and had built in 1960, and it's home, but I know it won't last forever either. What a comfort it is when I remember that a home is being prepared for me that WILL last forever - and it won't be crowded or destroyed by fire!

John 14:2 says, "In my father's house are many rooms; if it were not so I would have told you. I am going there to prepare a place for you." (ESV)

Mattie Lou Robinson has been married to Grover Cleveland (G. C.) Robinson, Jr. since June 27, 1954. They have four children: Timothy, Amy, Andy and Penny; and three grandchildren: Victoria, Quintin and Ransom. Mattie Lou is a homemaker and also taught school for 15 years. Mattie Lou turned 83 on October 9th, 2012.

Change

"Change" is an interesting word in the English language. As a noun we are likely to first think of "change" as coins. As an adjective, "change" often modifies a noun like "agent" (a "change" agent), signifying something that is a catalyst for change. It is as a verb that most of us know and use it. From changing a diaper to changing lanes on the interstate, "change" can go in many directions.

How many times has God changed people or events? Among many changes, scripture tells us that God changed water to blood, rods into serpents, leprosy to unblemished skin and vice versa, the sick to healthy, and the dead to life.

One of the most remarkable changes God orchestrated was changing Saul, the persecutor, to Paul, the apostle. When Paul went to Jerusalem, the Christians feared him, but Barnabas testified on his behalf because he knew of the change in Paul.

Who among us has changed? The Second Corinthian letter says that we are new creations when we become Christians. The old becomes new; transformed. We seldom think of the caterpillar that the butterfly once was, but we sometimes can't forget that someone who becomes a new creature in Christ was a sinner. The "bigger" the sin the harder it is to forget. When Paul wrote the first letter to the Corinthians he reminded them that they were sinners, and he enumerated a list of sins that left nothing to the imagination. He simply told them that those represented what they had been. Today, thank God that we are changed.

Conrad Slate graduated from Tennessee Tech, and was a member of the Air National Guard for 31 years, retiring as a Colonel. He holds a MS in Financial Services. Currently he is a principal in Slate, Disharoon, Parrish & Associates, a fee based financial planning firm. Married to Brenda for over 40 years, they have two children and three grandchildren.

Do Your Roots Run Deep?

There once was a father and son who decided to plant some trees on a hillside. The son wanted to have the most beautiful trees ever seen, so he planted his trees and carted water up to them every day. The father, on the other hand, planted the trees and left them alone. The son asked the father "Why don't you water your trees?" The father replied "I don't water the trees because the roots will grow deep and will find water beneath the ground. " The son didn't understand this and continued to water his trees. The son's trees grew quickly and were the most beautiful trees one had ever seen while the father's slowly grew looking scrawny at times.

One night a horrible storm raged through the area, causing damage with its severe winds. The son and father went out the next morning to survey their land and see what damage the storm had left behind. When they approached the hillside, they found all of the son's trees had been uprooted. Not a single one remained. The father's, however, stood firm. Why did the father's trees remain? It was because they had deep roots.

When a storm comes into our lives, are our roots deep enough in God's word to keep us upright? Are we more interested in how beautiful we look or how well-rooted we are? In the parable of the soils (Matthew 13), the seed that fell on rocky ground grew up, but was scorched by the elements because it had shallow roots. If we are deeply planted in God's Word, we can withstand the storms of life.

Katie Pruett has been a member at Karns Church of Christ for 14 years. She has a passion to teach and is heavily involved in the Bible School Program. Her interests include spending time with family, watching the UT Vols and Green Bay Packers, and reading.

I Picked Up Snakes

I was the kid in the neighborhood they looked for when a snake was found. The kids in the "hood" knew I would pick one up; all they had to do was do the finding. For whatever reason, I just picked them up. Fortunately, I got over that before one of them got me.

Looking back, I wonder, "What was I thinking?" I suppose a case could be made for my just not having any better sense. I did manage to do more than my share of less than smart things back in the day. I think, however, I have figured it out. The reason I grabbed the snakes up was because I didn't really think there was anything to be afraid of.

In a spiritual sense, I think this curious fearlessness of mine can go two very different ways. First, we need to learn the things in life we truly need to fear. Scripture tells us some things are to be avoided at all costs (Matthew 5:29-30). Sin is not a game; it has a bite. On the other hand, we must be courageous in living for Jesus (John 16:33). Even death should not intimidate us when we stand for what is right (Matthew 10:28). A timid Christianity is no Christianity at all (2 Timothy 1:7). The Serpent of old fears the day when God will crush him under our feet (Genesis 3:15; Romans 16:20).

The Devil would back us off in fear. He will offer many ways for us to rationalize ourselves out of a courageous stand. At such times, the little children have it right, let us "run right over him!"

Edwin Jones has been with Karns and the school of preaching for almost 27 years. Currently he is the Dean of Students with the school. Edwin and Sara have three children and four grandchildren as well as a variety of "adopted" family members they have incorporated into their mix over the years.

Trust God

Years ago I bought a charm necklace that said "Faith." What I didn't know at the time was that it was incomplete. Years later a second charm that said "Trust" was placed on that necklace.

If I were to ask you (a Christian) "Do you trust God?" You would most certainly say, "Yes, of course I do!" But do you really trust God? When I found out that I was pregnant with our second child after many years of difficulty achieving a viable pregnancy, a sonogram revealed that our baby had something wrong with his heart. I prayed to God asking for Rowan's life to be saved if it was in accordance with His will, acknowledging that in all of His great knowledge and wisdom He knew what was best. With two defective heart valves, the options were not good.

For three months Rowan went through various procedures and surgery. Many times every day I offered up the prayer and let God know how I trusted Him. Weeks after his surgery, Rowan died after being rushed to a hospital emergency room. Nothing can compare to the feeling I had walking out of that hospital without my son.

I now long for Heaven more than ever, looking forward to the day we are reunited. The test of my faith revealed something beautiful - I truly trusted God, even when it meant losing my precious son. I was blessed to never feel angry at God or ask "why me?" I thank God that His Spirit has helped me trust Him and view my life on Earth in light of eternity. Whatever happens here, it's only this life.

Gerri Nath has been a member at Karns since 2009 and has been a Christian since 1977. Gerri is married to Michael and they have a daughter, Elliana Grace. She is the Vice President of Accounting Services at Marriott International, Inc. , and enjoys spending time with Ellie, watching her play softball, photography, traveling, scrapbooking, reading, and writing.

It Is Enough

It seems we are always wanting more. No matter the subject, and no matter how much we already have, we seem to always want more. But when is enough, enough? Can we be content with "enough?"

Is it enough to have a car, or must we have the latest model? Is it enough to have a house, or must we have a "nice" house? Is it enough to clothe ourselves and our children, or must we have a certain brand of clothing? Is it enough to meet our financial obligations, or must we have additional money to "play" with? Is it enough to be a servant of God, or must we be in the spotlight?

It's really this last point I want you to consider. Have you ever heard of Quartus? He's probably unknown to you by name, but he's mentioned in the Bible. What the Bible records about him is not remarkable. He had no particular fame. He didn't slay a giant or survive a fiery furnace. In fact I know of nothing that this man did that would cause him to be remembered. But here's what the Bible says about him:

"Gaius, my host and the host of the whole church greets you. Erastus, the treasurer of the city greets you, and Quartus, a brother" (Romans 16:23).

Did you catch that? "Quartus, a brother." Nothing more; just a brother. But that's enough, isn't it? Whatever else I may or may not be able to achieve in life, if I can just be remembered as "a brother in Christ," it will be enough!

Steve Higginbotham has been the pulpit minister for the Karns church of Christ since 2010. Steve is married to Kim and they have four children, Kelli, Michael, Matthew, and Anne Marie. Steve enjoys writing, playing golf, and is a fan of the Pittsburgh Steelers, the WVU Mountaineers, and the Andy Griffith Show.

He Wags His Tail Real Good

My family used to live on a rather desolate road in Alabama; the kind of road people would use to get rid of their unwanted animals. One day my girls heard something whimpering in the grass alongside of the road. It was a dog that had been thrown out, having been beaten or injured in some way. Being tenderhearted, they brought him to the house and put him on the porch. They called for me to come see him. As soon as I saw him I was very upset. There he was—covered in blood, fleas, and ticks. It upset me that they had brought him to the house instead of just leaving him alone. So, I said, "Get that dog off my porch. Look at him. There's not one good thing about that dog." My words cut them to the heart. My oldest started to cry and looked at the dog. The dog caught her eye and began to wag its tail. She then looked up at me and said, "Well, Daddy, he wags his tail real good. Can we keep him?"

When I could not see one good thing about the dog, my girls could at least find something good in him. They looked beyond the blood, fleas, and ticks. The good they saw far outweighed the bad I saw. Many times we look at others and only see that which is bad in people and fail to see the good. God made every one of us and, as we have heard it said, "God does not make junk." There is good in every person. Look for it today.

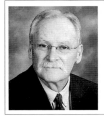

David Lipe was born in Charleston, MS and is married to his wife Linda (Wilson). They have three daughters and five grandchildren. David presently serves as the Director of the Southeast Institute of Biblical Studies.

Thank God for Every Remembrance

My grandmother was born in 1903. She was the oldest of thirteen children. She helped to raise her siblings, even as she was establishing her own home and family. She and her mother, twice, were with child at the same time. Granny valued her family unity. She and Granddaddy raised four children, all who became Christians and established Christian homes. Many have remained so, unfortunately some have not.

As for myself, I learned to be respectful of my elders, I honor their commitment in having those values passed from them to my parents, on to me and my family, which continues to be passed on today to my children and grandchildren.

When our children were born, Granny gave each one a small blue or pink Bible with their name engraved on the outside. Inside each Bible was inscribed Philippians 1:3, "I thank my God for every remembrance of thee."

We never know from time to time how many days we will have to spend with our loved ones. We must daily be thankful to God, our parents, spouse, family and friends. Keep in mind that every second and all actions of remembrances, whether good or bad, may be your last encounter with them.

Always be respectful of your actions towards others, especially to those who have or who are helping you to establish an everlasting Christian family and lifestyle. They too will remember to thank God and you!

Barbara "Bobbie" Lynch Martin is married to Vascoe Stephen Martin, Jr. Bobbie and Steve have three children, Gabe (Sarah), Leah (David), and Cory, (Rose Anne); 8 grandchildren; and her parents are Red & Helen Lynch. All 4 generations attend church at Karns. She enjoys arts, the beach, antiques, grand kids plus Oak Ridge History & WWII.

I Feel Loved

A few years ago I was diagnosed with breast cancer. No one wants to hear the word "cancer," but there was a lot of good that came with having cancer. From the time I was diagnosed until I had surgery was about 6 weeks. During that time and after, I received over 300 cards, emails and phone calls. I have kept all of the cards and emails. I was very thankful for the love shown to me and for the many prayers sent to God on my behalf.

The love that was showered on me during a difficult time was overwhelming and very encouraging. Since that time, when someone in our church family has been diagnosed with cancer, I tell them of all the love that will be showered on them by their Karns Family. Believe me, the feeling of being loved by so many and to know that they were all praying for me was a blessing.

But why do we wait until someone is diagnosed with a life threatening disease before we tell them how much we love and appreciate them? I am also guilty of this. I am sure that we tell our spouse, parents and children that we love them on a regular basis. Our brothers and sisters in Christ also need to be told that we love them and that we are praying for them. Imagine the difference it could make in our own Karns Family if you started telling your Christian brothers and sisters how much you love and appreciate them. Don't be surprised if I tell you "I love you!"

"Love one another" (John 15:12).

Sherrye Woodall is married to Gregg. They have 4 children: Stephanie Harder, Tiffany Dresser, Benjamin Woodall and Jonathan Woodall. They have 4 grand-children: Wrigley Harder, Walton Harder, Adalynn Dresser and Brooklynn Dresser. Sherrye has taught the 3 years old class at Karns for over 32 years.

I Can Do That

In one of the lesser studied books of the Bible, there is a sentence - just a single sentence - that is like a shaft of bright light in a dark, dark corner.

"...Amasiah the son of Zichri, who willingly offered himself to the LORD, and with him two hundred thousand mighty men of valor" (2 Chronicles 17:16).

Here we are introduced to this man who lived nearly 3,000 years ago. He seems to have been an officer in the army of good King Jehoshaphat. He had under his leadership 200,000 soldiers. Here, in this one sentence, is all the record that the Bible gives of him. His whole life has been shrunk into a single sentence, just as yours and mine will be in a generation or two, three at the most. The few people who will even remember we were on this earth will have pretty well shrunk our lives into a single sentence. "He was..." and they might say a dozen words about us. Here is what is said about Amasiah, he "willingly offered himself unto the Lord." There is not a finer compliment in the Bible about anybody - not one of the apostles, not any of the prophets, priests or kings who ever lived had a better thing said of him.

Now, Amasiah (and you and I could put our names there) willingly offered himself to the Lord. I could say "I can do that." I could stop sitting here just passing time, and I could offer myself unto the Lord. Yes, I can do that. That's something we all can do if we want. We can offer ourselves willingly unto the Lord. Will you?

Wendell Agee was born and raised in Pikeville, TN. He served 20 years in the USAF and was a successful business man for over 30 years. Wendell has served the Lord as a missionary to Cuba, Jamaica, Honduras and other countries. He's a member of the Karns Church of Christ.

Silence Is Golden

Silence is golden... or so the old saying goes. But do we really believe that? In the course of the day, we are constantly surrounded by noise. It might be the TV, co-workers, kids, or a spouse, but there is always something, or someone demanding our attention. Giving our time and focus to others isn't necessarily a bad thing, but how often do we make a focused attempt to be in silence, even if for a small amount of time? And not only to be somewhere just because it's quiet, but to use that time to focus on God?

In Psalm 46:10 we are instructed to, "Be still and know that I am God." The beginning of chapter 46 discusses struggles that surround us and can distract our focus from remembering that God is, and always will be in control. What a comforting thought!

Christ even took time away to spend in silence with God. In Mark 1:29-35, Jesus spent an evening healing those who were sick and possessed by demons. He rose early the next morning to spend time in prayer with God. Notice that this was probably not the most convenient time for Jesus. It was so early in the morning that it was still dark outside (v. 35). Considering that the whole city was outside the night before (v. 33), he probably wasn't able to get much sleep; however, Jesus knew that time with God would be well spent to refocus for the day. For us, it may not be first thing in the morning, but we need to make time in silence with God part of our everyday routine.

Lynlee Robinson has been a member of the Karns congregation since 2006. She was born and raised in Texarkana, TX and has been married to Lee Toothman since July 2007. She is employed at Kimberly-Clark Corporation in the transportation department. Lynlee enjoys scrap booking, playing the clarinet, and spending time with family.

All You Need Is Love

John Lennon of "The Beatles" wrote a song in 1967 entitled, "All You Need Is Love." The song was written to represent the United Kingdom during the world's first live global television link, "Our World." The link was watched by 400 million viewers in over 26 countries via satellite on June 25, 1967.

Jesus was the first person to use this catch phrase over 2,000 years ago in order to help us understand what being a Christian is all about. Love is spoken of throughout both the Old and the New Testaments. Here are just a few verses that we can ponder on to see just how much our Heavenly Father loves us, and how he expects us to love others: Exodus 20:8; Psalm 136:1-26; Matthew 5:44; Matthew 19:19; John 13:34; John 15:13; Romans 13:10; Galatians 5:22; 1 John 3:16; 1 John 4:16.

Just as The Beatles wanted to send a clear message to the world that love was everything, God has been singing His song of love to the world through the Holy Scriptures.

So the next time you hear The Beatles' #1 hit from the 60's, remember that God's message of love is still all we need, and his #1 hit, "Jesus Christ," tops the charts still today.

"For God so loved the world that He gave His only begotten Son, that whoever believes in Him should not perish but have everlasting life" (John 3:16).

Adrian Marsh is a retired Navy veteran and is married to his high school sweetheart Lisa Marsh. He enjoys family time, traveling, cooking, sports and serving God.

God Answers Prayers, This I Know

"Confess your trespasses to one another, and pray for one another, that you may be healed. The effective, fervent prayer of a righteous man avails much" (James 5:16).

I am so thankful that there are so many righteous people who prayed for Sherrye and me during her battle with breast cancer in 2007. The multiplicity of tests and the myriad of criteria that can affect the severity and criticality of her cancer always came back on the low side. Her surgery went well and her recovery has been amazing. I know that God answered those prayers and we are so very thankful to God for His goodness. Even though we were put through a distressing ordeal we have been blessed all throughout this trial in life. We are now so thankful to be celebrating 5 years of being cancer free. God is so good and He does answer prayers.

Several years back when our daughter Tiffany was a teenager and was dealing with a bad day, I asked her. "What should you do when life hands you a lemon?" and she remarked, "Make a sour face!"

We laughed so hard and then we explained that the correct answer is to make lemonade. James put it this way: "My brethren, count it all joy when you fall into various trials, knowing that the testing of your faith produces patience" (James 1:2-3).

When we are faced with difficulties in life, remember to pray, ask for prayers, and be assured that God answers prayer. This I know.

Gregg Woodall is an elder of the Karns Church of Christ. Gregg is married to Sherrye and they have four children, Stephanie, Tiffany, Benjamin, and Jonathan. They also have four grandchildren, Wrigley, Walton, Adalynn, and Brooklynn. Gregg enjoys golfing, dirt bike riding, spending time with family, and is a fan of the Tennessee Volunteers.

Honest Living

Diogenes, the cynic philosopher of ancient Athens, is reported to have appeared upon the streets of the Grecian city with a lit lantern one day at noon. Upon being questioned as to the why of this peculiar action he replied that he was looking for an honest man.

A wise teacher used to always tell his class, before giving them a test; I'm giving you two tests today—one in trigonometry and one in honesty. I hope you pass both of them, but if you can pass only one, be sure it is the test on honesty, because there are a lot of good men who don't know trigonometry, but there are no good men who are not honest.

"Have regard for good things in the sight of all men" (Romans 12:17; 2 Corinthians 8:21). Honesty is a three-lane street. First, there is honesty to God. "When men cease to be faithful to their God, he who expects to find them so to each other will be much disappointed" (Bishop Horner). Second, honesty to our fellowman. Third, honesty to oneself. "A man cannot be dishonest with others until he is first dishonest with himself" (Joe Barnett). "To thine ownself be true, and it must follow, as the night the day, thou canst not be false to any man" (Shakespeare).

"Failures in self-honesty are at the root of almost every emotional and mental disturbance" (Psychotherapist Dr. Albert Ellis).

James Meadows was born March 10, 1930. He graduated from High School in 1949, and Freed-Hardeman College in 1955. He later attended Union University and Harding Graduate School. He has done local work in Tennessee, Kentucky, and South Carolina. He served as Director of ETSPM from 1996 to 2006, and presently serves as Dean of Students.

Thankfulness

The ultimate love that has been given to us, as God's children, is a gift that our entire being should be continually thankful for each day. Our brother Paul said in 1 Thessalonians 2:3, ". . . we thank God without ceasing. . . "

Remember the ten lepers? The one that returned and thanked Jesus always impressed me. Why did he return and thank Jesus? He had a thankful heart and was touched by the kind gesture Jesus had made. I imagine the others were also grateful, maybe in their excitement they didn't think to return and give thanks. Jesus asked where they were. He expected them all to thank Him. Did they not receive the same blessings the one did? Yes, they did. Paul also says in 1 Thessalonians 5:18, "In everything give thanks, for this is the will of God in Christ Jesus concerning you."

Have you ever seen the ugliness of ingratitude? I imagine God sees this a lot. Why? Do we expect the blessings of God? God loves a humble and contrite heart.

We are so very blessed! We have forgiveness and a home in Heaven, just to name a couple blessings for which to be thankful.

Our thoughts and hearts should continually overflow with gratitude and thanksgiving to God the Father, our Lord Jesus, and the Comforting Holy Spirit.

Is your heart a thankful one? I hope you will contemplate having a thankful heart each day.

Kim Gill is a long time member of the Karns Church of Christ. Her parents were James & Mae Gill. Kim has taught the 2 & 3 year-olds as well as 2nd grade. Kim oversees care of her brother, Jim, who is bedfast with MS. Kim also is guardian to her great niece, Chloe Gill and great nephew Collin Baker. She enjoys Scrabble, genealogies, meeting people, and loves children.

I Should Have Done More

In the aftermath of the Penn State tragedy, the once iconic football coach, Joe Paterno, was quoted as saying, "In hindsight I should have done more."

I thought there was a great lesson to be learned from these few words. If we are honest with ourselves, we could all probably look back throughout our lives and say these words. I know at times I am guilty of not doing enough myself. So while we are able, why not do what Paul said in Colossians 3:17, "Whatever you do in word or deed, do all in the name of the Lord Jesus, giving thanks to God the Father through Him."

They say hindsight is 20/20. Let us not get to the end of our road with regret, saying, "I should have done more." Instead, hopefully we can say as Paul did in 2 Timothy 4:7-8, "I have fought the good fight, I have finished the race, I have kept the faith. Finally, there is laid up for me the crown of righteousness, which the Lord, the righteous judge will give to me on that day, and not only to me but also to all who have loved his appearing."

Let us all strive to do our best. "...for now is the day of salvation" (2 Corinthians 6:2).

Jeremy Stiles is a Telecommunications technician for the University of Tennessee. Originally from PA. Jeremy moved to Knoxville in 2001. He married Heatherly Stiles and is the father to baby Avery. He is also a Pittsburgh Steelers fan. Go Steelers!

Too Good to be True

There is an old adage that if something seems too good to be true, it probably is. I routinely follow this advice when I get offers of free airline tickets or free weekends at a resort. I don't bother calling or following up on such offers, as I am sure there are "strings attached."

There is one free gift that seems too good to be true but it is absolutely true. That is the gift of salvation through our Lord and Savior Jesus Christ. Consider Ephesians 2:8-10, "For by grace you have been saved through faith and that not of yourselves; it is the gift of God, not of works, lest anyone should boast. For we are His workmanship, created in Christ Jesus for good works, which God prepared beforehand that we should walk in them."

The Bible tells us here and in other Scriptures that is impossible to earn our way to Heaven. Instead, God sent his Son to be that perfect sacrifice for our sins. We can accept the free gift through obedience to God's word.

Of course Christians undertake good works, but not with the goal of earning our salvation. Instead, we are doing the good works God prepared for Christians. The primary good work is spreading the gospel as described in the Great Commission. "Go therefore and make disciples of all the nations, baptizing them in the name of the Father and of the Son and of the Holy Spirit, teaching them to observe all things that I have commanded you; and lo, I am with you always, even to the end of the age" (Matthew 28:19-20).

Dave Benner is married to Sue and they have three children. Dave retired after 40 years with USDA. He and his wife, Sue moved back to TN in 2012. He enjoys hunting, fishing, and is a fan of the Pittsburgh Steelers.

Turning the Other Cheek

My twin sister, Cathy, and I were very lucky to have each other to play with every day when we were young. We seemed to have a daily ritual of playing, getting into a fight, and then getting a whipping. We would then play, fight, get a whipping, play, fight, get a whipping, etc., etc.

One Sunday afternoon we had finished playing and had moved on to our daily fight. I have no idea what we were fighting about, but I know we were in the living room, and I had just delivered my first left hook. Cathy gave me a serious look and announced, "I'm going to do what we were taught in Sunday school this morning and turn the other cheek!" After a brief moment of hesitation, I let loose a right hook and knocked Cathy to the floor. Apparently our Sunday school class had talked about Matthew 5:39 where Jesus said, ". . . but whoever slaps you on your right cheek, turn the other to him also." The class may have also talked about Luke 6:29 where Jesus said, "To him who strikes you on the one cheek, offer the other also. . ."

Maybe I was distracted by a granddaddy longlegs during class (we had lots of those in the basement classrooms), or maybe I was just the evil twin that day! Let's just say the whipping I got from my mother was far more memorable than most!

However, although the whipping certainly hurt physically, the guilt I felt from that occasion haunted me a very long time. (Actually, I still apologize to Cathy for that second blow every now and then.) Remember, actions that take but a moment can have consequences that last a lifetime.

Becky Cagle was born in Oak Ridge Hospital in 1960 and grew up in Karns. She is the youngest of six children. Becky's identical twin, Cathy, is four minutes older than her. Becky has a degree in Nuclear Engineering and currently works in Oak Ridge.

Walking in the Light

I remember when I was much younger, my family took a trip to Mammoth Cave. The tour was amazing! It was like a whole city underground with the tall ceiling tops and the stalagmite and stalactite pillars seeming as if they were holding everything up and keeping it from crashing down on us. It was beautiful to see all the shadows the lights made against the jagged walls of limestone.

At one point in the tour, the guide gathered everyone into a huge chamber and instructed us to turn off all electronics, cell phones, flash lights, and my light-up sneakers. Then they turned out the lights! It was so dark you could feel the blackness creeping in on you. The saying is true about not being able to see your hand in front of your face. It was so dark I was not even sure if I had a hand let alone a body any more.

In that split second I felt alone, lost, and hopeless. Alone and lost because no one was to be seen and even if I could have found them there was no hope of getting out without light. Even if I wanted to, with every fiber of my being, it would have been humanly impossible to make it down the path without light.

In Psalm 119:105 God's word is called a lamp - one that will guide our path. Just like in the cave, if we do not use light as our guide, we will be lost in darkness. Let's not start a day of spelunking or life without making sure we have light in which to walk. 1 John 1:5-10 has a lot to say about being a light walker. Take time to read it today.

Wayne Begarly has been a member of the Karns Church of Christ since 2011. Wayne graduated from UT in 2007 with a Bachelors in Communications. Wayne is involved with the local United Way and American Cancer Society. He enjoys sports and the outdoors in his free time.

When the Answer is "No"

Have you ever had a situation where you were asking God to help you make an important decision? Maybe it was concerning a new job. Maybe it was a relationship that you hoped would lead to marriage. Maybe it was about moving to a new location. There are times when you want something and ask God to make it happen, if it is according to his will.

Most of the time, when I fervently prayed for something to happen, things worked out the way I wanted. When everything was finalized, I was grateful and made sure I expressed to God how much I appreciated his help. However, what about when God says, "No?" Maybe the job you wanted was given to someone else. Maybe a relationship broke up. What is our reaction then? Do we go to God in prayer thanking him for answering our prayer or do we pout that he didn't do what we wanted him to do?

If God always answered "Yes" to our every request, where would we be? As for me, I wouldn't be married to Steve. I wouldn't be where I am today. I wouldn't have the wonderful life that I do.

It's easy to thank God for all his blessings when he gives us what we want. Just don't forget that he is seeing the big picture of our lives. He loves us and knows what is best for us all the time. Always pray for his help and his will to be done. Just don't forget to give him just as much thanks for his care when the answer is "No."

Kim Higginbotham grew up in Poplar Bluff, MO. She is married to Steve and has four children: Kelli, Michael, Matthew, and Anne Marie. Kim teaches children with multiple disabilities for Knox County, a ladies' class at SEIBS, conducts teacher training seminars, and maintains two blogs, "Teaching Help," and "Relative Taste." She enjoys teaching and cooking.

Sin Separates

It was just the usual January day in the courtroom. Inside the courtroom folks were coming in for judgments, sentencing, hearings, probation matters - the usual court routine.

Mr. Ross was one of the inmates in the courtroom jail facility that day. He was very happy to be back in Knoxville. You see, his family was going to be in the courtroom to see him.

Mr. Ross had been in prison for several months. Sin had separated him from his family. However, Mr. Ross had a gleam in his eye because he was going to see his sisters and mother. He was so eager - he must have asked me twenty times, "Are my people in the audience yet?"

One by one, we took each inmate out to stand before Judge Mc-Gee. Each time I would bring out an inmate and take an inmate back to jail, Mr. Ross would ask, "Do you see anyone for me? Are my people out there?"

"Yes," I told Mr. Ross, "I see people for you." He smiled and thanked me for telling him. Mr. Ross' case came up about 1:00 p. m. He was the last one to go before Judge McGee. Mr. Ross didn't care that he was the last one - you see, he knew his sisters and mother were going to be there! Indeed, his sisters were there for him! His mother was not. You see, Mr. Ross' mother died on Wednesday, the day before.

So sad. Friends, don't let sin separate you from your earthly mother and father. But even more importantly, please don't let it separate from your Heavenly Father!

Mark Cawood has been attending the Karns Church of Christ since 1954. He was baptized in 1970. Mark's mother, Joyce Cawood, was one of the original members of the Karns congregation. Mark has served on the Knox County Commission from 1986-2008. He loves to travel in the USA and he's been to every state. He's also a fan of the Andy Griffith Show.

Leroy

My parents told me the day Laura was born that it was my job to protect my little sister. It was the same when Lisa came along. For a short time, we three walked to school together. Because Laura was closer to me in age, I walked with her for more years. When I started to drive, Laura rode with me. Her penchant for leaving at the last minute did not set well with my "always arrive early" policy.

I called her Leroy. I was the only one she would allow to use that name, a term of endearment between us. Our relationship was special in many ways. I always knew that I could talk to her about anything. She would listen; really listen to me, offering suggestions, but never in a way that put me down. She was only interested in lifting me up.

She did that for a lot of people, judging by the crowd that came for her visitation and funeral. The young people at the high school where she served as a secretary especially appreciated her tender heart and a soft shoulder to cry on.

I finally got around to throwing out all the sympathy cards. It is like a chapter has closed and I must move on, but it will not be without Leroy. Her memory will always challenge me to be kind to others and listen.

Will you join me in honoring Leroy? Remember, "He who covers a transgression seeks love, But he who repeats a matter separates friends" (Proverbs 17:9). Also, "A friend loves at all times, And a brother is born for adversity" (Proverbs 17:17).

Gary Hampton is the former director of the East Tennessee School of Preaching and Missions. He has preached for more than 30 years in AR, AL, GA, and TN, He and his wife, Teresa are currently living in Jackson, MS where Gary is preaching.

Even so the Tongue

In our daily walk we are in a constant struggle with several stumbling blocks. Controlling our emotions is one of the difficulties we deal with. The book of James is filled with the most valuable advice that relates to human emotion. James said, "For we all stumble in many things. If anyone does not stumble in word, he is a perfect man, able also to bridle the whole body. Indeed, we put bits in horses' mouths that they may obey us, and we turn their whole body. Look also at ships: although they are so large and are driven by fierce winds, they are turned by a very small rudder wherever the pilot desires. Even so the tongue is a little member and boasts great things. See how great a forest a little fire kindles" (James 3:2-5).

Christians who would never consider expressing anger through physical violence nevertheless can lose control and express their anger through sharp words and insults. This shows a clear lack of self-control, and is not appropriate for any who would wear the name Christian.

Again in James we find some of the most prudent advice: "So then, my beloved brethren, let every man be swift to hear, slow to speak, slow to wrath, for the wrath of man does not produce the righteousness of God" (James 1:19 20).

We can tear apart with our tongues, but remember the consequence. "But I say to you that for every idle word men may speak, they will give account of it in the day of judgment. For by your words you will be justified, and by your words you will be condemned" (Matthew 12:36-37).

Tony Williams is originally from Chattanooga and was baptized at the East Ridge congregation. He is married to Deanna, and they have three daughters, Claire, Maggie, and Ella. Tony has a Bachelor's and Master's Degree from UT. Tony and his family have been at Karns since 1999, and during that time he has served as a deacon, and currently as an elder.

Gott Mit Uns

That's right, it's German. Gott=God; Mit=With; Uns=Us. "GOD WITH US."

These are the words that were stamped on belt buckles of every WWII 3rd Reich German soldier. There was a young US Army Military Policeman during WWII. He was charged with processing German POWs off the battlefield, and confiscating uniforms. One day, a young German prisoner removed his belt and handed it to the American. This American could read and speak German. When he saw the words, he gave a puzzled look to the German and said, "GOTT MIT UNS?!" The German, surprised one spoke his language, pointed to himself saying, "Nein, Gott mit UNS!" The American argued, "Nein, GOTT MIT UNS!" Finally, the German stated with fervor, "GOTT MIT UNS!" and pointed to his own chest. This was a turning point lesson for the young American.

Sometimes our enemies are like us. We forget we are but humans with different lives which sometimes clash for reasons outside our control. We cannot expect to understand fully God's purpose for our trials except only for His glory.

"In Him also we have obtained an inheritance, being predestined according to the purpose of Him who works all things according to the counsel of His will, that we who first trusted in Christ should be to the praise of His glory" (Ephesians 1:11-12).

Steve Aragon is married to Susan and is the father of 2 boys, John and Joseph. Steve is originally from Sitka, Alaska. He works as a Project Manager for GE and is also an officer in the TN Air National Guard. He enjoys many outdoor activities, flying airplanes, and playing guitar. Steve and Susan have been members of the Karns church of Christ since 2007.

Family

Have you ever met the child of someone you had always revered or loved? Maybe it was someone you hadn't seen in years or had lost touch with over time. But when you first met their children, it made you instantly have warm feelings toward them because you admired their parent first.

The best example of this was after the death of David's best friend, Jonathan, in 2 Samuel 9. David wanted to show kindness to Jonathan's son, Mephibosheth, for the sake of Jonathan.

In the book of 1 John, Christians are called the "children of God."

"Beloved, let us love one another, for love is of God; and everyone who loves is born of God and knows God. He who does not love does not know God, for God is love. In this the love of God was manifested toward us, that God has sent His only begotten Son into the world, that we might live through Him. Beloved, if God so loved us, we also ought to love one another. If someone says, 'I love God,' and hates his brother, he is a liar; for he who does not love his brother whom he has seen, how can he love God, whom he has not seen? And this commandment we have from Him; that he who loves God must love his brother also" (1 John 4:7-9, 11, 20-21).

How can we read these verses and not have love for our Christian brethren? If we truly love God, we will love and care for each other. Jesus said that the two greatest commandments were to first love God, and second to love one another (Matthew 22:37-39).

Hannah Cox is married to Chris and is a homeschool mom to Samuel and Rachel. She teaches Bible classes and enjoys working with children. In her free time, Hannah likes reading, riding bikes and spending time with her family.

My Boy Is Fine

The personal blessings that I experience each day of my life have strengthened my faith in the Lord Jesus Christ. I will share one of the most glorious blessings and experiences that I have received from God. I have been a member at Karns since age 15. My mother and my 6 brothers and sisters were baptized at the same time. We attended a gospel tent meeting and my mother studied the Bible with Brother Frank Huber and Brother Harold Duncan.

I have three children: two sons, Fredric and Gregory, and a daughter, Kimberly. When my middle son, Greg, was in college, he was recruited to join the Navy. His ship was the U. S. S. Saratoga. I was very proud.

In 1990, during the Gulf war, I heard the news that there had been an accident involving the U. S. S. Saratoga. Oh Lord, I cried because that was Greg's ship. I called the Red Cross, but they couldn't tell me anything. My daughter, Kim, and I began to cry. I went into my bedroom and got on my knees. I began to pray for Greg. This is when a calmness came over me.

Saturday went by with no word about Greg. Sunday morning, before church, I got a call from Greg; he was safely aboard the ship, working. My boy was fine!

Aren't we so blessed to have the avenue of prayer and the peace that it can bring to our lives in the midst of so much uncertainty? "casting all your care upon Him, for He cares for you." (1 Peter 5:7).

Betty Jones has been a member of the Karns congregation for 44 years. She has 3 grown children and 8 grandchildren. She enjoys walking and spending time with her family and friends.

The Goalie

Today I was the goalie for two soccer games. I haven't played since I was 6 years old. The girls are bigger now, and the rules are different and hard to follow.

When I play as a goalie I have several jobs to do. I have to move with the ball. I have to run quickly to defend the goal and keep the other team from scoring. I am the last line of defense between the other team and the goal. Today, I even threw myself on the ball to keep it away from the goal I was protecting. The coach taught me today that I have to support the rest of my team and even direct them.

Sometimes playing goalie can be like life. Life gets harder as you get older. There seem to be more rules as you get older. Just like the ball, in life you have to stay focused on the narrow path, no matter how many distractions there are. Satan is like a fast moving player. You have to pay attention to keep him out of your heart. My parents, my sisters, and the rest of my family, my friends, and my church family are all trying to protect me. They are my team. If you pray to God for help and read your Bible to hear what He wants you to do, you will have a better chance of defending your heart from Satan. You have to support your Christian family and help them to stay on the right path.

As a goalie, you have to be willing to sacrifice and put yourself on the line for the team. You can't be all about yourself. Following God is the same. Jesus's example in John 3:16-17 showed us how we should be. "For God so loved the world, that He gave His only begotten Son, that whoever believes in Him shall not perish, but have eternal life" (John 3:16).

Emily Seibel attends the Karns Church of Christ with her parents, John and Christy Seibel, and her three sisters. Emily is active in the Karns Youth and Family Programs, including Bible Bowl participation in Knoxville, TN and Cookeville, TN. Emily enjoys swimming, classical ballet, soccer, dribbling a basketball, sleeping, and being with her sisters.

Psalm 100

I like Psalm 100 because it is a good scripture. It helps me know how to behave. It makes me happy when I read it. I am going to memorize this one.

"Make a joyful shout to the Lord, all you lands! Serve the Lord with gladness; Come before His presence with singing. Know that the Lord, He is God; It is He who has made us, and not we ourselves; We are His people and the sheep of His pasture. Enter into His gates with thanksgiving, And into His courts with praise. Be thankful to Him, and bless His name. For the Lord is good; His mercy is everlasting, And His truth endures to all generations" (Psalm 100:1-5).

When I read this from my Bible, I know:
• "All you lands" means everybody.
• We should be happy to serve God.
• God is the ruler over the universe.
• God is the one who watches over us like a shepherd and we are his sheep.
• We must enter His presence with thankfulness.
• God always tells the truth.

If I can remember this every day, I won't worry so much about the hard times - like when I got my stitches out. God took care of me! I won't worry about when I had a friend problem and it seemed like it never would end. God took care of me! I won't worry so much anymore, because I know that God will always take care of you and me! God wants the best for us. I am glad that God loves me so much!

Jeanne Seibel attends Karns Church of Christ with her parents, John and Christy Seibel, and her three sisters. Jeanne is active in the Karns Youth Programs, including Bible Bowl participation in Knoxville and Cookeville. She enjoys swimming, basketball, soccer, baseball, spending time with her sisters and friends, watching movies, playing the Wii, and sleeping.

Prayer

I recall a story told by a preacher whose daughter lost her son to a devastating illness. Many prayers were said on his behalf while he was alive but, in the end, his small body was taken in death. The daughter went to her father and said, "Teach me to pray."

I have thought about this story many times throughout the years. Is prayer something we do in repetition each night? Is "Now I lay me down to sleep" enough? We teach this prayer to our children as a beginning night time prayer, but as we grow, prayer should take on a different meaning.

Prayer for the Christian is a personal way of communicating with God, always giving God the glory for what He has done for us. Pray through faith. We know God hears all of our prayers and will answer them in His own time. Confess your love for God in prayer. God loved us so much He gave us the greatest gift of all, His son (John 3:16). We should do no less than to love God with all of our being.

I used to think that prayer was the last thing to do before going to bed. I have since learned that prayer is an ongoing process in life.

Quoting from the hymn, "Ere you left your room this morning, did you think to pray?" Ask God to help you through the day in this world we live in.

Give God the glory and don't forget to pray.

 Anne Anderson is a long time member of the Karns Church of Christ. She is a mother, grandmother, and great-grandmother and, she is an avid sports fan of the Chicago Bears and the Chicago Bulls.

Memory Verses

As I was growing up, we lived on a farm and walked a mile to church services every Sunday morning and evening. We did not have Bible classes because our building was only one big room.

Each Sunday morning we were to say a memory verse from the Bible and tell where it was from. Today, I can still remember many of those verses that I learned as a child. This is why it is important to memorize verses at a young age so that when you get older you still have them.

Matthew 16:18 says, "And I also say to you that you are Peter, and on this rock I will build My church, and the gates of Hades shall not prevail against it." Mark 16:15-16 says, "And He said to them, "Go into all the world and preach the gospel to every creature. He who believes and is baptized will be saved; but he who does not believe will be condemned." These are two examples of verses that I had to memorize. Another verse I had to memorize is found in 2 Peter 1:8, "For if these things are yours and abound, you will be neither barren nor unfruitful in the knowledge of our Lord Jesus Christ."

As a young child, my parents would choose the verses for me to memorize. The verses that were chosen, I now realize, were verses that would help me in my Christian life. Today I am thankful for having godly parents who required me to learn these verses from the Bible. That is why I really enjoyed the memory work here at Karns.

Rachel Anderson grew up in north Alabama, and attended Freed-Hardeman where she met and married Bill Russell. Bill served as a minister and Rachel taught Bible classes. Bill passed away in 1987 then In 1990 she married Bob Anderson. Rachel retired as a banking officer in 1990, and because of her health she has had to stop teaching classes.

Discipline

Through the years since my childhood I have had many occasions to reflect on the discipline administered then, compared to today.

My mother kept a fine willow-tree switch handy to correct our misbehavior. She also would warn us, "Your daddy will take care of you when he gets home." If that action should be required, we children would be bawling before he removed his belt from his pants.

For misbehavior at school teachers usually required us to stand in a corner for a prolonged period, write a sentence 100 times saying how we would not again perform the dastardly deed, or rap our hands with a ruler. For even more egregious deeds we would be sent to the school principal. He would perform stern lectures; perhaps prepare notes to be taken to our parents. For more dastardly deeds the ominous paddle or belt were available or perhaps dismissal from school for a short period.

Yes, we were sinful little people who were subjected to correction that would be considered physical abuse by today's standards. Nevertheless, I am not now aware of any that suffered permanent emotional or physical harm.

I am thankful that these corrections for childish behavior were effective for my sisters and me. Yes, all chastening for the moment seems grievous, but isn't it wonderful beyond comprehension that our Lord Jesus suffered the sentence that we who are mature deserve. Correction that results in faithful obedience is the foundation for our hope in the Lord.

G. C. (Grover Cleveland) Robinson, Jr. has been married to Mattie Lou Geer since June 27, 1954. They have four children: Timothy, Amy, Andy, and Penny; and three grandchildren: Victoria, Quintin and Ransom. G. C. is a retired mechanical engineer. He turned 86 December 1st, 2012.

Patience

In the "now generation," I had to learn patience at an early age. So many of us young people today desire to have a certain thing and then want it right now. We live in a "now" generation. We think we must have everything immediately.

Once I went to a store to buy a pair of shoes and to my surprise they did not have my size and would not have them in for another two weeks. Well, I was disappointed to say the least. I thought I had to have them right then. This taught me I had to practice patience. Many times since then, I've had to practice patience.

James 1:2-4 says, "Consider it all joy, my brethren, when you encounter various trials, knowing that the testing of your faith produces endurance (patience). And let endurance have its perfect result, so that you may be perfect and complete, lacking in nothing."

The Scriptures teach us to grow in grace by adding to our faith, moral excellence, knowledge, self-control, perseverance (patience), godliness, brotherly kindness, and love (2 Peter 1:5-7).

When one becomes a Christian, one must have faith that Jesus is the Son of God. To this faith we must begin to study more of God's Word which will help us to develop our patience and the other graces that are mentioned by Peter in 2 Peter 1.

During our early years our parents teach us many things that we need in this life, one of these things is to have patience.

Sasha Russell is the daughter of Steve and Becky Russell. Sasha is a 14 year-old Freshman in high school. She enjoys band and is currently in the Color Guard.

Los Niños

This past June I traveled to Honduras with 34 other Christians on a medical mission. My job was to teach Bible lessons to the children (niños) while their parents received medical treatment. We expected to have 10 or 12 at a time followed by a short break to prepare for another 10 or 12. Church members at Karns helped prepare materials for teaching the creation story from Genesis, Jesus the Good Shepherd, and basic Bible facts, as well as crafts designed to reinforce these lessons.

What happened was both challenging and exciting. Instead of 10 or 12, we had up to 90 children at a time with only a break for lunch. Many of the children did not even go home for lunch and just waited for us to begin teaching again. It would be a daunting task to teach that many in English but I had to teach in Spanish! Fortunately we had an interpreter and several sisters-in-Christ who helped. It was gratifying to see many of the same children every day. We were essentially holding a Bible School for the Honduran children in Villa de San Francisco.

The niños' enthusiasm for the Word of God reminded me of Christ's Sermon on the Mount. In Matthew 5:6, Christ says, "Blessed are those who hunger and thirst for righteousness, for they shall be filled." These children were hungering and thirsting for God's word and it seemed that they could not get enough of it. The Bible is available to all who seek Him. May we all be blessed with such hunger, and I pray that the niños we taught in Honduras will continue to hunger and thirst for the Word.

Sue Benner is a retired elementary teacher. She and her husband Dave are the parents of three children. She has taught Bible classes for over 40 years in PA, MD, DE, MN, and TN. Her hobbies are reading and working on Bible class materials.

Helping or Honking?

You've probably heard the story of the lady whose car broke down in the middle of a busy intersection. Of course, that would be a nightmare for any of us. But this lady kept her head and was doing her best to restart her car.

However, after several unsuccessful attempts at restarting her car, the driver immediately behind her began to mercilessly honk his horn. His honking just escalated an already stressful situation.

So, after enduring several moments of his incessant "honking," this woman exited her car, walked back to the man in the car behind her and politely said, "Sir, I seem to be having trouble starting my car. If you would be so kind as to help me get my car started, I would be more than happy to sit here and honk for you." Well, needless to say, the honking stopped!

Friends, how would you characterize yourself and your relationship to the church? Are you a "helper" or a "honker?" Sure, problems will arise from time to time. That's just part of dealing with imperfect people. No church is without problems. But more than likely, where you see a problem or an inefficient program at church, you'll also find godly men and women at wits end doing the very best they know how to fix the problem.

Next time you see a problem at church, please don't honk. It really doesn't help, and usually frustrates those who are trying to fix the problem. Instead, of "honking" why not lend a hand and help?

Steve Higginbotham has been the pulpit minister for the Karns church of Christ since 2010. Steve is married to Kim and they have four children, Kelli, Michael, Matthew, and Anne Marie. Steve enjoys writing, playing golf, and is a fan of the Pittsburgh Steelers, the WVU Mountaineers, and the Andy Griffith Show.

Someone to Watch Over Me

Songs flow through my mind continually, both the rhythm and the words, right along with the memorable tunes and lyrics. A song filled my day dreams as a girl. I was not realizing what a difference the words would make in my life. I whispered them as if in prayer. We are unaware of how deeply the words of songs are etched on our hearts as tunes run through our minds, both deliberately and casually.

Now, I have realized that the tune of Ella Fitzgerald's rendition of "Someone to Watch over Me" conveys for me a very different meaning. It reminds me of the answered prayers and blessings in my life with a godly husband and Christian family. My life in Christ, within God's family, keeps me singing new songs of joy and eternal life.

What songs go through your head, implanting the words deeply in your soul? Scripture is filled with the promise that we will no longer be alone as God's child in Christ. "Perfect love casts out fear," (I John 4:18) including the fear of being alone. The only perfect love we will ever find is in Christ Jesus. In Him, we will always have someone to watch over us. Consider these messages from God's word: Psalm 121; John 3: 16; Acts 2: 38, 39; and I Peter 5: 6, 7. God promises His watchful care and love to those in Christ who walk steadfastly in His ways. Pray that we may continue to follow His lead that we may sing a new song together forever.

Rosemary Cameron Spivey attends Karns Church of Christ with her youngest daughter's family, John and Christy Seibel and their four daughters. Rosemary is the widow of the late George Spivey, an educator and minister for 53 years. She is a retired teacher and is also the mother of Cameron Spivey and Cathy Haynes. She enjoys spending time with her family.

You're Invited

It's a fact that I was in the gym at UT for a Lady Volunteers' basketball game when the attendance count was under 250. Mom, Dad and Sadie, our neighbor, were fans in the early days. I'm telling you, we could sit anywhere, even right behind the bench. The best part for Dad was immediately after every game. The Boosters were invited to the Hospitality Room where folding tables held a buffet with plenty of good food. Dad loved it. All the players and coaches were in there and anyone could talk to them. It was not just a line for shaking hands. Naturally, Dad was telling them how to improve their game. Sadie was, too. I used to wait out in the hall because I was embarrassed to be standing around with the UT team. Can you imagine hardly anyone passing up the chance to talk to Pat Head Summitt now? She has an influence that's bigger than her chosen sport and bigger than Tennessee while her team averaged 14,000 in attendance for 2012. Because of my view of the Lady Volunteers' early days, I have this idea that much of Pat's success with people, teams, and programs came from her genuine hospitality, then and now. It's my theory.

Christian hospitality, God made clear, is accepted by Him in the simplest acts. However, where hospitality leads is in no way simple. In God's domain, hospitality is a catalyst which links vital spiritual areas. God draws the parameters very, very, very large when it comes to what He will do with our two fish and five loaves (Matthew 14:17).

Melea Nash Smith is married to Steve. They have four children, Jordan, Melea Jean, Bryan, and Sarah. Melea started her basketball career in the fourth grade on the Norris Optimist Club's orange team.

I Can Do This

"I can do all things through Christ who strengthens me" (Philippians 4:13).

This is one of my favorite verses in the Bible. It is a short little verse, but a very strong and reassuring verse. When dealing with my cancer, I had to undergo many tests. Some were MRIs, PET scans, and MRAs, just to name a few. I do not like to be in a confined area and left there all alone, because I tend to be claustrophobic. Twenty to sixty minutes inside of an enclosed machine can seem like forever. Every time I was put inside of one of these machines, I would say this verse to myself over and over again and I would sing hymns to myself, but I knew Christ was with me and helping me.

There are events and things in our lives we cannot handle alone and sometimes our loved ones cannot be there with us, but Christ is always there with us. He strengthens us above anything we can imagine. This verse not only says He will strengthen us, but we can do all things through the strength He gives us. I don't know about you, but I once considered myself a weakling.

After meditating on this verse during many difficult times, I now know I am strong because I have Christ by my side giving me strength. When you are enduring a hardship and you feel weak and alone, remember you are never alone and Christ will give you the strength you need to endure.

Sherrye Woodall is married to Gregg. They have 4 children: Stephanie Harder, Tiffany Dresser, Benjamin Woodall and Jonathan Woodall. They have 4 grand-children: Wrigley Harder, Walton Harder, Adalynn Dresser and Brooklynn Dresser. Sherrye has taught the 3 years old class at Karns for over 32 years.

Perspective

Glancing through a book of optical illusions, have you ever seen an image that can be construed as two completely different subjects, depending on how you look at it? Two people may look at the same picture; one sees an old lady and the other sees a young lady. In another image, you see a duck, but if you make the bill an ear and adjust your perception a bit, it begins to look like a rabbit.

The picture, the actual splotches of ink on the page, never changes, but our perception does. The only change is in the way we look, see, and process.

Occasionally, through history we will go through a revolutionary "paradigm shift," at which point the framework of thought changes. For a long time, the earth was thought to be the center of the universe. Then, following Galileo, a radical paradigm shift took place and suddenly the sun "became" central. Nothing about the universe changed, only the way people viewed it.

As a Christian, trying to reach others through example and attitude, I should strive to work under a framework of optimism because, after all, I am forgiven. Some of life's circumstances may be beyond our control and if you're moving through life looking for reasons to have self-pity or doubt, you will certainly find them. But what if, instead of seeing hardship, maybe I can see opportunity; instead of great earthly pain, a reminder of the coming comfort of heaven?

"For our citizenship is in heaven, from which we also eagerly wait for the Savior, the Lord Jesus Christ" (Philippians 3:20).

Kelli Boitnott is the librarian at the Southeast Institute of Biblical Studies and a speech-language pathology graduate student at the University of Tennessee. Upon graduation, she would like to work in a medical setting and become involved in research. When not in school, Kelli enjoys hiking in the Smokies, keeping up with her cooking blog, and web design.

Cherish Children

Most, or at least many of you came from homes where you were loved and cared for. How blessed you are! Today you are raising your children in that same way and teaching them to love the Lord. Unfortunately, I was not raised like that. I was fostered until I was 5 1/2 or 6 years old; bombed out of my bed while in my foster home and shortly afterwards sent to live in the country with many other children in an orphanage. This was during the years of World War II.

I never had a happy home life. I say this, not for sympathy, or "poor you" sentiment, but to remind you all to cherish your children, and give them good memories. Let them see that you love each other. Teach them early how to work, even if it's just making a bed. Teach them to obey your authority. If they don't learn this early, they will buck against all authority as they grow. As teenagers they will test this to the utmost, but you just have to continue to parent wisely.

Make your home a happy refuge. Tell them, and tell them again how much you love them, even when they're not the best behaved, even when they're being punished. Because you love them you will discipline them. Your girls will learn from their mothers how to mother, your boys will learn from their fathers how to become great dads. As you worship they will imitate you, so set a great example.

Above all - teach them to love God.

June Agee was born and raised in the UK and came to the United States when she married Wendell and became a U. S. citizen in Santa Fe, NM. June and Wendell have four living children and five grandchildren. June is a member of the Karns Church of Christ.

Can He Still Feel the Nails?

"Can he still feel the nails every time I fail? Can He hear the crowd cry "Crucify!" again? Am I causing Him pain when I know I've got to change? 'Cause I just can't bear the thought of hurting him." - Ray Boltz.

After reading the crucifixion accounts in the gospels, then watching "The Passion of Christ," how do we honestly answer, "Can He still feel the nails when I fail?" Is pain present to Christ? What is our mind-set when we meet on the first day of the week to break bread and sip the fruit of the vine? It takes no time at all to read about Jesus being arrested after praying in John 17, tossed between Pilot and Herod, the violent beatings and ridicule, Jesus' sentencing, the journey to the mount with the cross on His back, then Jesus on the cross. All of these processes took time.

Physically, we know He does not feel the pain, but I believe there is a greater pain. God became flesh, and experienced physical pain as an example of what He was willing to do for us. He experienced loneliness, shame, guilt, discouragement, separation, and temptation. He experienced these at a far higher degree than any of us. He had all sin placed upon Him. Every weight of every sin was placed on Him. When we stumble, I believe it hurts Him, but He understands we are not perfect. When we fall away or deliberately turn our backs on Him to quench our own desires, a far greater pain occurs: disappointment.

"Be faithful until death, and I will give you the crown of life" (Revelation 2:10).

Corey Moore is from Knoxville,TN. Corey enjoys studying the Bible, debating, working out, traveling, good food, working with teens and playing video games.

Be Nice

Often we may hear a mother telling her young child to "Be Nice" when they may have said or done something rash to another child. As adults, we are no less reminded to "Be Nice." We may be quick to make comments or point out our own observations about things that others have done or decided to do. We are all limited in our knowledge as to whatever facts and circumstances may have gone into someone else's actions. James says in James 1:19, "This you know, my beloved brethren. But everyone must be quick to hear, slow to speak and slow to anger;"

The words we use and the manner in which we deliver them can cause either great hurt or be wonderfully uplifting; it depends greatly upon each one of us. Paul reminds us in Colossians 4:6, "Let your speech always be with grace, as though seasoned with salt..."

Let's all resolve to keep ourselves in check so that no one needs to tell us "be nice," but rather we will be doing so already. Paul said in Ephesians 4:32, "Be kind to one another, tender-hearted, forgiving each other, just as God in Christ also has forgiven you."

The many good thoughts and words that you have written on the cards you have sent to the elders from time to time are very encouraging and uplifting. I keep them by my bedside and occasionally pull one out to read and remind me how blessed I am to have such a wonderful and nice church family.

Gregg Woodall is an elder of the Karns Church of Christ. Gregg is married to Sherrye and they have four children, Stephanie, Tiffany, Benjamin, and Jonathan. They also have four grandchildren, Wrigley, Walton, Adalynn, and Brooklynn. Gregg enjoys golfing, dirt bike riding, spending time with family, and is a fan of the Tennessee Volunteers.

Outdoing Each Other

You know that feeling you get when you outdo someone? Maybe you received the highest grade, or you ran up the score against your opponent in a sporting event. Perhaps your joke received the loudest and longest laughs, or all the women just had to have the recipe for your latest and greatest potluck dish.

Growing up with three brothers, there were many opportunities to compete with and outdo each other. When it came to academics, they had no choice but to compete against me. They had to go to school, had to take the tests, and had to bring the scores home to show the family. Each time their report cards came home, they got to be outdone by me once again.

One day I decided to decorate my wall with my academic awards and certificates. My brother, not quite the academic that I was, didn't particularly care for my choice of decorations. The next day I returned home to discover that he had permanently inscribed the phrase "the nut" in between my first and last name on several of my certificates.

That has been one of the strongest lessons I have learned in life, and it was well worth the price. The lesson is that I need to consider how the other person might feel when I outdo them. Paul inverts the whole outdoing others thing when he challenges us to outdo each other (Romans 12:10). I realized that day the effect my "trophy" display had on my brother. Just imagine the love others would have for us if we would outdo them in the way Paul recommends!

Chris Cox serves as a deacon at the Karns congregation. He is also a computer programmer and small business owner. Chris is married to Hannah, and they have two children, Samuel and Rachel. Chris enjoys gardening, reading non-fiction, learning new things, teaching others, and spending time with his family.

Strong Heart

"You also be patient. Establish your hearts, for the coming of the Lord is at hand" (James 5:8).

On December 22, 2005, Matt Long, a member of the New York City Fire Department was riding his bike to a training session when he was hit by a twenty-ton bus. The bus didn't just knock Long down; it ran OVER him. Long was impaled by his bike and suffered numerous other traumas. Amazingly, he was not killed even though the injuries he sustained were almost unspeakable. Rescue workers extracted his body from the wreckage and transported him to a hospital where he received 68 units of blood and had 22 surgeries before his release five months later. The doctors working on Long were astounded that his heart was still pumping until a family member explained that Long had just qualified for the Boston Marathon and was attempting to qualify for the Ironman Championship in Kona, HI. Because he was in top physical condition, Long's heart was strong enough to keep pumping even though the rest of the body was broken.

Your physical heart is important, but how strong is your spiritual heart? Are you exercising it daily through prayer and study so you can survive the wrecks Satan sends your way? If we strengthen our spiritual hearts as Long did his physical heart, Satan cannot send anything big enough to stop it from beating for God. Matt Long is still competing because his heart was strong. Is your heart strong enough to keep you in the race that ends in heaven (2 Timothy 4:7-8)?

Brad Alsup serves as a deacon at the Karns church of Christ. He is married to Jennifer, and they have two children, Evan and Allie. Brad is a hunter, a cyclist, and an avid reader.

Love Your Neighbor

During the Great Depression, my grandmother was suddenly widowed with eight children to house and feed. She was in her late 30's and had a third grade education. Her oldest child had recently graduated high school; the youngest was still in diapers. Faced with caring for children ranging from toddlers to teenagers the future looked bleak. They were poor tenant farmers in the Appalachian hills of Tennessee. They had no car. They had no horse. All they had was one milk cow–the family's only source of milk for the children and cooking. Their home had no electricity, no inside running water, no phone. They were isolated.

After my grandfather's funeral, the mortuary came knocking on Grandma's door demanding payment for the burial services. Grandma had no money. The milk cow was her only asset. The funeral home was going to take the family's only source of milk when a neighbor saw the commotion going on and came over. She told the bill collector to leave the poor lady alone and the good neighbor paid the money owed to the funeral home.

The Bible tells us to love our neighbors as ourselves. This good neighbor certainly took matters into her own hands and did what she could to help save this family from certain disaster. What kind of a neighbor are you?

"And the second, like it, is this: 'You shall love your neighbor as yourself. ' There is no other commandment greater than these" (Mark 12:31).

Sharon Cawood is an Executive Sales Coordinator with N2 Publishing. She recruits for the State of Alabama and owns and manages two publications in the West Knoxville area. Both of Sharon's children are grown and gainfully employed. She has 3 grandchildren and 4 granddogs.

In the Bleachers or In the Game?

There is nothing wrong with being a sports fan as long as you are bringing glory to God. I loved to watch sports of all kinds with my father. I've played on the field and court, been team manager, taken game statistics, kept official game books, and have even cheered on the varsity cheer squad.

Sitting in the bleachers is VERY different from suiting up to play. In order to play you have to prepare both mentally and physically. You have to learn the game and show up for daily practices, whether you are too tired or not. You have to put in extra time to work on your skills outside of practice. You have to agree to work with the team instead of only for yourself. You have to run the plays called by the coach. You have to build your confidence through hard work so that when the time comes, you'll be ready. Anyone can learn to play if they faithfully prepare for the game.

Following Christ requires the same type of commitment. You have to dress out, clothed in the spirit of Christ and full armor of God. You have to learn the game plan, show up, and work within the body of Christ, His church. You have to prepare mentally and build your faith by studying the Bible, meditating on His word day and night, and pray without ceasing.

In 1 Peter 4:7-11, we are called to a life of service and involvement with the purpose of bringing glory to God through Jesus Christ. Let's all decide today to get off of the bleachers and get in the game!!

Christy Seibel attends the Karns Church of Christ. Christy is married to John and they have four children, Lindsey, Mary Beth, Emily, and Jeanne. Christy enjoys spending time with the family and friends, hiking, reading, cooking with the family, watching family movies, and John's homemade hot fudge sauce!

Where's the Whisky?

I started a new job in the fall of the year. One of my first trips was to a customer in Johnson City, Tennessee. He was already talking about Christmas and how each salesman that called on him was to give him a bottle of whiskey for Christmas.

I told him that I too was excited about Christmas because I had three small children who enjoyed the Christmas season. On my next visit to this particular customer, he again talked about Christmas. I don't think he was celebrating the birth of Christ but was more interested in receiving gifts. Again he indicated that he would not buy products from a salesman who did not give him a fifth of whiskey for Christmas.

I called my boss and related this to him. He indicated that giving whiskey as business gifts was sometimes done. I thought about it and decided that if I had to give him whiskey for his business I probably didn't need his business. Christmas came and afterward I visited this customer. Although I was apprehensive, the subject never came up about my lack of the Christmas gift. He continued to purchase my products.

The Bible tells us to be in the world but not of the world in Romans 12:1,2, "Do not conform to the world but be transformed by the renewing of your mind."

Today try to do God's will because it is good, pleasing and perfect.

Ken Couch is a sales representative for Royal Brass and Hose, an industrial hose and fitting supplier in Knoxville Tn. He regularly travels in his job throughout East Tennessee, Eastern Kentucky and Southwestern Virginia. He enjoys high shool football and following the Tennessee Volunteers.

God's Remedy for Depression

Elijah was one of the great prophets of the Old Testament. He had met and overcome the four hundred fifty prophets of Baal and had them all put to death (1 Kings 18:22ff). When Jezebel heard about it she swore that Elijah would be dead by tomorrow (1 Kings 19:1-2). Elijah became so depressed that he went and set down under a juniper tree and asked God to take his life (1 Kings 19:4).

How did God take care of Elijah's depression? First, he took care of his physical needs. He told him to "arise and eat" (1 Kings 19:5-8). Depressed people are usually physically and emotionally exhausted.

Second, he dealt with him gently by asking questions to get his mind off of himself. "What are you doing here, Elijah?" (1 Kings 19:9, 13). This led Elijah to express what was happening in his life and how he felt about it (1 Kings 19:10, 14).

Third, God gave him something to do. "Go, return on your way to the Wilderness of Damascus; and when you arrive, anoint Hazael as king over Syria. Also you shall anoint Jehu the son of Nimshi as king over Israel. And Elisha the son of Shaphat of Abel Meholah you shall anoint as prophet in your place" (1 Kings 19:15-16).

Fourth, he gave him a friend. Elijah found Elisha, cast his mantle over him, and Elisha then arose, went after Elijah, and ministered unto him (1 Kings 19:21b). Everyone needs a friend, but especially when depressed. God's remedy for depression should be helpful to those who are depressed.

James Meadows was born March 10, 1930. He graduated from High School in 1949, and Freed-Hardeman College in 1955. He later attended Union University and Harding Graduate School. He has done local work in Tennessee, Kentucky, and South Carolina. He served as Director of ETSPM from 1996 to 2006, and presently serves as Dean of Students.

Be Still and Know that I am God

Daddy was a quiet man. He could spend hours upon hours by himself. As he grew older and as disease riddled his body, he spent more and more time in his paradise of a back yard. There seemed to be more to his little paradise than just dirt. This is where he felt his hurt, cried his tears, and where he spent a lot of time in conversation with God. I never heard him complain much; he chose to leave his burdens outside and with God.

Through the years, Daddy learned to know his land and the soil that comprised it. We always had a garden to eat from through the summer and, through his and Momma's foresight and work, were able to continue eating good stuff right up until the next season when his wonderful garden would produce for him again.

Daddy not only knew his garden and the soil in it, but he knew his Creator as well. He spent many hours studying his Bible and getting to know God. He had a personal relationship with both that could easily be envied by those on the outside looking in.

I remember seeing Daddy reading his Bible at night. It was on his bedside table, but, no dust could be found on top of it. He knew his Bible and would have an answer if you cared to ask a question. He had a way of asking you questions that would spark a desire in you to find the answer.

We too, have the opportunity to know God just as my Daddy did. Daddy did not give God the time he had left over in a day; he made time for Him. His knowledge of what made God who He is did not happen by accident. When I grow up, I want to be just like him!

Jean Thomas is married to Lloyd and they have 3 daughters, Dana, Amanda, and Casey. They are blessed to have 4 granddaughters, Jayde, Heidi, Lily, and Mya, and one on the way. Jean loves spending time with Lloyd, having sleep-overs with her grand-daughters, and crafting of all kinds, especially sewing.

Jesus Says

Have you ever played "Simon Says?" If you haven't, here's the idea: one person stands in front of two or more people and says, "Simon says. . . ." and that person might say, ". . . stand on one leg." Everybody does it and if they don't, then they're out.

Jesus is our Simon. He asks us to do things we don't always want to do and may not even think are very reasonable. However, if we don't do what He asks, we won't stay in the game. Once we're out, it can be tough to make yourself get back in. God's word says that if we follow Jesus's example and obey His commands, we will have eternal life with Him. In John 3:36, we read that, "He who believes in the Son has eternal life; but he who does not obey the Son will not see life, but the wrath of God abides on him."

Along the way, we can help others and be a stepping stone instead of a stumbling block for them on the road to salvation. Consider Romans 14:19, 21, which says, "Therefore let us pursue the things which make for peace and the things by which one may edify another...It is good neither to eat meat nor drink wine nor do anything by which your brother stumbles or is offended or is made weak."

It may take a while to finish, but let's be able to say as Paul said in 2 Timothy 4:7-8, "I have fought the good fight, I have finished the race, I have kept the faith. Finally, there is laid up for me the crown of righteousness, which the Lord, the righteous Judge, will give to me on that Day, and not to me only but also to all who have loved His appearing." Let's make sure that we are doing what Jesus says.

Mary Beth Seibel attends the Karns Church of Christ with her parents, John and Christy Seibel, and her three sisters. Mary Beth is an active member of the Karns Youth Group and enjoys pandas, purple, eating chocolate, playing with her dog, Bella, and spending time with family and friends.

Shrewd

Each year, Apple hosts the WWDC (Word Wide Developer's Conference) at which time they roll out their newest and coolest upgrades and gadgets. This conference is the culmination of a year's worth of dreaming, planning, research, and development by the people at Apple. And as a result, each year I am "wowed" at some of the new technology.

In Luke 16:1-13, Jesus commends this steward, not for his dishonesty, but for his shrewdness, and then says, "For the sons of this world are more shrewd in their generation than the sons of light" (Luke 16:8). In other words, could it be that "the world" dreams bigger, plans better, works harder, troubleshoots longer, and advertises louder for things that will perish than God's people do for that which is eternal?

Friends, what "wow" moments are we creating for the kingdom of God? What have we done to cause people to sit up and take notice? How much time are we spending as individuals or collectively in dreaming, planning, and troubleshooting for the kingdom's sake? Can you remember the last time you got together with fellow Christians for the purpose of brainstorming about the work of the church? Have you ever done that?

Without changing the gospel, can we not; should we not; must we not tweak, streamline, jettison, and enhance how we do what we do as the church? Paul instructed Titus to "adorn" the doctrine of God (Titus 2:10). To adorn something is to make something more beautiful or attractive. Let's be shrewd and do what we can to adorn the doctrine of God.

Steve Higginbotham has been the pulpit minister for the Karns church of Christ since 2010. Steve is married to Kim and they have four children, Kelli, Michael, Matthew, and Anne Marie. Steve enjoys writing, playing golf, and is a fan of the Pittsburgh Steelers, the WVU Mountaineers, and the Andy Griffith Show.

God's Gifts

Throughout the Bible we see many examples of God's love demonstrated through Him giving gifts. When the Jews were brought out of Egypt and were wandering in the desert, we read of the manna being given from heaven. This gift from God not only included manna, but quail as well. Although these gifts were from God, we read that the people of Israel had to rise up early to gather the manna. If they did not gather it early, it would spoil. It was a gift from God, but they had to do something in order to receive the gift.

When the Lord gave the city of Jericho to the people of Israel, he promised to deliver it into their hand. However, there were certain conditions that had to be met. They could not simply do nothing and receive the city. We read that they had to follow specific instructions from God to march around the city for seven days before the city would be delivered into their hands.

So it is today; God has given us a gift far above any gift that could be given. However, there is nothing in God's Book that God promises to give us without action on our part. Christ died for us, He has provided salvation, and God is willing to give us remission of our sins, but there are certain things that we must do in order to appropriate that gift. We must ask ourselves: are we sitting and waiting for the walls to fall down?

Tony Williams is originally from Chattanooga and was baptized at the East Ridge congregation. He is married to Deanna, and they have three daughters, Claire, Maggie, and Ella. Tony has a Bachelor's and Master's Degree from UT. Tony and his family have been at Karns since 1999, and during that time he has served as a deacon, and currently as an elder.

Do Something Small Today

The story of Naaman, the commander of the Syrian army, who was cured of leprosy by dipping seven times in the Jordan River as recorded in 2 Kings, chapter 5, is one of the more well-known stories in the Bible. The principle message of the story is the necessity of trusting God and being obedient to his commands. An important but less emphasized lesson is the role of servants in Naaman being cured.

It was a young captive girl from Israel, a servant of Naaman's wife, who informed Naaman of a prophet in Israel who could heal him of his leprosy. A letter from the king of Syria on behalf of Naaman to a king in Israel accomplished nothing, but it was a servant of the prophet, Elisha, who told Naaman what he must do to be cured. When Naaman refused to do as he was told because it was not what he expected, it was Naaman's servants who convinced him to do what he was told. A young servant girl was responsible for getting this powerful man started toward being obedient to God and cured of his leprosy.

Sometimes, we may think if we cannot do something big that gets headlines or if our deeds don't get noticed, it is not worth the effort. Little people, as the world sees them, doing small things can have a big impact on the spiritual lives of people. Zechariah said, "For who has despised the days of small things?" (Zech. 4:10). Do something small today!

Don Denton serves as an elder of the Karns Church of Christ. He is married to Margaret Rymer and they have three children, Richard, Jeffrey and Leigh. They also have eight grandchildren, Clifton, Micah, Caitlin, Hunter, Sara, Denton, Joshua and Quincy. Don enjoys hiking, travel and Tennessee football and basketball.

Love as Seen Through a Small Boy's Eyes

This is an essay written by a little boy:

Love is something that makes two people think they are pretty when nobody else does. It also makes them sit close together on a bench when there is plenty of room on both ends. Love is something that young people have, but that old people don't have, because it is all about dimples, and star-like eyes, and curls that old folks don't have. It is something that makes two people very quiet when you are around; also very quiet when you aren't - only in a different way. When they talk, it's all about dreams and roses and moonbeams. When I grow up, I'm not going to fall in love. But if I do, she's got to let me say what to do and let me run everything. And that's what I know about love until I grow up.

Where do you suppose he got his ideas? Love is a friendship that has caught fire. It is quiet understanding, mutual confidence, sharing and forgiving. It is a loyalty through good and bad. It settles for less than perfection and makes allowances for human weaknesses.

Love is content with the present, hopes for the future and doesn't brood over the past. It's the day-in and day-out chronicle of irritations, problems, compromises, small disappointments, big victories and working toward common goals.

If you have love in your life, it can make up for a great many things you lack. If you don't have it, no matter what else there is, it's not enough. If your children or friends wrote an essay about your love, what would it say?

Doris Finger was born in Knoxville and has lived in Knoxville all her life except for 3 years. She is currently retired and enjoys spending her time helping others. Doris has taught primary classes for 45 years with 42 of those years here at the Karns congregation!

Fighting Through the Pain

The past few years have been very rough for me. I think it was three years ago when I found out I had ulcerative colitis. It hit me so suddenly that I did not know how to act. I have been in and out of the hospital quite a few times. It sometimes got to the point that I couldn't stand it anymore.

I've really prayed when I was sick. My family and many of you prayed for me to get better. At times I just wanted to give up, but I didn't because I knew that because I am a child of God, He could heal me just like he heals many others, or he could use to reach others through my illness.

My illness really prevented me from doing some things, such as going to school, being on the swim team, eating my favorite foods and, most importantly, it prevented me from going to church.

Last year at school I missed approximately sixty-eight days. It was very hard for me to catch up on all of my school work, but the good thing is that I ended up passing the eleventh grade. I don't know how I did it. Wait, of course I know how I did it. I did it with God's help.

Never doubt that God can heal the sick. Through all of my hard times, I've known that He can. Deuteronomy 32:39 says, "Now see that I, even I, am He, And there is no God besides Me; I kill and I make alive; I wound and I heal; Nor is there any who can deliver from My hand."

Allen Walling is 18 years old and is currently a senior attending Bearden High School. Allen moved from Gettysburg, PA to Knoxville about five years ago, and has been attending Karns church of Christ ever since. Allen is involved in chorus and theater at school.

Fear of God

While our God is a tender, merciful and loving God, He is also a God to be feared. Consider the testimony from a few of the experts. Adam ate from the tree and was afraid (Genesis 3:10). David's flesh trembles for fear of God (Psalm 119:120). Moses taught the Israelites of God's willingness to destroy. There was fear in every soul in the days of the early Church (Acts 2:43) and there was great fear following the death of Ananias and Saphira (Acts 5).

Clearly, it is a good thing to be afraid of God, but why? Here's a short, but motivating, list of reasons from scripture:

Fear of God is part of working out our salvation (Philippians 2:12).

It, in part, brings about complete holiness (2 Corinthians 7:1).

Psalm 19:9 says that "the fear of the Lord is clean."

Proverbs 9:10 says "the fear of the Lord is the beginning of wisdom."

Equally persuasive is the description of people who don't fear God from Romans 3:9-18. They are liars, shedders of blood, unrighteous, worthless and in their paths are ruin and misery.

A proper fear of God is a healthy thing!

Don Scott was recruited to Knoxville from his home state of Virginia by his wife of 20 years, Amy, who is also responsible for bringing him to Christ. Don works from home as an engineer and Amy stays busy as a homeschooling mom. The children love to volunteer with various camps, little leagues, and scouting organizations.

Thinking Problem

When faced with a problem, I think. Ok, I over-think. I'll think in the box, out of the box, on top of the box... whatever it takes. I'll wrestle with the problem until I look as though I was in a street fight. And I lost.

Our ability to think through problems is a gift. But sometimes, we start believing that if we haven't solved every problem that we face, well, we just haven't "thought hard enough." We start believing we can and should handle everything life throws at us.

Then comes "that day." A crisis that hits you in the gut. You try to "figure it all out." You wonder how in the world you're going to solve this thing. But you can't. Despite everything in your soul, you just can't. It's too big. What do you do then?

I've been to this point. But I have learned something wonderful. Ephesians 3:20 says "Now to Him who is able to do exceedingly abundantly above all that we ask or think, according to the power that works in us."

God is bigger than I am. He can deal with things that I just can't handle. If it's too heavy for me, I can cast my care onto him. I may not understand all of God's ways, but I know they are bigger than mine. He will make it all work out in the end.

And during those moments when I understand this, I can rest just a little... and not think so hard.

Alan Goins is a 53 year-old Corporate Financial Analyst here in Knoxville. He is from the mountains of Eastern KY. He would rather sing for a living than count numbers, but he just can't figure out a way to get paid for his voice. At least not yet.

Prayer

I was mad. I knew it was wrong but there it was. My husband had just buried his grandfather, and he and his mother were taking his recently widowed grandmother to a new home. I was in the old home, cleaning it out, and I was mad. I didn't begrudge cleaning out the house; it was the least I could do. I wasn't alone however, my daughter and my niece were with me. Thankfully they did not require all my attention but neither could they commiserate with me or help me.

I was lying awake one night fully aware of my anger and that it was inhibiting me from doing what I needed to do. I sat up and opened James and still struggled. I realized I had not asked God for help with my burden. I opened my mouth and prayed out loud for God to take over. I told Him I knew that I could not do this job, that anger was the barrier and that He's the only one I could trust to help me get through it. I asked Him to take the anger from me so I could be who I needed to be and do what I needed to do.

After saying "Amen," the most incredible feeling of peace came over me. It was sudden and complete. God had answered my prayer. I was able to complete what others were counting on me to do, and I did so with a joyous heart. When the heart is sincere, God answers prayer (Psalm 37:8-9).

Mary Lindner has been a member of the Karns congregation since 2011. She is married to Kyle and they have one child, Kathryn. Mary likes traveling, reading and knitting; often managing to do the last two at the same time. A recent transplant from Minnesota, Mary is enjoying the lush scenery and temperate weather of her new home.

Trust

At some time in our lives we have all had to trust someone or something that we didn't necessarily want to trust. It might have been when climbing a tree as a child and trusting that a small limb wouldn't break. It might have been trusting that our doctor would make the right moves when we were on the operating table. Regardless, trust is something all of us have had to display at one time or another.

What makes trusting difficult? Often it is because we trust ourselves, because we think we know our capabilities, but we aren't so sure about someone or something else. Maybe it is because the person we need to trust has not displayed consistent trustworthiness.

Do you remember the comfort of nestling next to your mother or father when you were small and a thunderstorm came roaring through? What was it about them that made you feel secure? It's likely because they were always there, no matter what, to reassure and comfort you in times of stress or fear.

God is our comforter. He promised that He would never, never forsake us, but we frequently do not really trust Him. Often, rather than having faith that God will provide what we need, we want to be in control. James wrote that we should not be so sure about this life because it may not be here tomorrow. Today, let's trust God in every way knowing He is who He says He is.

Conrad Slate graduated from Tennessee Tech, and was a member of the Air National Guard for 31 years, retiring as a Colonel. He holds a MS in Financial Services. Currently he is a principal in Slate, Disharoon, Parrish & Associates, a fee based financial planning firm. Married to Brenda for over 40 years, they have two children and three grandchildren.

Decisions, Decisions

When you have decisions of real significance it can be very daunting if you believe you must make them on your own. There have been two occasions where the decisions that I made had a lifelong impact: choosing my husband and being the caretaker for my son.

In college I prayed for God to help me find the right person to marry. At a public university in Ohio, this was no easy task. There were times when I thought that a different path was the one God had in mind for me. I never expected I would meet my husband the way that I did. My senior year, I was pursuing a job in the South in hopes of meeting a Christian there. God had another path for me. Mike and I sat next to each other on exactly the right day, when our teacher asked us to keep our seats for the remainder of the semester. The rest is history.

When my son was born with two heart defects, every day of life was a gift. While he was home, I was his caretaker and the responsibility was enormous. I prayed that God would guide every decision I made, knowing that with this guidance His will would be done. Rowan lived to be three months old. Had I not asked for God's guidance, I would certainly doubt the decisions that I made the night Rowan died.

I am so blessed to have the peace of knowing that God guided me during these times of great decisions. If God is in it, your decision will always be the right ones.

Gerri Nath has been a member at Karns since 2009 and has been a Christian since 1977. Gerri is married to Michael and they have a daughter, Elliana Grace. She is the Vice President of Accounting Services at Marriott International, Inc. , and enjoys spending time with Ellie, watching her play softball, photography, traveling, scrap booking, reading, and writing.

Evidence of Things Not Seen

The preservation of the Bible to this day is, to me, evidence that it is the sacred Word of God.

- The fact that the theme of the Bible is harmonious, though written by so many over such a long time, is evidence of divine inspiration.
- The fact that the words within it have changed the minds and lives of persons over centuries is an evidence that it is God breathed.
- The fact that scribes trembled at the possibility of adding or subtracting from Scripture is evidence that we have preserved for us today the very thoughts of God in language plain enough for all to understand.

This is in no way a complete list of reasons. However, the attempt here is not to convince anyone of the inspiration of Scripture by facts or evidences. God requires us to have the faith that what he has revealed to us is truth. "Your word is truth" says John 17:17. We were, after all, not present for the creation or the resurrection. Yet, Scripture challenges us to credit God because of the evidence we do see.

"For since the creation of the world His invisible attributes are clearly seen, being understood by the things that are made, even His eternal power and Godhead, so that they are without excuse" (Romans 1:20).

When all the evidence is in, faith is essential, but not blind. I wrote this to give a friend some years ago. You may have a friend to share this with as well.

Sara Terlecki is married to her husband Bill. They moved to Knoxville from Ohio. Sara has worked in the church office since 2010. They have two grown children. Gerri married Michael Nath and blessed them with granddaughter, Ellie. Bill Jr. married Hope Whittington and blessed them with two grandsons, Allen and Evan.

Does Our Name Really Matter?

I was recently in a Bible study with a married couple and during the conversation the question was asked, "Why does the name of the church matter?" I have often been asked this question and I use the illustration of marriage to answer, "Why does it matter?"

I asked the woman, "When you got married to this man, whose name did you take?" I have always received the same answer: "My husband's name." Then I asked, "Why did you do such a thing?" Her explanation was, "As part of the marriage ceremony. He gave me his name to wear to show that I belonged to him."

I agreed with her explanation and asked her what she thought her husband's reaction would be if she decided she did not really care for his name and chose a name like "Jones" that is easier to pronounce. I have always received a "have you lost your mind" look which, eventually, takes the conversation back to the church.

The Bible teaches that when we are baptized into Christ, we become a part of His church and the church is described as the bride of Christ (Ephesians 5:22-32). We take on or wear His name to show that we belong to Him. Let us wear the name of Christ faithfully and actively! As Christians, we must be willing to do the work of the church wherever we find ourselves and remember that the truth is all about Christ and not about the individual. May God bless you as you continue on your Christian journey.

Jeremy Gillentine is married to Amber Gillentine (13 years) and has four children Sidney (11), Hutson (9), Raegen (7), Linden (4). He is currently a student at the Southeast Institute of Biblical Studies.

The Doctor with Credentials

While sitting in the doctor's office awaiting a routine checkup, I felt a searing pain in my side. I became somewhat concerned, until I looked up on the door leading into the clinic and noticed nine names all followed by the letters, MD! I felt immediate relief knowing that however this pain manifested itself, I could have nine capable doctors caring for me in a matter of seconds!

As Christians we can draw even more comfort knowing that we have the "Great Physician" always available to help in time of need. Isaiah writes, "Behold, the LORD's hand is not shortened, that it cannot save; nor His ear heavy, that it cannot hear" (Isaiah 59:1). Peter adds, "casting all your care upon Him, for He cares for you" (1 Peter 5:7). Most assuredly, there is no pain that God cannot heal, emptiness that He cannot fill, or worry that He cannot silence. He knows our thoughts, is mindful of each concern, and yes, is familiar with each painful flare-up, for He is our Creator!

I am certainly glad I have a qualified personal caretaker whose name is followed by MD. However, I am more grateful to be acquainted with a higher being whose name is Jehovah, followed by the letters, G-O-D! This "Great Physician" is always "on-call," always has an appointment available, and needs no referral. That referral has already been delivered, having been written in blood by His only begotten Son over 2000 years ago!

John Hoffarth has been a Christian for over 20 years and enjoys sharing the faith with friends or those seeking a stronger relationship with God. He also likes trying any new activity that challenges his fears or physical endurance. To relax, he enjoys the opportunity to travel abroad or spend quality time at home with his wife Karen and son Austin.

Smile Power

Tired and weary, I had started home from the hospital to have a pity party. It had been a long day sitting with a sick friend. Going out into the crowded lobby, I noticed a black man, pushing a dolly, entering through a side entrance. His facial expression indicated that he was tired and having difficulty maneuvering through the crowd. I smiled and spoke as he passed. He acknowledged me with a slight nod but the expression on his face never changed.

I had almost reached the outside door when I heard some-one yell "Hey, lady." I turned and looked back, as did others, and saw him weaving his dolly back through the crowd in my direction. When he reached me he said, "Thank you. This has been a rough one but your smile just made my day, and I wanted you to know."

As he turned to leave, I noticed that he was smiling. For a moment, I stood there in amazement; then, it hit me. I had just witnessed "smile power" in action.

I have read that a smile is a blessing when you give it away. It was truly a blessing for me for it completely changed my attitude about my whole day. It revived my spirit, put a song in my heart, and made me happy knowing that my smile had made a difference in the day of a stranger.

Gloom and doom were never meant for display on the fac-es of children of the King. Put a smile on your face and don't be choosy about a recipient for all people smile in the same language.

Jane Higdon is a widow of 28 years and a retired Administrative Secretary. She has a daughter and a son, three grandchildren and five great grandchildren. She enjoys cooking and eating; watching sports, especially Tennessee football and Braves baseball; eating; grading Bible Correspondence courses; and get-togethers with her church family.

The Peace of God

"Be anxious for nothing, but in everything by prayer and supplication, with thanksgiving, let your requests be made known to God; and the peace of God, which surpasses all understanding, will guard your hearts and minds through Christ Jesus" (Philippians 4:6-7).

This is one of my favorite passages in the Bible because it shows the power of prayer to calm our troubled lives. But what is the peace of God? One event in my life best describes the feeling you have when the peace of God guards your heart and mind.

I was a young officer in the Army during Operation Desert Storm. My unit was the lead unit for the ground phase of the war and engaged in heavy combat. The last night of the ground war was the worst of all. There were explosions all around and bullets flying in every direction. I should have been scared out of my mind, but was not. A complete sense of calm washed over me and I felt no fear. It was like being surrounded by a protective sphere. I knew that nothing would happen to me and was able to complete my mission.

When you earnestly pray to God, and look to him for comfort, you are in the protective sphere of God's arms. The peaceful feeling you have cannot be explained, but you know that God will take care of you. So, in everything by prayer and supplication, with thanksgiving, let your request be made known to God. In that way you will know the peace of God.

Tony Turner is a retired Army officer who has been a member of the Karns Church of Christ since May 2011. He works at the Oak Ridge National Laboratory. He is married to Kathy and has three children: Richard, age 17; Joel, age 15; and Brigitte, age 9. He enjoys watching high school and college football, playing golf, and officiating soccer.

Rejoicing and Weeping

"Rejoice with those who rejoice and weep with those who weep" (Romans 12:15). Over the last 2 years, we have had many babies born, many weddings, many graduations, many anniversaries, many baptisms and many who have been restored to the Lord. All of these give us reasons to rejoice with our brothers and sisters in Christ. It is easy to rejoice with those who rejoice and encourage each other. But we also have had many who have passed from this life leaving behind spouses, children and friends. Some have divorced, some have suffered with health problems or personal problems and some have turned away from Christ. These brothers and sisters are weeping and sometimes we are weeping with them. Every Christian has times of rejoicing and times of weeping, we as their church family should share in the rejoicing and weeping.

Christ attended weddings and rejoiced with these people. He also wept over the death of His friend, and was saddened by those who betrayed or turned away from Him.

For us to weep and rejoice with our church family, we have to know our brothers and sisters in Christ. In order to truly know them, we must spend time with our church family. The elders have arranged many opportunities for us to have fellowship with one another outside of the worship services. Take advantage of these opportunities, open yourself up and let someone who loves you in. When was the last time you rejoiced with a brother or sister? How about weeping with them? "Bear one another's burdens, and so fulfill the law of Christ" (Galatians 6:2).

Sherrye Woodall is married to Gregg. They have 4 children: Stephanie Harder, Tiffany Dresser, Benjamin Woodall and Jonathan Woodall. They have 4 grandchildren: Wrigley Harder, Walton Harder, Adalynn Dresser and Brooklynn Dresser. Sherrye has taught the 3 years old class at Karns for over 32 years.

Where Everyone Knows Your Name

Several years ago there was a program on television that had a rather catchy tune and lyrics. Over lunch one day a friend of mine remarked, "You know that song is talking about the Church." Over the years and with every move our family has made, I've reflected on my friend's statement. It is an amazing blessing to be a child of God and part of His family. Everywhere we have ever lived there have been brothers and sisters welcoming us into the fold; sharing our burdens as well as our triumphs; always ready to lend a supporting hand, or perhaps just an ear!

Scriptures like Ephesians 4:2, I Thessalonians 5:11 and James 5:16 help us understand some of the tremendous benefits of being in the body of Christ. Ultimately, our sincere love and appreciation for one another will impact the lives of those around us and lend credence to the Lord's words in John 13:35. That theme song (from decades ago) was based on a TV show far removed from the ideals of God's word. However, I think the lyrics of that song can be applied to the Church family.

"Making your way in the world today takes everything you've got. Taking a break from all your worries, sure would help a lot. Wouldn't you like to get away? Sometimes you want to go where everybody knows your name, and they're always glad you came. You wanna be where you can see our troubles are all the same You wanna be where everybody knows your name. You wanna go where people know people are all the same. You wanna go where everybody knows your name."

Phoebe was a faithful servant in the church at Cenchrea (Romans 16:1-2). However, in this case, Phoebe is the pen name of one of our sisters in Christ here at Karns.

In All We Do

One of my favorite scriptures is Mark 12:30: "Love the Lord your God with all your heart and with all your soul and with all your mind and with all your strength."

Love the Lord with all your mind—This is what we think. Do we think on things such as complaining, crude jokes, gossiping, what the girl in the next office is wearing or should we say not wearing. . . or do we see the good in the person next to us, the sunset, the laughter, the new Christian?

With all your heart—This is what we feel. How do we feel about our neighbors, our co-workers, our family, the sinner living next door, the books we read, what our children are being taught in school, what we see and hear on TV and radio?

With all your strength—This covers what we do daily. Do we stand up for what is right? Do we dress modestly when others are dressing immodestly? Do we turn off the television when others just "overlook" the bad language, sexuality, violence, crude humor, and the degrading of those things which are good? Do we stop the gossiper in their tracks or turn the other way?

With all your soul—This encompasses our deepest being; the immortal part of man; that part which will one day be in heaven or hell.

This passage reminds us that everything we think, everything we say, everything we feel, and everything we do is to be God-centered. Strive this day to make our thoughts, our words, our feelings and our actions to always be as God commands.

Terry Albert is a home-school mom of two teenagers and a 4-H volunteer leader with a BS in Animal Science and MS in Rehabilitation Counseling. Her hobbies include reading and sharing the family's many animals through a variety of 4-H, school, and community activities.

Wanted: Faithful Fathers

A few years ago, a family went searching for a new congregation. They left the comforts they had known for nine years in search of something different. As they visited various congregations, a pattern emerged that was alarming. After each visit, without exception, they would ask the question: Where are all the fathers?

At what point did a large number of men in the Lord's church decide it was time to shirk the responsibility of leading their families? Furthermore, how many men are physically present, but check their spiritual leadership at the door on the way out of worship?

Eddie Watkins, in the August 2010 edition of Christian Worker, wrote, "A father is a walking, talking, breathing, and living object lesson for his children. Children learn what to think and believe [...] from their fathers. [...]It's walking with them and showing them how to live." Mr. Watkins' words seem to dovetail nicely with what we see in an Old Testament passage–an intense walk-along, talk-along relationship between a father and his children (Deuteronomy 6:7). It is important for fathers to teach their children and encourage them as they grow to "set their hope in God" (Psalm 78:7). We need to live our lives so that future generations will not remember us as being "stubborn and rebellious...whose heart was not steadfast, whose spirit was not faithful to God" (Psalm 78:8).

Fathers, accept the responsibility God has given you!

Jason Jarrett is married to Amber and they have three children, Maddy, Tyler, and Daniel. Jason grew up in Benton, KY. Jason has a B. S. Degree in Computer Science from FHU, and is currently a student at SEIBS. Jason enjoys gardening, home improvement projects, genealogy, basketball, and spending time with his family and friends.

A Cross With Wheels

A few years ago, I passed two men along the side of the road carrying crosses, followed by a crowd of about 30 or 40 people. As I passed these two men, I looked at the crosses they were carrying and I couldn't help but notice that both crosses were accessorized with wheels!

Now, I understand why they placed wheels on their crosses. The wheels made the crosses they were carrying easier to carry. The wheels made the crosses more convenient to bear. But that's the impetus for this article. You see, there's nothing convenient about a cross! In fact, it was designed to be an inconvenient, excruciating, and humiliating means to kill someone.

Convenient crosses? They don't exist. . . or at least shouldn't. But from my observations, more than a few people have attempted to accessorize their cross. Unwilling to reject Christ completely, they have attempted to fashion a cross of convenience - crosses with wheels.

However, the cross is more than an icon we wear around our necks, dangle from our ears, or even tattoo on our bodies. The cross represents selflessness, sacrifice, obedience, dedication, and self-denial.

My advice to those who wish to gain public attention by carrying a cross - take off the wheels! Those wheels are incongruous with the message of the cross.

May God give us strength to embrace all the sacrifice and self-denial required to daily "take up our cross."

Steve Higginbotham has been the pulpit minister for the Karns church of Christ since 2010. Steve is married to Kim and they have four children, Kelli, Michael, Matthew, and Anne Marie. Steve enjoys writing, playing golf, and is a fan of the Pittsburgh Steelers, the WVU Mountaineers, and the Andy Griffith Show.

Doing Good

"You know of Jesus of Nazareth, how God anointed Him with the Holy Spirit and with power, and how He went about doing good and healing all who were oppressed by the devil, for God was with Him" (Acts 10:38).

One of the simplest and yet most powerful descriptions of our Lord and Savior while He was here on earth was that He went about "doing good." We understand that the doing of good works does not merit our salvation, but we also know that in Hebrews 13:16 we are told, "And do not neglect doing good and sharing, for with such sacrifices God is pleased." There are many other reasons why we should become actively involved in doing good works. Our good deeds will bring glory to God, prepare unbelievers to be more receptive to the gospel, demonstrate the living nature of our faith, and are necessary if we are to be Christ-like.

Remember the words of the apostle Paul to our brethren in Thessalonica: "But as for you, brethren, do not grow weary of doing good" (2 Thessalonians 3:13).

Even if we do not do enough to grow weary, let's resolve to at least do enough to get really tired. We have much to do and we need everyone's help to accomplish our responsibilities to God. If we have been lacking in our service to the Lord, let's resolve that now is the time to give the Lord His due. Today is the day for us to do good and help be the hands and feet here on earth for our Lord.

Gregg Woodall is an elder of the Karns Church of Christ. Gregg is married to Sherrye and they have four children, Stephanie, Tiffany, Benjamin, and Jonathan. They also have four grandchildren, Wrigley, Walton, Adalynn, and Brooklynn. Gregg enjoys golfing, dirt bike riding, spending time with family, and is a fan of the Tennessee Volunteers.

A Light in a Dark Place

Growing up in Norris, Tennessee, it was standard practice to make spending money selling fireflies to the Oak Ridge scientists. I thought every American kid did this but I have been told that's not so. Saturday mornings we would carry our plastic baggies of frozen fireflies up to the Town Center where the scientists would sit at a card table with a little set of scales, sort our bugs, and pay the going rate of that particular summer. I could get enough money to buy a candy bar, some would get enough to buy a comic book. However, my friend, Gloria, and all her family went out with dedication every night below Norris Dam and caught them in pillowcases! They could fund their Myrtle Beach vacation!

So how have decades of research done regarding fireflies? What do we know about their lights? Still not sure. There's an Oxygen Control Theory and a Neural Activation Theory among others. A firefly chart is marvelous, ranking degree of biolumi-nescence and proportion of different enzymes in chemical re-action. Charting their Morse code communication is still inex-act. What I love is when some design of God's keeps working away, in this case, blinking away, despite mankind's inability to understand it fully.

When Jesus was coming into the world, He was foretold as a light to shine in a dark place (Matthew 4:16). 1 John 1:9 calls Him the Light of the World. All through scripture are unsearch-able truths about the ways and the excellence of Jesus the Light. We can spend the rest of our days contemplating His Light and our part in this wonder.

Melea Nash Smith is married to Steve. They have four children, Jordan, Melea Jean, Bryan, and Sarah. Her favorite firefly is the species Photnus, which produces the soft green glow.

'Tis So Sweet to Trust in Jesus

Webster's Dictionary defines the word trust as "Confidence; a reliance or resting of the mind on the integrity, veracity, justice, friendship or other sound principle of another person." Trusting in Christ and His work on the cross involves more than accepting it as a historical event. It is a resting of the mind.

Think about a roller coaster. When we walk up the stairs to partake in this type of enjoyment (or torture depending on your interpretation) we are putting our trust and our lives in the hands of the makers of the roller coaster. We trust that the frame is well built, the mechanics are functioning properly, and the seat belts and harnesses are without defect. Our lives depend on it!

In the same way, we must trust in and rest our minds on the work of Christ on the cross because our lives depend on it. When we realize our sinfulness before God, we have no option for self-redemption. We missed the mark (Romans 3:23). We can't shelter enough homeless, feed enough hungry, or adopt enough orphans to cover our trespasses. Only the blood of Christ is sufficient to cleanse us and set us free (Romans 5:9, Hebrews 9:23-28). If we have put our trust in anything else (including ourselves), we will come up empty-handed on the day of judgment.

In addition to believing Jesus Christ died on the cross, we should believe that He is God's Son; however, the demons also believe (James 2:19). Our trust in Christ involves more than belief in these facts. We should rest our minds on the fact that the blood of Christ is sufficient to cover our sins and rest our souls in His grace through obedient faith. "Blessed is the man who trusts in the Lord. . ." (Jeremiah 17:7).

Amber Jarrett met her husband, Jason in the Christian Student Center at the University of North Alabama. She has a B. S. degree in Education from the University of North Alabama. She and her husband have three children, Maddy, Tyler, and Daniel.

Food or Faith

Some time ago, my family and I went out to eat with another Christian family at a local Mexican restaurant. We all ordered our food, and one of the members of the family ordered their particular dish without sour cream. When the food finally arrived, the person's dish contained sour cream. Now, the dish was not a burrito or anything, so it would have been quite easy to simply put it to the side and eat around it; however this person did not do that. They demanded that the dish be taken back and a new one be given to them.

I cannot count the number of times I have seen things of this nature happen when eating out with other Christians. Well, you might say, "What's wrong with that? That person paid good money for that dish, they have the right to expect their food done the way the ordered it." Let me ask you a question: do you think the waitress would have wanted to have a Bible study with that person after they did that? I think not. Now, I'm not saying it is wrong to have food taken back; I understand if you have a food sensitivity, or if you really dislike something, but most of the time that's not why people do it.

In Matthew 5, starting in verse 40, Jesus says, "If anyone wants to sue you and take away your tunic, let him have your cloak also. And whoever compels you to go one mile, go with him two." We should be more concerned about other people's souls than our rights. Yes, that person had the right to expect their food to be cooked right; however, consideration for others is far more important. Christians should seek to live their lives so that anyone who knows us would love to have a Bible study with us, because they know we really care about their souls.

Andrew Jensen is a student as SEIBS. He is 19 years old, and comes from Angels Camp, CA. His parents and brother and sister live in CA as well. He enjoys hiking, camping, and playing Angry Birds.

Soul Saving

Many times when we think of soul saving, we think of mission work, Bible correspondence courses, jail ministry, etc. However, there is a way we can save souls, which is sometimes overlooked - teaching at church. James tells us in James 3:1 that teachers will receive a stricter judgment than others. Why would this be the case? It is because teachers share the word of God with others and have a responsibility to represent His word accurately. This is not only applicable to adult teachers, but also to those who teach school-age or preschool.

If teaching is a way to save souls, and if it brings upon us greater judgment, then how can we ensure we are accurately teaching the word? We must take the responsibility of teaching seriously. It's easy to agree to teach but it's much more difficult to commit to teach. With commitment comes preparation, and we must prepare for each and every class. Skimming over a lesson 5 to 10 minutes prior to teaching does not classify as preparation, but rather procrastination. If we need to represent God's word accurately, then shouldn't we study it so that we know it? As we teach, remember that we have an awesome responsibility to save souls. If we ever doubt the importance of teaching, look to the examples given to us in the Bible. Ananias took the time to teach Paul, Lois and Eunice taught Timothy, Peter and the other apostles taught the Jews on the Day of Pentecost, etc. Most importantly, remember that someone took the time to teach us so we too might have a home in Heaven.

Katie Pruett has been a member at Karns Church of Christ for 14 years. She has a passion to teach and is heavily involved in the Bible School Program. Her interests include spending time with family, watching the UT Volunteers and Green Bay Packers, and reading.

You Can Do Anything but Play Football. You're Just Too Small.

What discourages us? When we are afraid, do we look for a grand intervention by God, like the arrival of Commander of the Lord's Army in Joshua 5:13-15?

When I start something new, a new challenge, or even a new task in my job, I get nervous. I'll even assume God is too busy for my little insecurities. I think we need to change our focus. We need to see the power is within us. We need to grow stronger by knowing that God will take care of us as we follow Him. We need not allow fear to limit us. A good example is Caleb, Joshua, and the sending of the 12 spies.

Looking in Numbers 13, Moses had sent out the 12 spies; one of each tribe, to enter the land of Canaan and report back about the land and those who inhabit it. In Numbers 14:8, Joshua and Caleb said, "If the Lord delights in us, then He will bring us into this land, and give it to us." Meanwhile, the other spies were consumed by fear.

And why not? God is proud of us. He wants us to be comforted. The 23rd Psalm reads, "I will fear no evil, for you are with me; your rod and your staff, they comfort me."

So, next time you are facing that fear of something new, or of something others say that you can't handle, just remember Joshua and Caleb. They saw the positive and knew God would provide.

Al Linn is married to Angie Linn and the dad of three wonderful young women. He spends most of his time travelling while selling equipment to Papermills but would rather find a way to fish for a greater portion of his life. AL did spend a little time in the Army and is a graduate of N. C. State University.

Forgiveness

Forgiving others is difficult to say the least. Many times we are faced with situations where we have been hurt by those we are not close to (co-worker) or by a loved one (relatives, or close friends). Forgiveness is spoken of throughout the Bible and we are charged with forgiving others as we have been forgiven. We all know it cannot be done on our own, but the Holy Spirit is in place to help us accomplish what seems to be impossible (Ephesians 4:30-32). Simply put, we must display God's love in our lives and extend His mercy to others, as he has done for us.

Releasing hurt and pain is critical for us to maintain a strong and fruitful relationship with our Heavenly Father. If we choose to hold grudges or justify our actions that are not in alignment with God's Word, we are saying that our way is best and I have the right to handle things in a manner that makes me feel adjudicated. This is not submissive to God's Word and keeps us from enjoying true fellowship with Him (1 John 2:9-11).

Ways to obtain a forgiving spirit:

- Conduct a self-assessment (Is there an area in your life that requires forgiveness)?
- Read and meditate on God's Word daily.
- Pray for those who have hurt you and wish them well.

Pray that the Holy Spirit helps you to overcome your hurt and live by God's Word to bring Him the glory (Matthew 5:43-48).

Adrian Marsh is a retired Navy veteran and is married to his high school sweetheart Lisa Marsh. He enjoys family time, traveling, cooking, sports and serving God.

Going Out for Christ

In today's world, it is easy to become complacent. Gone are the days when you had to go out to visit with your friends. I remember when I was younger I would go outside and actually do things with my friends. Now when people want to see what their friends are doing they just go to their computers. It makes me wonder what Christ would think.

Christ told us to be the light of the world in Matthew 5:14-16. This is hard to do when we spend most of our time in front of a computer carrying on conversations with people we may have never met in real life. They cannot see if the actions of our lives match up with the words we are telling them. The absence of our physical presence lessens the impact of our words.

Christ knew the power actual personal interaction has. This is why he spent so much time with people. He could be found having a meal with the Pharisees (Luke 7:36ff) or with known sinners (Matthew 9:10-13). He also made this perfectly clear to his followers when he sent them out to tell the Jews about Him (Matthew 10:5-7). To reinforce His desire he issued what is known as the Great Commission, found in Matthew 28:19-20 and also in Mark 16:15.

Christ wants us to be people who show other people his love. He was the perfect example of what we need to be. Therefore, if our true goal is to be more like Jesus, then we need to find ways to be where the people are so they can see Christ through us.

Clint Turek is from Rockwood, TN and he came to Karns as a student at the Southeast Institute of Biblical Studies (formerly East Tennessee School of Preaching and Missions). Clint is presently preaching for the church in Spring City, TN.

Aging with Acceptance and Dignity

The aging process begins the minute we are born. Growing older is inevitable, so why is it so hard for many to accept? Many people today spend much time and money trying to look and feel younger. It has become an obsession in our society. In our culture, age is feared and dreaded rather than revered and respected.

In Bible times this was not the case. Old age was not only accepted but even welcomed. It was associated with favor from God. There was no obsessive concern with the changes brought by aging as there is in today's society.

Aging is said to bring wisdom and understanding (Job 12:12). We are instructed that the older women are to teach the younger women (Titus 2:3-5). Elders are to lead the flock and make wise decisions for the congregation (1 Timothy 5:17; Titus 1:5-9). In the early days of Israel the elders would sit at the city gates to make wise judgments (Numbers 11:16-17). The aged in Bible times were treated with great respect (Proverbs 1:8-9), (1 Timothy 5: 1-2). The younger would honor the aged by rising in their presence (Leviticus 19:32).

Today's attitudes that view those who are aging as less portant, less valued, less useful, or less worthy are contrary to the message found in God's Word. Spiritual beauty transcends time; it does not fade with age. As Christians we should learn to accept, enjoy, and appreciate every stage of the aging process. Each age holds unique and valuable opportunities and experiences that should be appreciated rather than feared or dreaded.

Sara Jones was born in Camden, AL and became a Christian in 1969. She received her education at Alabama Christian College where she met and married Edwin S. Jones. They have three children and four grandchildren. Sara is the manager of Evangelist Bookstore and teaches women's classes at SEIBS. Her hobbies are interior decorating and gardening.

Pictures

I love to see the pictures of the people from the Honduras mission trip. The one face I remember from the recent presentation was the face of a lady who refused the Bible tract, but wanted her picture taken. It was sad to think that she was proud of herself enough to have her photo taken and shown to others, but she didn't want to spend any time learning about God's word. Perhaps I am judging her situation without knowing it, because maybe she couldn't see or read. But assuming that wasn't the case, it reminds me of how we spend so much time on the outside of our bodies, but so little time on our souls.

In Luke 11:39-41, Jesus says, "Now you Pharisees make the outside of the cup and dish clean, but your inward part is full of greed and wickedness...Did not He who made the outside make the inside also?" We spend a lot of money and time making our outsides more attractive and appealing to others, but that part will be dissolved. It is our eternal soul that will live forever (2 Peter 3:10-11). Colossians 3:2 says, "Set your mind on things above, not on things on the earth."

Are we more willing to let people see our outward appearance than our hearts? I hope that this lovely Honduran woman gets another chance to study God's word, and I hope we will take advantage of our daily opportunities to grow in the grace and knowledge of our Lord and Savior Jesus Christ (2 Peter 3:18).

Hannah Cox is married to Chris and is a homeschool mom to Samuel and Rachel. She teaches Bible classes and enjoys working with children. In her free time, Hannah likes reading, riding bikes and spending time with her family.

What Would You Do?

One day the kids were talking about the fire department, asking if they had ever been to our house. So I decided it was the perfect opportunity to bring up the subject of our fire safety plan. So I asked my 3 year-old, "What would you do if our house caught on fire?" I was thinking she would respond with "call 911," "get out of the house," or "yell for you, Mom." No! Her response was very matter-of-fact: "I'll go see Jesus!"

I have learned so much from my children. They have such a pure love for God and complete devotion to please Him and others. My children are a gift from God (Psalm 127:3) and I want to learn to be more like them. Christ has told us that we are to be like the little children. In Mark 10:15 he says, "Assuredly, I say to you, whoever does not receive the kingdom of God as a little child will by no means enter it."

Is your faith like a child? Do you have total belief and hope in God?

My daughter loves to sing "Blue Skies and Rainbows," and I know she believes every word of the song. As you go throughout the day, what song does your soul sing?

Leah Baldwin has been a member at Karns church of Christ since 1988, and is a teacher for the 2 year old class. She is married to David and they have 3 children, Victoria, Eli and Charlotte. Leah is a stay at home mom and enjoys sewing, reading and spending time with her family.

Self Portrait

My mother was a faithful Christian and served the Lord until He called her home. After her death, a friend and her little five-year old son came to visit me. As he came in, he handed me a sheet of paper on which he had drawn a picture for me.

Among the many colorful objects on the paper were two stick figures—one was his best friend and the other one was him. Not wanting me to miss anything, he pointed to another stick figure in the "sky" and said, "That's your mother going to heaven in her red hat." From the mouth of babes timely thoughts are often sparked and I began to take inventory of my life.

By our lifestyle, we are painting a picture. Does it say that we are Christians or does our speech betray us (Colossians 4:6)? Does it say that we refuse to participate when an innocent conversation turns into gossip, or do we feel compelled to add our two cents also (Proverbs 26:20)? Does it say that we dress modestly or that there is a shortage of material in our country (1 Timothy 2:9)? Is your claim to Christianity legitimate or are you mimicking the chameleon and hiding your identity as you blend in with the world?

What does the world see in the picture you are painting - a "Christian" trying to have the best of both worlds or a Christian preparing to go to heaven in her red hat?

"Be careful how you live; you may be the only Bible some people will ever read" (Apples of Gold).

Jane Higdon is a widow of 28 years and a retired Administrative Secretary. She has a daughter and a son, three grandchildren and five great grandchildren. She enjoys cooking and eating; watching sports, especially Tennessee football and Braves baseball; eating; grading Bible Correspondence courses; and get-togethers with her church family.

Enough Already!

Have you ever considered that Jesus was the most exasperating man who ever lived? Yes, you read me correctly; He was the most exasperating man who ever lived. He never let up. He totally, uncompromisingly, relentlessly expected excellence. He was untiringly committed to the Father's will (John 4:34).

Well, who would want a Savior like that? I mean, really, isn't that all just a bit much, especially knowing we are all a bunch of sinful mortals? Indeed, who would want a Savior like that?

I would! I don't want a compromiser. An enabler wouldn't be useful to me. A "let's all just get along" Jesus is of no use as a model of true holiness (Romans 8:29). Yes, I need a Savior who will lovingly, caringly, nurture me in righteousness. But I need patience, not a pass. Games and spins may at times appear to be godly, but they are not—we all know that! I want a truthful Savior (Mark 12:14; John. 14:2b).

Please don't get me wrong; I desperately need all the grace I can get (Luke 17:10). The compelling character of Jesus relies heavily on grace; but grace without holiness is not attractive, it is ungodly (Romans 12:22a).

As I challenge myself, daily so I challenge everyone, "read the Gospels every day." The exasperating, merciful, righteous, and loving Jesus we find there is just what we need to inspire us to eagerly reach for Christ-likeness. Yes, though we need all the love we can get, we need an exasperating Savior!

Edwin Jones has been with Karns and the school of preaching for almost 27 years. Currently he is the Dean of Students with the school. Edwin and Sara have three children and four grandchildren as well as a variety of "adopted" family members they have incorporated into their mix over the years.

Ambassadors for Christ

After the shooting that took place in a movie theater in Colorado, the President of the United States went to visit the surviving victims and families of those who were affected by this senseless act. Also, Peyton Manning, America's favorite quarterback, called the hospital to encourage the injured.

When I heard this, I thought to myself, "Wow, the President of the United States and Peyton Manning!" Both men are bringing to those families the love and support of our nation. There will be more visits by recognized role models and men and women in high places.

I think, "What about me?" As Christians, we represent the Creator of this world and the most influential man that ever walked on the earth, Jesus! We are "Ambassadors for Christ." It is Christ who gave, by example, how we are to care for one another (Matthew 25:35-36). In scripture we read that we are to do good to all, especially to those of the household of faith (Galatians 6:10). We are to visit (James 1:27). We are to show brotherly affection and bear another's burdens (Romans 12:10, Galatians 6:2).

It is because of God's love and comfort towards us, that we are able to extend our love and comfort (1 Corinthians 1:4). Jesus said, "By this all will know that you are My disciples, if you have love for one another" (John 13:35). The ultimate love and concern for our fellow man is sharing the good news of Jesus Christ. It is the great commission (Matthew 28:19-20). It is because of Christ we have purpose and influence to represent Him on a daily basis sharing His love and care. Thank you Lord!

Steve Smith is married to Melea Nash and they have four children, Jordan, Melea Jean, Bryan, and Sarah. Steve serves as deacon for the Karns Church of Christ.

He Being Dead, Still Speaks

Over the past year, I became interested in genealogy. I never knew relatives on my mother's side of the family and my grandparents died when I was very young. Aunts and uncles were scattered all over the country.

In my research, I scanned pictures and letters to share with my sister and children. Among those letters, I have over 60 pages of letters written from my grandmother to my parents. You see, my grandparents became Christians when they were in their 50's. My mother, the eighth child of eleven, was 16 years old and had no interest in church at that point in her life, nor did most of the other siblings. However, my grandmother persistently and consistently wrote letters to each of her children. Those letters are full of scripture teaching every aspect of the plan of salvation, the church, worship, and many other Bible topics.

Approximately seven years after my grandparents became Christians, my parents obeyed the gospel as did five other siblings. In time, my father became a Bible class teacher, deacon, and elder. My sister and I married Christian men and have six Christian children between us.

My grandparents were simple people living on a farm in Missouri. My grandmother was not a public speaker or author, yet she had influence that she never lived to know! I believe that once she knew the Truth, she was desperate to share that truth with those she loved the most.

I am reminded of Hebrews 11:4 which says of Abel, "He being dead still speaks." What will our lives say when we are gone?

Kim Higginbotham grew up in Poplar Bluff, MO. She is married to Steve and has four children: Kelli, Michael, Matthew, and Anne Marie. Kim teaches children with multiple disabilities for Knox County, a ladies' class at SEIBS, conducts teacher training seminars, and maintains two blogs, "Teaching Help," and "Relative Taste." She enjoys teaching and cooking.

Keep the Book

"You shall love the LORD your God with all your heart, with all your soul, and with all your strength. And these words which I command you today shall be in your heart. You shall teach them diligently to your children, and shall talk of them when you sit in your house, when you walk by the way, when you lie down, and when you rise up. You shall bind them as a sign on your hand, and they shall be as frontlets between your eyes. "You shall write them on the doorposts of your house and on your gates" (Deuteronomy 6:5-9).

These words from Deuteronomy chapter 6, verses 5-9, list the greatest commandment from God to the people of Israel as they were to cross over into the land given to them by Him. These words in strong and repeating language convey the desire of God to the children of Israel that He wanted his Word to be a priority.

We read also in the book of Joshua where God is telling Joshua after the death of Moses to be courageous and above all to keep the Book, to not depart from it to the left nor to the right (Joshua 1:7-8).

Do we "keep" the Book? Do we let the Word depart from our mouths? Do we teach the words diligently to our children when we walk by the way? Do we teach the words diligently to our children when we lie down? Do we teach the words diligently to our children when we rise up?

Tony Williams is originally from Chattanooga and was baptized at the East Ridge congregation. He is married to Deanna, and they have three daughters, Claire, Maggie, and Ella. Tony has a Bachelor's and Master's Degree from UT. Tony and his family have been at Karns since 1999, and during that time he has served as a deacon, and currently as an elder.

The Lord Reigns

There are things in this life that seem to just about defy description. I admire, and might even confess to just a little twinge of envy of those who can sit down to write. Words just seem to flow from their pen. To write beautiful phrases seem to just come naturally to them.

Many years ago while on a mission trip to the Island of Tobago, I witnessed the most beautiful sunrise there could possibly be. I had gotten up early that Sunday morning because I was teaching the adult Bible class and I needed to study my lesson. I went out on the porch. It was pitch black, heavy dark clouds obscured the sky, no moon, not a star could be seen. For some reason, I sat down and in just a few minutes something started to happen in the east. At first just a faint glow appeared, but soon beautiful red and golden rays from the sun came into view.

The brilliant rays from the sun bouncing off those dark clouds just defy description. Those dark clouds were no match for the sun and soon the whole earth (that I could see) was showered in bright, early morning sunshine. I believe that was one of the most beautiful sights that I have ever witnessed.

"The heavens declare the glory of God; And the firmament shows His handiwork" (Psalm 19:1). "Let the heavens rejoice, and let the earth be glad; And let them say among the nations, "The LORD reigns" (1 Chronicles 16:31).

Wendell Agee was born and raised in Pikeville, TN. He served 20 years in the USAF and was a successful business man for over 30 years. Wendell has served the Lord as a missionary to Cuba, Jamaica, Honduras and other countries. He's a member of the Karns Church of Christ.

Faith Like the Centurion

I have been a student of history since I was young. One of my interests is the Roman army in the early 1st Century. Most of us have heard the story of the Centurion from scripture but few of us know what a centurion really was.

A centurion was in charge of a century of 80 men, 1/6th of a cohort of which there are ten in a Roman Legion. All members of a legion were Roman citizens and served for an enlistment of 20 years. To gain the rank of centurion was a great honor and was difficult for the average soldier. The Greek historian, Polybius wrote: "In choosing their centurions the Romans look not so much for the daring or fire-eating type, but rather for men who are natural leaders and possess a stable and imperturbable temperament..."

Centurions could also be tasked in peacetime with other duties such as overseeing the local interests of Rome. This could involve providing a security force for an area, diplomatic missions, special construction of structures, or collecting taxes.

This gentile man referenced in Matthew 8:5-13 and Luke 7:1-10 had never met Jesus, but after hearing about Him from others, his faith was so great that it impressed Jesus. The centurion believed that Jesus could heal his servant with only a word.

We, too, can learn from this man's faith - even though we have never seen Jesus, He can still be with us from afar and affect our lives in so many ways. A faith such as the centurion's is a powerful testimony from a man in power to our Lord who has the ultimate power to forgive our sins and bring us home to Heaven.

Todd Guthrie is married to Yvette, and they have two sons, Ethan and Daniel. Todd and his family have been members at Karns since 2002.

Bible Class

I have taught the 3 year-old class since 1980. I love teaching this age because they are so eager to learn. Every week we work on learning the books of the New Testament. We start out with Matthew, Mark, Luke and John adding one or two books as they master the previous ones. By the end of the year, my class leaves for the 4 year-old class able to say, not sing, all of the books of the New Testament. We also spend the year studying Joseph, Moses, David and Daniel. We spend a quarter (sometimes more) on each Bible character. Each week, I retell the story from the beginning to where we are currently.

The year that the movie The Prince of Egypt (the story of Moses) came out, I had a student who stunned his parents. His family went to see the movie and on the way home they were discussing the movie. This 3 year-old spoke up and said "That movie was not right!" He pointed out what he believed to be wrong and what the Bible said about that. His parents told him he was not right, but agreed to look it up when they got home. Well, guess who was right - my little 3 year-old Bible student! He had been paying attention in class. His parents were eager to come and tell me this story, and were thankful that he knew what the Bible had to say about Moses.

As adults and teens are we paying attention in class and learning what the Bible has to say?

Sherrye Woodall is married to Gregg. They have 4 children: Stephanie Harder, Tiffany Dresser, Benjamin Woodall and Jonathan Woodall. They have 4 grandchildren: Wrigley Harder, Walton Harder, Adalynn Dresser and Brooklynn Dresser. Sherrye has taught the 3 years old class at Karns for over 32 years.

That Has to be a Mistake

Have you ever watch Bob Ross paint? You know who I'm talking about, the artist on TV with the fuzzy hair? I understand that he passed away a few years ago, but his television programs continue to be shown. on TV.

Mr. Ross's show simply consisted of him standing in front of a blank canvas with his color pallatte and paints, and as he painted, he would give instructions to the "would-be" painters watching.

While I could do without his comments about "happy clouds" and "happy trees," I have been amazed at his abilities. In a period of 20 minutes, this man could transform a blank piece of canvas into a beautiful work of art. On many occasions, I would see him make a stroke with his brush and think, "Aw, he's really made a mess with that stroke," only to be proven wrong. What seems to be mistaken strokes, eventually blend into something beautiful.

Don't you think it would help us if we could remember this when it comes to the working of God in our lives? At times, God allows things to happen to us that appear to us as though no possible good can come from it. Sometimes events may even make us feel that God has blundered with our lives. But as a skillful artist, He eventually brings first one and then another influence to bear upon it until something purposeful begins to emerge.

When life is difficult and a bit ugly, hang in there. Don't change the channel on God too soon. If you do, you may miss something beautiful.

Steve Higginbotham has been the pulpit minister for the Karns church of Christ since 2010. Steve is married to Kim and they have four children, Kelli, Michael, Matthew, and Anne Marie. Steve enjoys writing, playing golf, and is a fan of the Pittsburgh Steelers, the WVU Mountaineers, and the Andy Griffith Show.

The Domino Effect

Have you ever been in an environment where something extraordinary happens, and soon everyone knows about it in what seems like half an hour? If so, you probably realize the speed and power of word of mouth. One amazing thing about mass communication is that it can be started by just one person.

There is an example of this in John 4:39-40. In John's account, Jesus met a Samaritan woman at a well and told her about living water. She then believed in Him and returned to town and told everyone about her amazing encounter with Jesus. Because of her testimony, many people believed in Him, and because of their belief, they anxiously welcomed Him when He came.

Now you may tell yourself, "this setting is very different than the setting at my school or workplace." Well, actually, it isn't. If you glorify Christ in your actions and openly share your enthusiasm for what Christ has done for you, those around you might become more interested in and receptive to the gospel of Christ. Others may even decide to accept your invitation to join you for worship service or another congregational event. As we have previously stated, word of mouth spreads when news is extraordinary. Because you made that first move, inviting someone to church or a church activity, you brought someone to Christ and they, too, may get equally as excited and help spread the word.

We need to help bring people to "the well" so they may come to a full appreciation of Christ. Every soul counts. Here is my challenge for you: the world is trying to block out Christ - we need to let Him shine!

Austin Hoffarth has lived in Tennessee all his life. He attends high school at Webb School of Knoxville. He likes to draw, play tennis, go camping and hiking. He became a Christian in 2011 and enjoys the activities within the youth group at Karns and area-wide churches.

Salvation

Salvation is extremely important. What's great about it is how simple it is! There are just a few steps: hear, believe, repent, confess, and be baptized. We know that's what we need to do, because there are verses to back it up.

For hear, Romans 10:17 says, "So then faith comes by hearing, and hearing by the word of God." First, we have to hear the word of God.

Next for believe, John 3:16 says, "For God so loved the world that He gave His only begotten Son, that whoever believes in Him should not perish but have everlasting life." Now we know that we must hear the word, and believe it.

Next is repent. Repent means to turn away from sin and to do better. One verse that shows this is Acts 3:19, which says, "Repent therefore and be converted, that your sins may be blotted out, so that times of refreshing may come from the presence of the Lord."

And now, confess. When you confess, you are admitting that Jesus is the son of God. Romans 10:10 says, "For with the heart one believes unto righteousness, and with the mouth confession is made unto salvation." So now we must hear the word, believe what we hear, start doing what's right, and confess our faith in Jesus.

Finally, we must be baptized. Acts 2:38 says, "Then Peter said to them, 'Repent, and let every one of you be baptized in the name of Jesus Christ for the remission of sins; and you shall receive the gift of the Holy Spirit.'"

Once we do that, we are saved from our sins. Are you saved from yours?

Anne Marie Higginbotham is the daughter of Steve and Kim Higginbotham. She is 12 years old and attends Karns Middle School. Anne Marie enjoys drawing, water colors, and photography.

A Better Book

The word, "better" appears twelve times in the book of Hebrews. In our study of Hebrews at "SEIBS," James Meadows pointed out some specific things of significance that are said to be better. I have taken a few of those and modified them for this article.

In Hebrews 1:1-4 we learn that we have received a better revelation. In times past God has spoken in various ways, but in our great age he has spoken to us by his son. We have a better priest. Christ is our merciful and faithful high priest who resides in heaven (Hebrews 2:16-17; 8:1-4). We have a better hope that is the anchor of the soul (Hebrews 7:19; 6:17-20). Christ is the mediator of a better covenant that is based on better promises (Hebrews 8:6). We also have access to a far better sacrifice (Hebrews 9:23-28; 10:4-10).

In my studies at "SEIBS" I have grown accustomed to looking for flag words. Teachers will often give us clues to various things that will judge our knowledge on test day. The Hebrews writer has done the same. The work is easy, but the test will be hard. We must be prepared.

What hope is there for anyone who neglects so great a salvation; who tramples underfoot the son of God, and counts his blood as just a common thing (Hebrews 2:3; 10:29)? The fact is, there is no hope for that person. Certainly it would be a fearful thing to go unprepared into the hands of the living God (Hebrews 10:31).

Doug Tooley is from Tompkinsville, Ky. He has been married to Carla Tooley since 1999. They have two kids, Logan and Aubrey. Doug enjoys studying the Bible, hunting, and playing golf. He is currently a student at SEIBS, and he preaches part time for the Wartburg Church of Christ. Carla works for UT Medical Center.

Trusting God's Will

Have you ever prayed for God's will in a situation and then been a little nervous about what His will might actually be? You know that God's will is going to be the best solution, but will it be painless? C. S. Lewis explained it this way:

"We are not necessarily doubting that God will do what is best for us; but we are wondering how painful the best will turn out to be."

God has taught me that it is at the point of total trust in His solution to our dilemma, whatever the cost, that His work is best accomplished in me. Did you catch that? I said, "In me." Yes, sometimes it is us he needs to refine in order to resolve the dilemma.

Can we be our own worst enemy? Can we hinder our own prayers? If we are not willing to entirely surrender our will to His will as Jesus did in the garden, are we actually telling God we don't trust him?

Trust is essential in any relationship. God has placed a trust in us to represent him by sharing his truth and his love with those who need both. Can we not have complete trust in the One who allowed His son to suffer the shame of the cross for our sake?

What is it you are having difficulty trusting God with today? Totally release it to God and trust the One who knows you and loves you anyway. He may just be waiting for you to get out of the way.

Sara Terlecki is married to her husband Bill. They moved to Knoxville from Ohio. Sara has worked in the church office since 2010. They have two grown children. Gerri married Michael Nath and blessed them with granddaughter, Ellie. Bill Jr. married Hope Whittington and blessed them with two grandsons, Allen and Evan.

A God-Sized Dream

All of us have dreams. From the time we are little until the day we die, we dream about the many possibilities for our lives. When I was a kid, I wanted more than anything to be a professional athlete. As you can probably tell, this dream didn't work out so well; however, this didn't keep me from dreaming. We've all had BIG dreams for our lives, and maybe you still do.

What about the dreams you have for your spiritual life? Do you have dreams for what you want to become - for what you hope to accomplish for the Lord? I'm afraid when it comes to dreaming about things of a spiritual nature, our dreams are too small. Why is it that when we dream about our lives we dream BIG dreams, but when we dream about our impact in the Kingdom of God we dream small dreams? I think it's past time for us to dream God-sized dreams. You say, "what is a God-sized dream?" A God-sized dream is a dream that is so big others might say, "You can't do that." God-sized dreams are what some might call, "ridiculously insane."

Christians need to start dreaming God-sized dreams. As long as we have God on our side, nothing is impossible (Mark. 10:27). The apostle Paul said, "Now to Him who is able to do exceedingly abundantly above all that we ask or think, according to the power that works in us" (Ephesians 3:20). Did you catch that?

Friends, the size of our dreams reflects the size of our God. How big are you dreaming?

Justin Morton has been in student ministry for almost 10 years. He has been the student and family minister for the Karns church of Christ since 2010. Justin is married to Miranda and they have one son, Caden. Justin enjoys spending time with his family, studying, teaching, writing and is a fan of the Tennessee Volunteers.

Now I Lay Me Down to Sleep

Gradually, through the years I've learned to appreciate the prayer that formerly was taught to little children, "Now I lay me down to sleep; I pray the Lord my soul to keep."

My family rather infrequently would visit my maternal grandparents. My sisters would enjoy the feather bed located in my grandparents' bedroom. I had the pleasure of enjoying sleeping on a corn shuck mattress located just below the wood shingle roof. The sound of rain dropping on the roof lulled me to sleep.

Associated with my entrance into the Navy, I shared a room with an engineer who regaled me with a tale about strange happenings in Anderson County. I later learned he was talking about the building of the Atomic City of Oak Ridge. Others working at the Atomic City then shared a bed on an eight-hour shift basis.

Working in the oil-patch country, I was fortunate to enjoy a variety of sleep arrangements. In one assignment I used a canvas cot located in tool-pusher's shack. In another case I roomed and boarded with a widow who entranced me with tales of the Dust Bowl Days. I was also temporarily housed on the top floor of an old hotel that used a rope and chain secured to the steam radiator for a fire escape.

Each new location, in which I lived, perhaps 30 of them, provided a new and rewarding view of life's circumstances. I've attempted to use these to develop spiritual character. Paul emphasized that godliness with contentment is great gain. I hope that my journey through life has succeeded in accomplishing this great aim.

G. C. (Grover Cleveland) Robinson, Jr. has been married to Mattie Lou Geer since June 27, 1954. They have four children: Timothy, Amy, Andy, and Penny; and three grandchildren: Victoria, Quintin and Ransom. G. C. is a retired mechanical engineer. He turned 86 December 1st, 2012.

Sow, Sew, or So

As we go through our daily Christian walk, we are encouraged to sow the seed of the kingdom. But I know that there are times where we sew or so and we need to be confronted about that at times because there could be a crucial opportunity to do the Lord's work that we are missing.

"Sew"ing is meant to take a thread or needle and either make or repair something, mainly to clothing. That is something we should be doing with ourselves on a daily basis. We should be sewing our relationship with the Lord to be sure that we stay firmly connected at all times. There will be times where we become disconnected for one reason or another but the Lord is always ready to repair that tear.

"Sow"ing involves spreading of a seed for growing. There are many in the world today that we need to help sow in the word of the Lord. We need to spread the Lord's seed so that his kingdom will grow.

Then there is "so"ing and that is something we as Christians should never be saying or doing. We shouldn't look at something or someone and say "so." There is a pretty good chance that there is an opportunity to help in some way in any situation.

So as your day goes, ask yourself, "Am I Sowing, Sewing, or So-ing?" We reap what we SOW and if we don't SEW our relationship with the Lord daily, the Lord could say SO when we plead for our eternal life.

Wayne Begarly has been a member of the Karns Church of Christ since 2011. Wayne graduated from UT in 2007 with a Bachelors in Communications. Wayne is involved with the local United Way and American Cancer Society. He enjoys sports and the outdoors in his free time.

How Will You Be Remembered?

How well do you remember Shammua, Shaphat, Igal, Palti, and Gaddiel? You say, "Who?" Well then, how about Gaddi, Ammiel, Sethur, Nahbi, or Geuel? Come on, you're telling me you don't know these men either? Oh, but you do. You know them well, and have probably heard sermons about them, read about them, and maybe even taught Bible class about them. Still don't know who I'm talking about?

These are the names of the ten faithless spies that Moses sent into the "Promised Land." These are the men who came back with a bad report, saying that they could not take the land. However, as you know, Moses didn't send 10 spies into the land, he sent 12. Interestingly enough, the two spies who came back with a good report, you probably remember by name. . . Joshua and Caleb.

Interesting, isn't it? The difference between being a hero that everyone knows by name, and a nameless blemish on the history of God's people is faith or the lack thereof.

Here's a question for you to consider. Judging from your present lifestyle, will you be remembered by name as a man or woman of faith, or will you fade away into obscurity?

After we're dead and gone, will our brothers and sisters in Christ who are left behind remember us for our great faith and be spoken of for years to come in fond remembrance, or will we be soon forgotten? Give it some thought.

Steve Higginbotham has been the pulpit minister for the Karns church of Christ since 2010. Steve is married to Kim and they have four children, Kelli, Michael, Matthew, and Anne Marie. Steve enjoys writing, playing golf, and is a fan of the Pittsburgh Steelers, the WVU Mountaineers, and the Andy Griffith Show.

Memorials

On April 18, 2012, I had the honor of going to Washington D.C., on the Honor Air Flight. The purpose of these flights is to allow veterans to visit the various military memorials.

Our first stop in Washington was at the Air Force Memorial (the newest). Here we had our group picture made. There were 129 veterans plus about 100 others. Next we visited the Korean War Memorial as well as the Vietnam War Memorial. This was very emotional for many of us because we were involved in these wars. This brought back many memories—some good, some not so good. Our next stop was the World War II Memorial. On one wall there are over 4,000 gold stars each representing 100 men and women who sacrificed their life for freedom.

The Vietnam War Memorial lists all of the names of those men and women who gave their lives for freedom. Freedom is not free. Freedom comes at a very high cost in lives and other causalities. One freedom is especially important: the freedom to worship the way we see fit. This freedom has come at a high cost.

There is another memorial that is more important, has come at a very high cost, and gives each one a higher dividend: *eternal life.* This is a memorial that our Lord and Savior set up at His last Passover meal with His disciples. This memorial is very simple and involves only unleavened bread and the fruit of the vine. This memorial is to be observed each Lord's Day (Acts 20:7).

Jesus said, "Do this in remembrance of Me" (1 Cor. 11:24).

Bob Anderson was born in Farmersville, TX and was baptized by V. E. Howard. He attended East Texas State Teachers College, then entered and retired from the Navy. He also retired from Oak Ridge National Laboratory and attended ETSPM. After school he preached for Spring Creek Church of Christ. Bob serves Karns as a deacon and a Bible class teacher.

What's On Your Mind?

Do you get the feeling that you're doing the same stuff day in and day out, with the exact same worries? Galatians 3:11-14 tells us that "the righteous shall live by faith." I think that I live by faith, but I wonder sometimes if I'm distracted. A friend gave me a list of questions that had a profound impact on me and I will ask them of you now. In a tangible-practical way ask yourself:

- What is your biggest concern at the moment?
- What was your biggest concern 1 month ago? A year ago? 5 years ago?
- What is the longest possible duration of your concern? Is it of eternal nature?
- What is the worst thing that could happen? Does God want that to happen?
- Do you trust that God will cause the best thing to happen?
- What actions do you think God wants you to take?
- How much time have you spent praying about the issue?
- Has God spoken about these issues?
- How much time have you spent studying about the issue?
- Have you sought the counsel/help/prayers of other disciples?
- Does your suffering help you identify with your Lord?
- Can you use your experience to help others?

When I find myself caught up in a concern or issue I go back to these questions. I remember that, "But we are not of those who draw back to perdition, but of those who believe to the saving of the soul" (Hebrews 10:35-39).

Angie Linn is married Al Linn and the proud mom of three wonderful young women. The daughters do monopolize most of her time, but she does enjoy various Bible studies and her new found home in East Tennessee. Angie is from Rock Hill, SC and attended Winthrop College.

A Leader for God

Want to be a leader for God? What kind of leader does God want? He wants someone who is zealous, excited and willing. In Isaiah 6:8 God asks, "Who shall I send?" and Isaiah quickly answered, "Here am I! Send me."

God wants someone with the right attitude; an attitude that's energetic, pure, humble, just, and kind. Colossians 3:12 says, "Therefore, as the elect of God, holy and beloved, put on compassion, kindness, humility, meekness and patience..." Colossians 3:23 states, "Whatever you do, do it heartily, as to the Lord and not to men." He wants a leader that keeps his commandments. In John 14:15, Jesus says, "If you love me you will keep my commandments." Most of all, God wants a leader that is real Luke 9:23 states "If anyone would come after me, let him deny himself and take up his cross daily and follow me."

How can I actively be a leader? James says to serve others and to keep yourself unspotted from the world. That means serving with a pure heart. Colossians 4:5 tells us to walk with wisdom toward outsiders and to make the best use of our time.

Make sure to get involved in the lives of your friends, especially your non-Christian friends. We can be an influence of good to them. Pray that you can be a positive influence. James 5:15 says to pray for one another, Matthew 5:44 says pray for your enemies and 1 Thessalonians 5:17 tells us to pray without ceasing. Let us be leaders with a fiery passion. Let us be leaders for God.

Catherine Albert is a home-schooled senior who trains and shows miniature horses. Her hobbies include playing the flute, piccolo, piano, and guitar, singing, reading, and caring for her menagerie of animals. She is active in 4-H and coaches the Horse Bowl/Hippology teams. She plans to attend college and major in Animal Science and Music.

Bedtime Stories

Every night when the girls were small we would have bedtime Bible stories and prayers. Then, later, one of us would go check on them before going to bed too. One night I went in, Julie was asleep but Casey was awake and feeling afraid. I sat with her and we started talking about all the reasons why she didn't have to be afraid. Casey thought for a minute and then looked at me and said, "Mom, how do we know that God is watching us, we can't see Him?" I looked at her and asked, "Well, can you see the stars when you're in your bed?" Of course she answered, "no," because the curtains were closed. So I then explained that we know the stars are still there, just because we can't see them doesn't mean they're not there.

That's how it is with God; we see all of His creation, we see His glory, but we can't see Him, because while we are living on this earth we have something like curtains over our eyes. It doesn't mean He's not here watching over us and loving us, because He is. Someday, I explained, the curtains will be pulled back and we will see Him! This was a very special moment for us, Casey slept very well after that little talk.

"Little talks" sometimes have the most meaning. It can be easy to lose sight of the fact that our Lord is watching over us. Casey may not remember that night but I will always remember. The moments that happen, the small windows of opportunity to help show our children that God truly exists and that He loves them, both scares me and humbles me. I pray that neither I, nor any other parent let those moments slip by, no matter how exhausted we feel.

Amy Jackson was born in Rome, GA. She is married to Gentry Jackson, celebrating 15 years together. They have two beautiful daughters Casey (age 12) and Julie (age 10). Amy is a registered nurse at a local hospital on weekends and a proud homeschool mom through the week. Amy and her family live in Karns, TN and worship at the Karns church of Christ.

Live Where You Are

I heard someone say, "God gave Abraham everything he wanted; because Abraham gave God everything He wanted." How many times have we wanted God to bless us or give us something, when we are not willing to give God what He wants?

We are too busy. We have worked too much and we are tired. We might think, "I don't have the money to do that;" "if I had this much money, I could do great things for the church;" or "if I had this much free time, I could do great things for God." What we have really become is great at making excuses. This is living outside our boundaries. Let us not be guilty of robbing God (Malachi 3:7-12).

Let us live where we are. We may not have much money; but what are we doing with the money that we do have? Let's live where we are and use what we have to the glory of God. Don't worry about the time we don't have, but rather redeem the time we have and live where we are. Do not worry about the talents we do not have; rather live where we are and use our talents as best we can to help the church to grow.

Great tasks have been accomplished with small things. The walls of Jericho fell because the people of Israel had faith in God and marched, blew their trumpets, and shouted. Dorcas made clothing for many people with a needle and thread (Acts 9:36-40).

Let us live where we are. Give God everything He wants and He will give us more blessings that we could ever imagine receiving.

Dale Tanner serves as a deacon at the Karns church of Christ. Dale is married to Barbara and they have 3 children, Brenda Patterson, Sarah Tanner, and Daniel Tanner. Dale and Barbara have a grandchild on the way. Dale's favorite place is Charleston, SC and the Isle of Palms.

Make God Proud

Is God proud of you or is He disappointed in you? Having raised 4 children, there were times that my children followed all of our rules, behaved themselves and made the right decisions and we were very proud of them and their accomplishments.

There were also times when they did not follow the rules or made wrong decisions and we were very disappointed in them. As a parent, these times of disappointment hurt us deeply. We knew they knew better but chose to do what they wanted. Our Father probably feels the same way about us. I am sure there are times He is proud of how we behaved or handled a situation. But I am also sure there are times when He is disappointed in our behavior.

When I stop to think about how I felt when one of my children disappointed me, it makes me think about how God must feel when I disappoint Him. Just as we love our children and they love us and want to please us, so also God loves us and we love Him and we should want to please Him. Even in times of disobedience, we still love our children and even when we have sinned God still loves us. We forgive our children and God forgives and loves us. John 14:15, "If you love me, keep my commandments."

Next time you are tempted to make the wrong decision, stop and think about how much you will be hurting God and do you want to disappoint Him!

Sherrye Woodall is married to Gregg. They have 4 children: Stephanie Harder, Tiffany Dresser, Benjamin Woodall and Jonathan Woodall. They have 4 grandchildren: Wrigley Harder, Walton Harder, Adalynn Dresser and Brooklynn Dresser. Sherrye has taught the 3 years old class at Karns for over 32 years.

Contracts

When I was signing a mountain of paperwork to join a gym recently, I casually asked, "So what's the cancellation fee, if I get a month into it and realize this isn't for me?" The sales rep smiled, looked me in the eye and said, "There isn't one." "Whew!" I thought. Then she continued, "You're obligated to fulfill your end of the contract and are responsible for the entire 36 months of fees, whether you decide to continue using our facility or not." I was shocked. I almost de-clicked my pen and walked out the door.

As I was leaving (after I did, indeed, make the 3 year commitment) I was struck by sadness at the idea that it is shocking when a contract is a contract—when our yes must be our yes and our no must be no. We are so used to being able to have an escape plan, a plan B, a cancellation fee, an "irreconcilable differences" clause that the concept of a binding contract is foreign.

The situation at the gym left me thinking how wonderful it would be if we all abided by our word no matter what—in marriage vows, in dealings with friends, at work, in becoming a member of the body of Christ. Would we give more thought to the words we utter, the promises we make and the commitments into which we enter? Would we be more determined to work things out, even when it means denying ourselves, and look to God for wisdom in doing so? Jesus kept His word for the benefit of others, though it cost Him dearly. Do you?

Jennifer Alsup has been a member of the Karns family for 19 years. She met, got engaged to and married her husband, Brad, at the Karns church building. They have been happily married for 8 years and have two children, Evan and Allie, whom she teaches at home. Jennifer enjoys sewing, baking, gardening, reading with her kids, and sipping coffee with friends.

Baptismal Buddies

My family and I were invited to attend Karns by Jill's co-worker, Valerie Sampson. We didn't know what to expect. The obvious things, such as a cappella singing and taking the Lord's Supper every Sunday, stood out. However, it was the teaching about baptism that really got our attention. I was "scared" into baptism at 10 years old after hearing a story of a boy who didn't go to heaven because he wasn't baptized and I didn't want to be like him.

After attending for about 2 weeks, Jill decided to be baptized on a Sunday morning. I remember being so excited for her and smiling all during church. The next week, we were visited at home by Edwin Jones and Tom Miller. I told them the story of how I was baptized at a young age and didn't feel like it had been for the right reasons. Immediately, they said that this situation could be corrected and we could go to the church right then. I didn't want to put them out, being that it was a Monday night, but they insisted that it was not a problem! Jill called Valerie to let her know what I was going to do and she and her husband met us there. Once they arrived, Valerie then decided that she needed to be re-baptized as she was baptized very young as well. We call ourselves "Baptismal Buddies."

I am thankful that Valerie invited us to attend church because I have learned so much that I never knew. I am now a worker for the Lord and who knows, you may see me on door number 4!

Daniel Cheatham is a graduate of Powell High School and attended Pellissippi State. He is married to Jill and they have two sons, Jonah and Conner. In his spare time, Daniel enjoys going to movies, playing basketball with his boys, and working on the field crew for the Powell High School Marching Band.

Lusitania

O n this day in 1915 during World War I, a steamship named the Lusitania was sunk by a German submarine as she was sailing from New York to Liverpool. Over 1,000 people lost their lives, including many Americans. The sinking came as a surprise to almost everyone since the Lusitania was known as the fastest ship above or below water, and it was believed that no German sub could sink the ship. One survivor later recalled, "I don't think we thought of war. It was too beautiful a passage to think of anything like war."

The sinking, however, shouldn't have come as a surprise to the passengers. Before departure, the German embassy ran ads warning that the ship would be attacked if it sailed into the war zone. The ads were even printed directly next to the ship's departure dates.

Revelation 22:20 says, "He who testifies to these things says, 'Surely I am coming quickly.' Amen. Even so, come, Lord Jesus!" Even so come Lord Jesus." Here is a warning of a future event, the return of Jesus Christ. What is your reaction to this warning? Some of us are like those on the Lusitania who completely ignored the clear warning. Others are like that one survivor who read the warning but believed that destruction could never occur in his beautiful, secure world. Let's not be so busy and preoccupied with the little things of life that we don't heed clear warnings. Instead, take a few moments to think and reflect about eternity and what Jesus has warned will occur. Then, I hope our response will be just as the apostle John's: "Even so, come Lord Jesus!"

Justin Boitnott is a second year law student at the University of Tennessee. He enjoys watching football, soccer, basketball, baseball, NASCAR, Formula 1, Indy car racing, golf, hockey, cycling, cricket, lacrosse, rugby, tennis, and curling. He also plays piano and enjoys cooking with his wife, Kelli.

Sippy Cups or a Big Gulp?

Question: Can a glass that is full hold anymore?
Answer: Yes!

Question: Can a person receive more blessings?
Answer: Yes!

Question: What is the difference between a person and a glass?
Answer: A person can grow; a cup is always the same size.

How can a cup hold more? Pour out its contents and it can hold more. How does a person receive more blessings? When we pour our blessings on others, we can hold more.

Sippy cups are for small hands, not yet experienced in the art of drinking from an open glass. You simply do not see the majority of adults drinking from Sippy cups, instead we have moved on to the "Big Gulp." The 96 ounce "supersize me" container! We want to have plenty to fill us up!

But that is not how it works with God's blessings. First, His blessings are bountiful; everyone can have what they can hold! Second, for us to receive more we do not fill our cup with them, we pour our cup of blessings on others. Third, to have more, we have to change from our "Sippy cups" to the "Big Gulp!" How? We grow in our understanding and knowledge of God. Should we expect to receive more of God's blessings if we fail to learn more about Him? Should we expect Him to bless us when we fail to live for Him? To do so is like drinking from an empty cup. Yes, God wants to bless us, but we chose our cups! So which will it be, a "Sippy Cup" or the "Big Gulp?"

Jeff Smith is married to Sherry and they have two children, Lauren and Hannah. Jeff and his family have been members at Karns since 2001. Jeff has served the congregation as an elder and is often referred to as "The Bible Bowl Man." He enjoys reading, writing, congregational singing, and passionate gospel preaching.

Count Your Many Blessings

All of us have problems and they can, at times, overwhelm us. One usually feels that his own problems are the worst of all. It is in this kind of situation that we need to pause and remember our blessings in order to see our problems in proper perspective.

An attitude of "count your many blessings, name them one by one" will change our basic life attitudes from negative to positive. If we can see our day-to-day problems and even our longer-range problems against a background of our blessings, our lives can be much happier and we will be much more constructive in facing our problems.

Let's focus our attention on our blessings. Let's think of what we do have instead of what we do not have. It would be a good exercise for each one of us to sit down and make a list of all our blessings, then post that list in some prominent place where we can see it daily as we go about our usual routine. We must let the positive dominate our thinking in order not to become negative-minded and pessimistic.

God has made us in His own image, giving us the realization that we are living souls and that we will live on eternally. Let's remember the words of James, "Every good gift and every perfect gift is from above, and comes down from the Father of lights..." (James 1:17).

If we want to live a happy life and be pleasing to God, we must take the time to count our many blessings and name them one by one.

Gregg Woodall is an elder of the Karns Church of Christ. Gregg is married to Sherrye and they have four children, Stephanie, Tiffany, Benjamin, and Jonathan. They also have four grandchildren, Wrigley, Walton, Adalynn, and Brooklynn. Gregg enjoys golfing, dirt bike riding, spending time with family, and is a fan of the Tennessee Volunteers.

God Has a Job for You

It was a cold January 21st, my birthday, and I was planning to travel to upper East Tennessee to work that day. About 10:00 that morning it started spitting snow and I decided to return to Knoxville. Later that day, I decided to go jogging at the high school track, although it was still snowing.

Making my first lap, I noticed that ahead was a pile of clothing, at least, that's what I thought. However, jogging on, I realized it was a person! I thought the man was stretching for a jog. Looking down, I realized that I knew this man. I said, "Hi, Glenn." He did not respond and as I stopped and went back, I realized that my Christian brother was in deep trouble. Glenn went to my church and was a very active Christian with our work.

Glenn was not breathing. I looked for help, but the students had all left except for one that was getting into his car. I ran to him and told him to go to the school and tell any coach that he saw to call 911.

I went back to Glenn and started CPR by myself. I finally got into a rhythm and was going pretty well, but he was not breathing yet. Two coaches came and one helped me. Yes, I was doing mouth-to-mouth.

Glenn was taken to the hospital and eventually recovered. He said the most beautiful prayers in our worship. God had a job for me that day. He also had a job for Glenn and He needed him a while longer. "For we are His workmanship, created in Christ Jesus for good works, which God prepared beforehand that we should walk in them" (Eph. 2:10). God has a job for you to do!

Ken Couch is a sales representative for Royal Brass and Hose, an industrial hose and fitting supplier in Knoxville Tn. He regularly travels in his job throughout East Tennessee, Eastern Kentucky and Southwestern Virginia. He enjoys High School football and following the Tennessee Volunteers.

One for the Record Books

Gloria lived at 58 Pine Road. I lived at 77 Pine Road. As a natural result of our avidly searching Gloria's copy of the Guinness World Record Book, Gloria decided that we would set a world record. She put a plank across a wooden sawhorse and secured pillows on either end. Gloria and I would break the world's longest see-saw record. Gloria always put action behind her ideas.

Ever persuasive, she talked me into her undeniably thorough plan. The key to our certain success was location. Gloria placed our see-saw of Destiny under her mother's kitchen window. We would lack for nothing. All we had to do was yell through the window. A bucket on a rope would lower to us any drink, snack or book we needed. The belief that her mother would be completely available for three days and nights clinched our resources.

When the shepherd of Psalm 23 said his cup runneth over, and when Jesus explicitly looked to His Father for His needs while on earth, and when Paul assured the sailors of safety despite shipwreck even as they tossed their own resources into the stormy sea, this principle was in place. We have the God who promised all His resources are available. As believers, we choose our location and trust in the ready availability of those resources. With a well-placed sawhorse and God's guarantees, we pray.

"My God shall supply all your need according to His riches in glory by Christ Jesus." (Philippians 4:19). "May the God of hope fill you with all joy and peace in believing. . ." (Romans 15:13).

Melea Nash Smith is married to Steve. They have four children, Jordan, Melea Jean, Bryan, and Sarah. Melea participated in the creation of the World's Longest Banana Split while I was a student at Freed-Hardeman College. She has photos.

It's Magic!

Many years ago, I learned a few "magic" tricks so that I could entertain the young people at church

On one occasion, I was "magically" pushing a pencil through my ear, and pulling it back out. Well, the kids were impressed. Their eyes opened wide, their mouth's dropped open, and I could even hear a few gasps. Mission accomplished.

However, after church that morning, I saw a little boy who had seen me do this trick, with a pencil in his ear, grimacing in pain as he was trying to push that pencil in his ear. Ouch!

It was at that point I decided not to do that trick anymore. I can just hear it now. . . The emergency room doctor talking to the parents of this boy saying, "He said the preacher told him to do it."

Something else I learned that day is that "Faith is only as safe as the object in which it is placed."

Blind faith is not only useless, but it can be dangerous. Friends, consider the things that you believe. In what have you placed your faith? We certainly don't want to find ourselves pushing pencils through our ears because of a misplaced faith.

Open your Bible and study it, for faith comes by hearing the word of God (Romans 10:17).

Steve Higginbotham has been the pulpit minister for the Karns church of Christ since 2010. Steve is married to Kim and they have four children, Kelli, Michael, Matthew, and Anne Marie. Steve enjoys writing, playing golf, and is a fan of the Pittsburgh Steelers, the WVU Mountaineers, and the Andy Griffith Show.

Is Your Christianity a Costume?

On October 31st each year, children of all ages dress up in costumes or put on masks and pretend to be something they are not. Some of the costumes are cute, some funny, some scary and others are flat out hideous. Yet, it does not matter how different each costume appears, they all have one thing in common; they are all used so people can pretend to be someone they are not.

Many times, I'm afraid we do the same thing with our Christianity. We dress up in a costume and pretend to be something we are not. Each week we put on our best clothes, grab our Bibles, put a smile on our faces and attend worship services. We try to trick people into believing we are devoted followers of Christ. We come to church and pretend to be someone different, hoping no one will notice our Christianity is nothing more than a costume.

When God sent Samuel to anoint one of the sons of Jesse as king, Samuel was sure God was going to anoint Eliab as king; however, God chose David, because He saw in David what Samuel could not see: his heart (1 Samuel 16:7).

When we come to church, we must remember that we may be able to trick most people, but we can't trick or fool God. He does not see as man sees, because God can see our hearts!

Friends, God knows whether our Christianity is genuine or simply a costume. Let's make sure the kind of lives we are living during the week match the kind of lives we live on Sundays.

Justin Morton has been in student ministry for almost 10 years. He has been the student and family minister for the Karns church of Christ since 2010. Justin is married to Miranda and they have one son, Caden. Justin enjoys spending time with his family, studying, teaching, writing and is a fan of the Tennessee Volunteers.

Best Friends

I know I am very blessed to be able to say that I have had a best friend for 42 years. Not a lot of people could say that. We have been the best of friends through thick and thin, and have seen a lot of changes over the decades.

Frances Redmon was there for me when my oldest son was killed in a car wreck, when I lost my daughter to cancer, and through the loss of my husband to cancer. It broke my heart when she had to move to Collierville. I didn't want to see her go.

We can find good friends all around us, especially in the church. We have deacons, elders, and all of our brothers and sisters in Christ, but another best friend we can find is Jesus, himself. He, too, is always with us everywhere we go and in all that we do: in all of our losses, He grieves with us. He helps us to make it through some of the hardest times in our lives. We would be lost without him.

What a great thing to have best friends here on Earth and in Heaven.

Thelma Teague is the mother of Gary Teague, grandmother to Heatherly Stiles, and the great-grandmother to baby Avery. Before retiring, Thelma worked for Bellsouth for 35 years.

Standing Out

Most of us who have children, or who are young enough to remember watching Sesame Street will remember a particular song that was sung on the show. This song was sung while children were shown a group of four or five items, one of which was different from the others, and they had to find the item that didn't belong. It was a fun game for the children.

Can the world tell that you are not like others; that you are somehow different? Does the world see Christ in you or do you just blend in? 1 John 2:6 says, "He who says he abides in Him ought himself also to walk just as He walked." Does this remind you of that popular saying from a few years back, "What would Jesus do?" "Therefore be imitators of God as dear children. And walk in love, as Christ also has loved us and given Himself for us, an offering and a sacrifice to God for a sweet-smelling aroma" (Ephesians 5:1-2).

Jesus was a perfect example of how we should live our lives and we should strive diligently every day to emulate Him in all we do. In Matthew 5:16 Jesus tells us, "Let your light so shine before men, that they may see your good works and glorify your Father in heaven."

Everywhere you go let your light shine so brightly that people can't help but notice that you are different.

Sarah Martin is a stay at home wife and mother. Sarah is married to Gabe and they have three children, Drew, Jackson, and Emma. Sarah stays busy teaching children's Bible classes, volunteering at her children's school, and serving on the PTA board. Sarah enjoys reading, sewing and crafting, and spending time with her family.

On Being Whole

There was once a manger, socially unacceptable shepherd witnesses, a poor person's dedicated sacrifice, and a blue-collar household. Among such things, Jesus learned a physically demanding trade, often did not have a place to lay His head, and, at His death, was stripped of everything He owned—the clothes on His back.

There is a message there. The message may comfort, it may embarrass, and it may perplex, but it cannot be easily ignored. Jesus was great because of His unadorned character. Without an "acceptable" education, no professional status, and in the absence of either worldly power or wealth He still stands as the greatest man to have ever lived.

He knew, in His humanity, where He came from. A young virgin girl raised Him in a town held in contempt. When His message hit too close to home, His past was dismissively remembered. He did not care. He knew who He was.

These things mean a lot to me. They help me remember where I came from. Old clothes, a run-down house, twenty years old and still in high school could give a guy a complex. I must admit, at times they did. Then one day, I read the Gospels and was introduced to Jesus. Things have never been the same!

You see, in Jesus every man and every woman can find meaning and acceptance. With or without the things the world covets, we can all be whole in the Christ!

Edwin Jones has been with Karns and the school of preaching for almost 27 years. Currently he is the Dean of Students with the school. Edwin and Sara have three children and four grandchildren as well as a variety of "adopted" family members they have incorporated into their mix over the years.

He Picked Me

My best friend throughout elementary school was a guy named Tony. Tony was more athletic than me, and knew more about all sports than me. During recess, we would play football with other guys. Tony and another guy were often the "captains" and would pick teams from among the rest of us who would gather on the playground. I was often picked last, but Tony would always pick me. I managed to get a first down on occasion (even though I really did not know what "first down" meant). Looking back, I know Tony could have chosen any number of reasons NOT to pick me, but he picked me anyway.

From mankind's perspective, there are any number of reasons why God could have chosen NOT to pick certain people to do certain tasks. When I am down on myself, I am reminded that I'm in good company. Moses had a speech impediment. David was an adulterer. Jonah ran away from God. Jeremiah was depressed. Lazarus was dead. However, God picked each of these people anyway, and gave each of these people the opportunity to overcome their weaknesses, to manifest His power.

The prophet records in Jeremiah 1:5 that before he was formed in the womb, God knew him, and had picked him to be a prophet. Though I am not a prophet, I was picked by God to be a part of His mission of reaching a lost world. Like a lot of people recorded in the Bible, there are any number of reasons for God to NOT pick me. He picked me anyway, and I am thankful.

Darren McCoy and his wife, Pam, joined the Karns congregation in 1997 (the year he moved to Knoxville and attended graduate school at the University of Tennessee College of Nursing). Darren works as a nurse practitioner, and his hobbies include outdoor activities such as scuba diving, fishing, and skiing.

Find Your Talent

As a young lady, I tried to have a happy home. I spent a lot of time cleaning, dusting and all my wifely duties. As the years went by it seemed like no one noticed my clean house, so I did more entertaining of those less fortunate and people I wanted to know better. I came to love entertaining in my home.

One young lady told me her thoughts about myself and my home. She had left home because she was so unhappy. I let her stay a couple of nights, after calling her parents and getting permission for her to stay. She told me she loved to come to my home because of the genuine love, understanding, and most of all, the peace. I have always remembered her words and tried to be more patient with others by having more love, laughter and peace in my home.

I recently had a chance to observe a lot of people. First the teens washed my car with much laughter and fun, then some came to the hospital for my surgery to sit with family and later still to visit with me in my hospital room. Many came to my home to bring food or offering the help in other ways from shopping to cleaning house. I really enjoyed all the many cards that were sent. I observed and saw the reaction of others to all these kind deeds. We all have time to make a call, send a card, or make a short visit. All these things remind me of how Jesus went about doing good and how even the small things bring joy.

Everyone has a talent. Find your talents. Whether they are big or small, you can bring glory to God and joy to others through them only if you use them. Purpose today to use yourself in service to others. It will bring joy to them and you.

Shelba Kennedy was born in Crossville, TN and raised in Elyria, Ohio. Shelba is a widow with two children and two grandchildren. She's been a member at Karns since 1981. She loves to entertain, cook, and meet members of the community while she works at the polling booths, which she has worked for the past 25 years.

In a Spirit of Gentleness

It was 2002 and we were on vacation in Florida when a television news report from Loxley, Alabama caught my attention. It seems that a local man was delivering the eulogy at the funeral of his wife's uncle. He recognized the life of the uncle as having not been a very good example to the rest of the family, so he chose this occasion to try to steer them in a better direction. He described the uncle as a "drunkard and a fornicator" and said that he was in hell and those in attendance were headed in the same direction. A vicious beating ensued and police were called to the scene.

The first thing I thought of was Acts 7 and Stephen's death by stoning following the biting condemnation he delivered in Jerusalem. I felt some admiration of this man for being ready to rebuke sinners with all authority in accordance with scriptures such as 2 Timothy 4:2 and Titus 2:15. But did he read those passages completely and in context? While our readiness to rebuke sinners is commanded, it's to be done with "complete patience and teaching" (2 Timothy 4:2). A reading of Titus 2 in its entirety reveals that we are to teach and rebuke - but with integrity and dignity. Stephen's cutting remarks made him the first recorded Christian martyr (Acts 7:60).

Yes, this man's zeal and courage are admirable, but I hope he read Galatians 6:1 during his recovery: "Brothers, if anyone is caught in any transgression, you who are spiritual should restore him in a spirit of gentleness. Keep watch on yourself, lest you too be tempted."

Don Scott was recruited to Knoxville from his home state of Virginia by his wife of 20 years, Amy, who is also responsible for bringing him to Christ. Don works from home as an engineer and Amy stays busy as a homeschooling mom. The children love to volunteer with various camps, little leagues, and scouting organizations.

A Worthy Woman

My mother was a true pioneer faithful Christian woman. She gave birth to my five brothers and four sisters and me in a bedroom at home. She had the first five of us in five years and the second five in ten years. I'm next to the youngest, born on October 9, 1929, a birthday I share with my brother!

After I married and had four children, one day I asked her how she ever managed with so many of us! She said she would rather have not had so many but she loved Daddy and wanted to be a good wife to him. She said, after knowing that she really was expecting again, she began praying and looking to the future. She asked God to guide her in the rearing of yet another child.

And life was hard. We had no inside plumbing until I was 22 years old. No electricity until I was 14. Yet she canned hundreds of jars of food on a wood burning stove, washed clothes on a scrub board, sewed for us on a treadle sewing machine, cooked and cleaned and countless other tasks. And she was happy! I remember her singing "church" songs quite often as she went through her day working. She and my daddy had devotionals with us at night, but if he were not at home because of some work-related reason, she read the Bible and prayed with us. I have such good memories of hearing her read.

How very blessed I am to have had her for my mother! Truly a worthy woman as in Proverbs 31!

Mattie Lou Robinson has been married to Grover Cleveland (G. C.) Robinson, Jr. since June 27, 1954. They have four children: Timothy, Amy, Andy and Penny; and three grandchildren: Victoria, Quintin and Ransom. Mattie Lou is a homemaker and also taught school for 15 years. Mattie Lou turned 83 on October 9th, 2012.

Teach Your Children to Show Kindness

There was a young mother who decided to take Thursdays to teach her little girls how to show kindness. One Thursday they set out, not knowing exactly what they were going to do, but sure an opportunity would present itself. Near noon, the girls were hungry and on the way to McDonald's, the mother noticed panhandlers at several intersections. The idea struck her that these people must be hungry too. At McDonald's she bought Happy Meals for the girls and ordered additional meals to-go.

At each intersection they would give the panhandlers a contribution and say, "Oh, by the way, here's lunch." There was no time for a reply, just a surprised look. As they came to the end of their route, they had one lunch bag left. They handed it and a contribution to a small lady on the corner. While they were waiting for the traffic light to change the lady expressed her amazement, "No one has ever done anything like this for me before." The young mother replied, "When will you eat your lunch?" The lady looked at her and replied, "Oh, I'm not going to eat this lunch. I have a little girl at home and she just loves McDonald's, but I can never afford to buy it for her, but tonight she is going to have McDonald's!" The mother had tears in her eyes. Many times she questioned if their acts of kindness were too small or insignificant to really effect change. I am sure at that moment she knew.

What a great example to her girls. Do you take the time to teach your children kindness?

Doris Finger was born in Knoxville and has lived in Knoxville all her life except for 3 years. She is currently retired and enjoys spending her time helping others. Doris has taught primary classes for 45 years with 42 of those years here at the Karns congregation!

Greatness

Michael Phelps began swimming at the age of seven and started competing around age eleven. On July 31, 2012, Phelps became the most decorated Olympic athlete ever, winning his 19th medal. He accomplished the feat at age 27. It is an impressive feat brought about by dedication and determination on the part of Phelps and his family over the course of twenty years. Phelps spent countless hours training, keeping a rigorous schedule to ensure he was in peak form. His family taxied him to practices and swim meets, and ultimately followed him around the world, as he became the dominant force in swimming, earning international stardom.

What if Michael Phelps had been introduced to the truths of the Bible at age seven? What if his family had spent all those hours immersed in God's Word instead of a swimming pool? What if the trips around the country and world had been mission trips instead of swimming trips? What if he had led nineteen people to Jesus instead of winning that many Olympic medals?

We can pursue greatness for ourselves or our children in almost any field imaginable, from sports to business to medicine, but God tells us to put our best efforts into His cause, seeking His glory and His will (Matthew 6:19-21, 33). Let us just make sure that we are giving our best to God each day. There may not be a medal stand in our future, but we will hear God's welcome home when our lives are over (Matthew 25:21). That's better than Olympic medals any day.

Brad Alsup serves as a deacon at the Karns church of Christ. He is married to Jennifer, and they have two children, Evan and Allie. Brad is a hunter, a cyclist, and an avid reader.

Why Do I Own a Pizza-Loving Dog?

As I threw a few slices of pizza on my plate and plopped down in the living room chair, I immediately became the best friend to my dog, Shadow. Odd as it was, he never gave me this kind of attention before when I called on him to play or snuggle! But now, with each savory bite I took, Shadow inched closer. Oh how sad and frustrated he must have felt when I resisted his gazing, sad eyes and weakening whimper. I certainly wished I could have somehow communicated to him that I wasn't trying to be mean or selfish. After all, I would have loved to share with him, but it wouldn't have favored him in the end!

In similar fashion, it's so easy to thank God when we receive those things we pray for and desire most. On the contrary, how often might we call into question, grumble or rebel when He doesn't seem to give us what we want or desire? Jeremiah 29:11 reminds us, "For I know the thoughts that I think toward you, says the LORD, thoughts of peace and not of evil, to give you a future and a hope." God certainly knows and desires what's best for us. For this reason alone, we should humble ourselves and appreciate God for His wisdom, insight, and loving care that is best for our welfare.

It certainly brings great joy and comfort. "Now this is the confidence that we have in Him, that if we ask anything according to His will, He hears us" (1 John 5:14). In those moments when God's response doesn't seem to align itself with our desires, when we look up toward heaven with sad puppy dog eyes and a whimpering voice, how joyful would be our song if we could faithfully respond, "nevertheless not My will, but Yours, be done" (Luke 22:42).

John Hoffarth has been a Christian for over 20 years and enjoys sharing the faith with friends or those seeking a stronger relationship with God. He also likes trying any new activity that challenges his fears or physical endurance. To relax, he enjoys the opportunity to travel abroad or spend quality time at home with his wife Karen and son Austin.

Keep Nothing Back

" And how I kept back nothing that was profitable unto you" (Acts 20:20).

The Lord always keeps up on His part. The words that the apostle stated long ago should bring great comfort to all who seek the Lord.

God and Christ have kept nothing back that would be profitable to men. They have done everything and provided all that is needed for salvation of mankind. Christ died on the cross after a perfect life, was raised from the dead, sent his apostles into the world to preach the gospel to men through the guidance of the Holy Spirit, and gave to man through that means all the knowledge that is needed to know concerning salvation.

The apostles kept nothing back that men needed to know. Everything they had received, they delivered to others that they may have knowledge and be convinced of the truth of the gospel of Jesus Christ. The text shows that these men endured all sorts of tribulations - even torture and death - taking the words of eternal life to men. They kept nothing back men needed to know, but preached Christ and him crucified. They were determined to know nothing except Christ and to proclaim the truth to men. They lived for Him and died for the truth.

Men who know the truth today should keep nothing back. They should not hold back or soften speeches in order to influence men. They should not refrain from speaking all of the truth. This type of hesitation to remark on sins would allow more sin to creep in.

Tony Williams is originally from Chattanooga and was baptized at the East Ridge congregation. He is married to Deanna, and they have three daughters, Claire, Maggie, and Ella. Tony has a Bachelor's and Master's Degree from UT. Tony and his family have been at Karns since 1999, and during that time he has served as a deacon, and currently as an elder.

Take Care of Your Own Dent

I have always liked cars, especially fast, classic cars. When I was 14 years of age, while driving a go-cart, I came just a little too close to a car and put a small dent in the side of a brand new '63 Ford Fairlane. My life went before me. I thought, I may as well end it all. I got sick at my stomach thinking about having to tell Daddy about this. I had learned long before not to try to hide things. So, the only thing I could do was to fess up—tell Daddy and suffer death with as much dignity as I possibly could.

I still remember the scene to this day. I had already gotten the estimate—$11. 50. Daddy was standing in the cow lot when I told him. Daddy was short on patience and meted out justice rather quickly, and generally according to deserts on my part. To my surprise, Daddy said, "Well, you'll just have to pay for it. You are responsible for the dent and you will have to own up to your responsibility. You must take care of your own dents." I was able to get the money by piling brush for 25 cents per hour.

We live in times such that many view themselves as victims. Frequently, we hear the cry, "It's not my fault." The best lesson I ever learned was to own up to my responsibility. This is a lesson better learned while young. One will go far in life by learning to be responsible. Don't whine about your plight, whatever it may be, but be responsible.

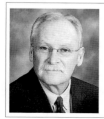

David Lipe was born in Charleston, MS and is married to his wife Linda (Wilson). They have three daughters and five grandchildren. David presently serves as the Director of the Southeast Institute of Biblical Studies.

You Play to Win the Game

The title quote was made by former football coach Herm Edwards. It might just seem to be for the few that appreciate football, but it can apply to our daily Christian walk.

What do we get if we win this game? A home in heaven. Jesus Christ drafted us when he died on the cross and we sign a lifetime contract with him when we are baptized and begin our walk.

Just like football, we face many different challenges throughout our game. Jesus doesn't want us on the sideline or just in the huddle. He wants us on the field making plays and making sure Satan doesn't cause a change of possession.

There are times where we are in a 4th down situation and thanks to Jesus, we can get a 1st down anytime needed from anywhere on the field. Of course, we won't execute the playbook exactly but the coach won't yell at us but pick us up and say try again.

Unlike football, there is not a halftime. There are no timeouts. The game is played continuously and challenging from end zone to end zone. There is not a time in the game where the starters are pulled to rest. We are in the starting lineup from beginning to end and expected to give 100%.

No matter what quarter of the game you are in, Jesus will not give up on his expectations for you. Jesus Christ is the head coach and our playbook is the Bible and if we execute the way God drew it up, we will win the game without worrying about a last second play.

Wayne Begarly has been a member of the Karns Church of Christ since 2011. Wayne graduated from UT in 2007 with a Bachelors in Communications. Wayne is involved with the local United Way and American Cancer Society. He enjoys sports and the outdoors in his free time.

The Light of the Word

God wants us to be a light to this world (Matthew 5:13-16). You may be the only way that someone ever hears the gospel (Mark 16:15-16)! Notice the consequences if one is not saved in verse 16 of Mark 16! We have to reach out to as many people as possible before it's too late. It's also very important that we live right and be examples to others.

There are plenty of different reasons why people choose not to become Christians, but there are two that we can definitely do something about.

1.   They don't know the gospel or any Christians.

2.   They know the gospel and they know Christians, but those Christians don't act right; they don't live how a Christian should live. Once again, we can do something about both of those! We can be a light and spread the gospel, and we can be an example to others of how to live a Christian life.

It will not always be easy. "Remember the word that I said to you, 'A servant is not greater than his master.' If they persecuted Me, they will also persecute you. If they kept My word, they will keep yours also" (John 15:20). There WILL be hard times. That doesn't mean you'll be killed like Jesus, but it won't be all easy-going either. God has promised those who are persecuted eternal life (Matthew 5:10-12).

No matter what happens to you on this earth, it will all be worth it in the end.

Samuel Cox is the son of Chris and Hannah Cox. Samuel is in the 8th grade and likes basketball, playing guitar and keyboard.

Judge Not

Matthew 7:2 has always been a classic passage on the issue of judging. There are many passages on judging. In fact, you could probably write many hundreds of thousands of words just on the topic of judging in the New Testament. The English word "judge" appears more than 54 times in the New Testament, even more if you widen parameters to include the equivalent Greek word - "krino." We judge, in a loose sense, every day of our lives. We discern whether we like the weather; we analyze the clothing of our coworkers and classmates; and we even critique our own actions. All of these actions are considered judging; some of them more innocent than others.

At what point are these judgments considered wrong on our part? In my estimation, it is when our observation or analysis becomes one that condemns or passes sentence upon another. Sin is often obvious, just as a beam would be obvious in the eye of another (Matthew 7:3–5; Luke 6:41–42). Sometimes we cannot help but notice when there is such a fault being paraded about in a public and noticeable manner. But, as these passages indicate, it is easier for us to find the beam, than to dig deep and refine our own specks. We are quicker to point out the obvious beam (often in the form of gossip to others) before we are willing to deal with our own issues and judge ourselves.

Is judging another truly love as Christ commanded?

Romans 14:10 says, "But why do you judge your brother? Or why do you show contempt for your brother? For we shall all stand before the judgment seat of Christ."

Spencer Clark is the son of Terry and Teresa Clark. He was born and raised in the Karns Congregation. As of December 2012, Spencer will have graduated from Freed-Hardeman University with a degree in Bible. He plans to continue onto graduate studies and begin work in the ministry.

Plowshares of Peace

Strong's Exhaustive Concordance defines a plowshare as "a hoe or other digging instrument." Most of us think of a hoe as something used to loosen dirt or dig up weeds in the garden. However, in the book of Isaiah it refers to a time of peace.

In Old Testament times, God's people were involved in many carnal wars at the direction of God (Deuteronomy 21:10). The enemies of Israel were trying to destroy them. However, the God of heaven protected them. At times, Israel was attacked and lost the war due to their sins. One example was the seventy years of captivity in Babylon (Jeremiah 25:11).

Isaiah 2:2-4 reads, "Now it shall come to pass in the latter days That the mountain of the LORD's house Shall be established on the top of the mountains, And shall be exalted above the hills; And all nations shall flow to it. Many people shall come and say, 'Come, and let us go up to the mountain of the LORD, To the house of the God of Jacob; He will teach us His ways, And we shall walk in His paths.' For out of Zion shall go forth the law, And the word of the LORD from Jerusalem. He shall judge between the nations, And rebuke many people; They shall beat their swords into plowshares, And their spears into pruning hooks; Nation shall not lift up sword against nation, Neither shall they learn war anymore."

According to 1 Peter 1:20 and Hebrews 1:2; 12:18-29, we are now living in the "last days." The Kingdom of God (the church of Christ) is not a Kingdom of carnal war. Carnal war cannot bring the type of peace described in John 14:27. The destructive power of carnal warfare has no place in the Kingdom of God.

 Gary Kelsey has been preaching the gospel for 35 years and is married to Chris (Banner). They have been married for 57 years and have 4 children. He has served congregations in Virginia, London England, Tennessee, Alabama, and Ohio.

The Blind Leading the Blind

While studying Literature, I came across a painting by Pieter Bruegel illustrating Matthew 15:14, which states, "...If the blind leads the blind, both will fall into a ditch." It shows a group of five blind men being led by a blind man. The first man falls into a ditch and one by one the others are headed into the ditch, as well.

When I saw this I thought how a "seeing" man should jump in front of those that hadn't yet fallen and save them from the ditch. There are many people that are being led astray by false doctrine. They are blind, because instead of studying the Bible themselves, they put their trust in others.

There are numerous religious groups including Christians, Jews, Buddists, etc., all teaching different things. Within "Christianity" there are many sects, all teaching different things. They can't all be right. God knows what He wants His followers to do and gave us His written Word and made it simple enough for even children to know. It is our responsibility to study that word and know it. Those who learn it and become Christians should work hard to jump in front of those who are blindly following the blind and help them onto the right path to heaven.

I don't want to blindly follow someone else. Have you studied God's Word yourself or are you following a certain path because your parents or grandparents or your preacher or friend says it is the right way? Don't leave going to heaven to someone else. "Study to show yourself approved unto God,. . . rightly dividing the word of truth" (2 Timothy 2:15).

Will Albert is 15 years old and a home schooled sophomore. He enjoys playing video games and tennis. He also enjoys playing with his sheltie, Miya. He plans to attend college and pursue a career in video game design or video game development.

From Faith, to Grace, to Glory

I do not know how to adequately describe the glory of springtime–the new life, the beautiful flowers. I do not know how to adequately describe a golden sunset in the winter. I don't know how to do justice in trying to describe the real worth and value of this life that we have been given in Christ.

I feel like David must have felt when he wrote in the book of Psalm 139:6, "Such knowledge is too wonderful for me; it is high, I cannot attain unto it."

In Galatians 2:20, Paul wrote "...the life which I now live in the flesh I live by the faith of the Son of God, who loved me, and gave himself for me."

Above anything else in the world, the Christian religion is a thing of faith. A faith which is not a blind, illogical thing, but a faith that is grounded and founded upon facts. Our faith has been tested and tried and is true.

In Titus 2:11 Paul wrote, "For the grace of God that brings salvation has appeared to all men." In the Bible there is the idea that God's grace is for all people, no matter the circumstances of one's life. 2 Corinthians 3:18 says, "But we all, with unveiled face, beholding as in a mirror the glory of the Lord, are being transformed into the same image from glory to glory. . ." Moses on top of Mt. Sinai was permitted, with a veil over his face, to see the glory of God. But Paul says that we, "With open face are able to behold the glory of God." From faith, to grace, to glory.

Wendell Agee was born and raised in Pikeville, TN. He served 20 years in the USAF and was a successful business man for over 30 years. Wendell has served the Lord as a missionary to Cuba, Jamaica, Honduras and other countries. He's a member of the Karns Church of Christ.

We All Need Encouragement

"Then news of these things came to the ears of the church in Jerusalem, and they sent out Barnabas to go as far as Antioch. When he came and had seen the grace of God, he was glad, and encouraged them all that with purpose of heart they should continue with the Lord. For he was a good man, full of the Holy Spirit and of faith. And a great many people were added to the Lord" (Acts 11:22-24).

The description "good man" is reserved for use only 10 times in the Bible. Barnabas was attributed with that description and for good reason as he exemplified the man of God who was always found encouraging brethren. He was a great source of encouragement to Paul and to the early church. Is it any wonder that the brethren in Jerusalem chose Barnabas to go out and encourage all of those who were new in the faith?

The first example of Christ-likeness we find is in Antioch. It was there that the disciples were first called Christians. The encouraging leaders they had were Paul and Barnabas. Let's set our sights on being encouragers just like Barnabas so that we, too, can be worthy to wear the name Christian.

If, like the church in Jerusalem, we selected an encourager to send out to those in need would it be you or someone else? It is not possible to have too many encouragers in the church, so let's all start today by encouraging someone. I know you can do it!

Gregg Woodall is an elder of the Karns Church of Christ. Gregg is married to Sherrye and they have four children, Stephanie, Tiffany, Benjamin, and Jonathan. They also have four grandchildren, Wrigley, Walton, Adalynn, and Brooklynn. Gregg enjoys golfing, dirt bike riding, spending time with family, and is a fan of the Tennessee Volunteers.

The Cello Man

One Saturday I felt like going on a road trip. A friend decided to come along and thirty minutes after planning it we were on our way to Nashville. While walking down Boulevard St. and passing by some street musicians surrounded by large groups of tourists, a lonely guy playing the cello called our attention. We literally sat down on the sidewalk and listened to him and talked to him in between songs.

I noticed that every time he finished playing a song, he would look around, not at his tips, but at how many people were standing around listening, and he would get so upset to see nobody or just a few other people listening, or tipping without listening. It saddened us, so we stayed there to encourage him and to get others to notice him. Then my friend made a touching comment. She compared this image to God and us. Just like this cello man played such beautiful songs hoping for people to notice him, so is God around us, giving us so many beautiful things hoping for the lost people notice him. But just like these people quickly passing by, minding their own business without even stopping to listen, people today get so busy with their own lives and don't take the time to notice God.

It was so good to stop and listen to this cello man, and it made me think... God is everywhere. We all need to stop our busy lives, see what's around us, and notice Him.

Helena Yegros was born and raised in Asuncion, Paraguay. She came to the US for college and attended Freed-Hardeman University. Helena graduated in 2011 with a B. S. degree in Biology and with a minor in Biochemistry. She worked for the year of 2012 at an Equine Hospital as a vet assistant in Knoxville, TN, and is currently living in Miami, FL.

Lost

It happened in January as our son was packing to go back to college: I washed some apples for him to take back to the dorm and I put them into his truck so he would not forget them. I finished up the lunch dishes and sat down - that was when I noticed it was missing! I looked everywhere. I frantically began retracing my steps. I was sick inside. I mourned and prayed and I kept looking. I looked when I was cooking, cleaning, or just sitting in my favorite chair (usually with my hands down in the cushions for the fourth time). There was a metal detector involved. The dog got x-rayed. Three places of business were on the look-out. Everyone knew it was missing. I even offered $100 reward to the family for whoever found it. Yes, I lost my wedding ring!

I thought about the woman who swept her house for her lost coins (Luke 15:8-10). Jesus told me to look for the lost to teach them the gospel. Do I search for the lost like I searched for that precious ring? Do I mourn and pray for the lost? It was a humbling lesson.

Five months, hundreds of miles and three mechanic visits later, I found the ring in my son's truck door when he returned home. I rejoiced and told everyone.

I now know how the woman felt when she found her coins. I hope I understand how the Father feels when we look and find His lost people.

Teresa Clark is the wife of Terry Clark and mother of Spencer and Seaver. Teresa works part time as a RN. She is a Bible class teacher to children, teen girls, and ladies. She enjoys outdoor activities, watching sports, and doing anything with her family.

Caught in the Undertow

I grew up in the "Great Lakes State," Michigan, and lived very close to Lake Michigan. If you know anything about the great lakes, you know that they are not your typical lakes. They are great in size and can become extremely violent due to high winds and shallow depths. Every summer I would hear news of several people who would get caught in an undertow and swept away from the shore. No matter how many warning signs were put out, people still chose to swim at their own risk in areas that were deemed unsafe. The power of the invisible current would overcome even the most advanced swimmers and sweep them out to their death.

We too can find ourselves at risk of being caught in the undertow of sin when we do not heed the warnings of the Bible. On the surface things look calm, but below the surface lies an invisible current of destruction that can carry us out to a point of no return. No matter how mature of a Christian a person may be, you can still be swept into a sinful circumstance and find yourself out of reach of our Heavenly Father's life ring of grace.

Read your Bible and take heed to its warnings. Here are a few scriptures that we can meditate on:

Proverbs 24:19-22.
Matthew 14:22-33.
2 Corinthians 6:14-16.
Colossians 3:1-25 & 4:1-6.
2 Peter 2:1-22.
The book of 1 John.

Adrian Marsh is a retired Navy veteran and is married to his high school sweetheart Lisa Marsh. He enjoys family time, traveling, cooking, sports and serving God.

The Body of Christ

Have you given much thought to what it means to be the body of Christ? Paul made a very profound statement in 1 Corinthians 12:27 when he said that we are the body of Christ. It is true when we say that Christians are members of the church and members of His body. However, it's very easy to be a passive member of something. It is easy to be a member of a gym, but never go to the gym. It is easy to be a member of the PTA at your local school, but never participate in any event geared toward improving the educational environment. When my kids were in the public elementary school, the school had more members of the local PTA than there were parents of the school. While they did have a high participation rate during meetings and activities, there were always more inactive members than active ones.

One of my favorite contemporary songs was written in 2003 by John Mark Hall. It is entitled, "If We are the Body." In this song, Hall reminds us that if we are the "body of Christ," then our hands would be used to heal, our lips would be used to speak the gospel of peace, and our feet would take us to those who need to be shown the way to Jesus.

We do some reaching, healing and teaching, but don't we have much room for improvement? Sometimes I ponder what will happen as our world becomes more and more hostile to Christianity. I know what Christ would do, and since we are His body, we'd better get moving!

Chris Cox serves as a deacon at the Karns congregation. He is also a computer programmer and small business owner. Chris is married to Hannah, and they have two children, Samuel and Rachel. Chris enjoys gardening, reading non-fiction, learning new things, teaching others, and spending time with his family.

My Brother's Keeper

I recently started volunteering in the women's prison ministry. This is one of the most rewarding services I have ever done. A recent class brought me to understand how much we impact each other in this life.

Romans 14: 7, 12-13 tells us, "For none of us lives to himself, and no one dies to himself. . . So then each of us shall give account of himself to God. Therefore let us not judge one another anymore, but rather resolve this, not to put a stumbling block or a cause to fall in our brother's way."

So often we hear people say, "It's nobody's business what I do." In reality, nothing is further from the truth. No person goes to heaven or hell alone. Therefore, what each one does is somebody else's business. This is a serious thought for everyone, especially for parents who have young souls within their care.

An unknown author writes:

"My life shall touch a dozen lives before this day in done,
Leave countless marks for good or ill ere sets the evening sun,
This is the wish I always wish, the prayer I always pray;
Lord, may my life help other lives it touches by the way."

This person could have not said it better for me. A smile, a handshake, a hug, a call, a text, a card, and words of encouragement speak volumes to a hurting soul. I'm a living ex-ample of the love I felt when I experienced personal loss in my family.

Lisa Marsh has been a federal employee since 1991. She is married to her high school sweetheart and they have one son together. Lisa enjoys traveling, family time, meeting new people, entertaining, reading and watching movies.

The Power of One

Things were not going well for the people of God. They were being oppressed by their enemies and the new government was not faring well. Their new king was constantly battling their enemies and the peace they longed for under an earthly ruler had eluded them. Something positive needed to happen and to happen soon before the whole nation fell into despair.

Given these circumstances, one man, not a group, not an army, but one individual took action. Jonathan rose up and said to his armor bearer, "Come, let us go over to the garrison of these uncircumcised; it may be that the Lord will work for us. For nothing restrains the Lord from saving by many or by few." (1 Samuel 14:6).

We may never face a garrison of uncircumcised Philistines, but God has a place for us in His battlefields. What are we waiting for, someone to lead the charge, someone to go with us, or just a more convenient time? How many souls are lost simply because we do not have the faith of action Jonathan had? Is our faith strong enough to trust God to lead us forward, to protect us, and to guide us as we do His service?

God has proven He is capable of doing so much with so little: Noah, and one ark; David with one stone; Mary, one faithful virgin; Jesus, the one and only begotten Son and his one cross. Come; let's go see what God can do with one faithful solider! Nothing can stop God.

Jeff Smith is married to Sherry and they have two children, Lauren and Hannah. Jeff and his family have been members at Karns since 2001. Jeff has served the congregation as an elder and is often referred to as "The Bible Bowl Man." He enjoys reading, writing, congregational singing, and passionate gospel preaching.

Occasion of Stumbling

How do we cause another to stumble? Maybe it's a careless word, or something intended in jest but misinterpreted by the other person.

I was reminded of this recently when my husband and I were leaving a restaurant. A small boy stopped suddenly in front of me and caused me to stumble. I had my husband's arm and my sturdy cane so I was alright. The father of the child scolded him saying, "Son, look where you are going." However barely out of earshot, I heard the mother say, "Honey, he was looking at her toenails." My big toes had red, white and blue banners on them celebrating the 4th of July. I do not go to that extreme generally, but two of my daughters dared me to.

By way of dressing could I cause others to stumble? What if my clothing were too short, too tight, too low cut in front, or with words on it inappropriate for a Christian to wear? If I were to wear that type of clothing, would it be a reproach on the church for others to say, "Oh, it must be okay to wear that to church?"

New Christians should be taught with loving kindness because their knowledge of God's Word is still limited. We, as older Christians are to be an example for them (Psalm 119:165; Proverbs 3:23). We are not to be a stumbling block for them, or others who are not strong in the faith. I am especially reminded of Paul's words to Titus in 2:3-5 where the older women are to be reverent, and teach and admonish the younger women as becometh holiness.

June Agee was born and raised in the UK and came to the United States when she married Wendell and became a U. S. citizen in Santa Fe, NM. June and Wendell have four living children and five grandchildren. June is a member of the Karns Church of Christ.

A Pitcher's Mound

I guess you have to know my dad to fully appreciate this devotional message, but for those of you who don't know him, I'll introduce you to one of his character traits.

My dad loves his lawn. He doesn't mow the lawn, he manicures the lawn. I have countless memories of my dad working in the lawn. My dad started training me to care for a yard when I was young. One of the early lessons I learned is that a yard was not really done properly if it wasn't trimmed every time it was mowed. Are you old enough to remember those hand-held scissor tools used for trimming? While my dad mowed, I would have to trim the edges all around our house and sidewalk, as well as around the church building. (I had the strongest grip of any 10 year-old in town!). I was never so thankful for the invention of the weed eater!

Anyway, our yard was pristine and beautifully manicured. . . except for one spot in the back. There was a bare spot in the middle of our back yard where no grass would grow. One day, someone visiting with my dad, who could obviously see that he took great pride in his yard, asked him why there was a bare spot in the back yard. My dad's response to him was simply, "Don't you know a pitcher's mound when you see one?"

You see, as much as my dad loved his lawn, he loved his son more. Dad wasn't raising grass, he was raising a boy. And I for one, am thankful for his perspective.

What about you? How's your perspective? Give it some thought.

Steve Higginbotham has been the pulpit minister for the Karns church of Christ since 2010. Steve is married to Kim and they have four children, Kelli, Michael, Matthew, and Anne Marie. Steve enjoys writing, playing golf, and is a fan of the Pittsburgh Steelers, the WVU Mountaineers, and the Andy Griffith Show.

Friends

The dictionary describes a friend as a person who has strong feelings for and trust in another person. To that I add, a person to whom you can pour out your heart, and it won't go further.

God blessed me with such a friend when I graduated high school, and we formed a friendship that spans several decades. What a graduation gift! She is the busy wife of a dedicated gospel preacher, a servant of our Lord, and her days have no closing time. When I am sick she calls me regularly, and I can feel concern for me in her voice. Through the years, however, time, miles and busy schedules have kept us physically apart, but love and prayers have kept our friendship strong. We communicate by phone and when we hang up, my phone reads "Recharge! Recharge!"

It's because of her love for our Lord and our friendship that I am a stronger Christian today. Proverbs 17:17 says, "A friend loves at all times..." and Proverbs 18:24 states, "...there is a friend who sticks closer than a brother." That's Jeane, my dear friend, and through her life, I see Jesus, the greatest friend of all.

Our choice of friends reflects our relationship with our heavenly Father. Choose wisely. They can help us get to heaven or lead us into the world, making us enemies of God (James 4:4). Jesus is the glue that bonds a friendship. Do you see Jesus in the life of your friends? Take heed. Be honest with yourself and consider their lifestyle seriously. You may need to do some purging.

Jane Higdon is a widow of 28 years and a retired Administrative Secretary. She has a daughter and a son, three grandchildren and five great grandchildren. She enjoys cooking and eating; watching sports, especially Tennessee football and Braves baseball; eating; grading Bible Correspondence courses; and get-togethers with her church family.

The Best Team Ever!

Have you ever decided to play on a sport team? Last year, I participated in a rowing class. Through involvement with this group, I came to realize how a sports team is like the church.

The most important member of a team is the head coach. The coach is the expert because he has done the same things we have as players. Similarly, Christ is our head coach because he has gone through what we have in life (1 Peter 2: 21, 24-25). In coming to the Earth to die for our sins and to be a role model, He established the church and set the guidelines for us.

The next most important individuals on the team are the team captains. In football, the team captains are always on the field, telling players where the coach wants them to position themselves for a play. The elders must know God's commands so that they can guide the church in the right direction (1 Peter 5:1-4).

Now, let us look at the responsibilities of strong team members. The team members must practice what they have learned so that they can perform well in a game. Likewise, as Christians, we must also practice what we have learned in order to mature in Christ. Through growth, we can help support each team member and thus strengthen the team.

If you just finished a season with a sports team and you really liked it, you would tell people about it. Likewise, we should rejoice in God's team; the team that has encouraging members, devoted team captains, and the greatest head coach of all time. I hope you will remember this: "The teams on Earth will pass away; but God's team, will last forever."

Austin Hoffarth has lived in Tennessee all his life. He attends high school at Webb School of Knoxville. He likes to draw, play tennis, go camping and hiking. He became a Christian in 2011 and enjoys the activities within the youth group at Karns and area-wide churches.

Listen Up!

Are you a good listener? At some time, most of us have been bad listeners. Ask yourself:

- Have you ever been so busy thinking about what you were going to say next that you missed what someone was saying to you?
- Have you ever been so upset about something that you hardly heard the offender's explanation?
- Have you ever been so focused on something else that you say, "That's nice" when your daughter runs to tell you that her brother is playing in the toilet?

You may not be a good listener.

Being a good listener is a rare quality. It shouldn't be. The Holy Spirit reminds us through James 1:19, "Everyone should be quick to listen." If listening is important enough for James to bring it up, why is it so rare?

Perhaps we are self-absorbed. Have you ever talked to someone so intent on passing on information about themselves they showed little interest in you? Or, could it be we are distracted and overrun by the stimuli all around us? Has your lunch with a friend been interrupted by frequent cell phone calls that couldn't wait to be returned later? I've asked a lot of questions. Our answers to them can help us.

God is speaking through James. Are we listening?

Sara Terlecki is married to her husband Bill. They moved to Knoxville from Ohio. Sara has worked in the church office since 2010. They have two grown children. Gerri married Michael Nath and blessed them with granddaughter, Ellie. Bill Jr. married Hope Whittington and blessed them with two grandsons, Allen and Evan.

I Never Heard Him Complain

When I was two years old, my father was diagnosed with rheumatoid arthritis. He was primarily affected in his hands and feet which was not easy for a man who made his living as a barber.

He had a stool that attached to his barber chair that enabled him to sit and work. He continued to work until I was twelve, just long enough for my sister to finish college. Then his health forced him to take early retirement.

When he taught Bible classes or filled in to preach, he had a kitchen stool he would sit on since he couldn't stand very long. His hands were twisted and terribly disfigured. Because of severe deformities in his feet, he could only walk short distances. I've heard my mother say that there were times when he was having a flare up that it hurt just for the sheets to touch his feet. While I knew he had arthritis (I saw his twisted hands and knew the trouble he had walking), his arthritis was never a burden to me.

He never complained at home, nor did he spend his time telling everyone else about his pain. He was a strong, quiet man who just appreciated all the ways that the Lord had blessed him. He never missed a school activity in which I participated. He never missed church because of his pain. He served as an elder for many years. He did all he could do for as long as he could.

May we follow his example and remember the Lord's words: "Do all things without complaining or disputing" (Philippians 2:14).

Kim Higginbotham grew up in Poplar Bluff, MO. She is married to Steve and has four children: Kelli, Michael, Matthew, and Anne Marie. Kim teaches children with multiple disabilities for Knox County, a ladies' class at SEIBS, conducts teacher training seminars, and maintains two blogs, "Teaching Help," and "Relative Taste." She enjoys teaching and cooking.

Nourishment for Body and Soul

In musing about life in America today, it is amazing about how much attention is devoted to our food. For example, we spend much time considering where we eat, home or restaurants, how we prepare, how to delight our tastes, how to deal with food addictions, how to organize to ensure health, how to manage ballooning costs, etc. Food obviously has always been essential for life. But the perspective during the depression years of America was far different. Only a small percent of people then, only the upper crust of society would obsess as modern Americans do.

My family lived in a moderately poor section of Chattanooga in a small 4-room house. However, the good Lord blessed our lives though we didn't have much.

We children were privileged to participate in Mother's canning operation. For example, we helped string and snap green beans or peeled and sliced fruit to place in Mason glass jars in a copper container placed on the coal-fired cook stove for cooking.

We were able to get by well enough to provide nourishment and growth to our physical bodies. But of far greater importance was the spiritual growth that our parents provided us. They were well aware of the Biblical admonition, "Man does not live by bread alone but by every word that proceeds from the mouth of God." I'm thankful for the memory that I have of being regularly walked to the little church building located about a mile from our home to participate in classes and worship.

G. C. (Grover Cleveland) Robinson, Jr. has been married to Mattie Lou Geer since June 27, 1954. They have four children: Timothy, Amy, Andy, and Penny; and three grandchildren: Victoria, Quintin and Ransom. G. C. is a retired mechanical engineer. He turned 86 December 1st, 2012.

Be Angry and Do Not Sin

Have you ever gotten angry or mad at someone? Silly question, right? After all, we are all human beings and we don't always agree with one another. We can't live with one another on a daily basis and not get upset with each other from time to time. The important thing is how we handle that anger. The Bible tells us in Psalm 30:5 that our Lord's anger is only for a moment, but His favor is for life. We should learn from this.

I've never understood how some people can get mad at someone, especially a family member, and stay mad for days or even months, sometimes, never speaking to that person again. I can't imagine the guilt that I would have if something happened to someone I loved and I was mad at them, never being able to tell them how much I love them again.

I was taught a valuable lesson as a teenager in Sunday school class: "never go to bed mad at someone you love." Ephesians 4:26 says, "Be angry and do not sin. Do not let the sun go down on your wrath." A dear friend taught me that lesson and I have since thanked her for it. Her reply was, "I always wondered if y'all were listening!"

Well, I was, and I have tried to pass this on to my children as well. Of course, I'll be the first to admit that I have a temper, and I do get mad, but I can't stay mad. It bothers me. So, I apologize and try to make it right. I was told that not being able to stay mad was a downfall of mine. I don't see it that way. I actually see it as a blessing. After all, what if God stayed mad at us and didn't forgive us of our sins when we asked? We would be in serious trouble now, wouldn't we?

Ethel Yates was raised in the Church of Christ. She became a member of the Karns Church of Christ when she and her husband moved to Tennessee in 2010. Ethel works as a Medical Assistant for Dermatology Associates of Knoxville and has two children, Adam and Megan.

Friendships

Friends can be one of the most uplifting things in life, but they can also tear us apart. We've all heard to "choose our friends wisely," but what does that mean? Who's a friend and who's not?

We as Christians should be kind to everyone, no matter what, but we need to be careful of who we let influence us because our friends shape who we are, especially at a younger age.

You know you have good friends when they uplift you daily. If you've had a bad day, they know just what to do to make you feel better. They support your decisions, but will correct you lovingly if you're doing something wrong. Proverbs 19:20 says, "Listen to counsel and receive instruction..." because they're usually right.

You aren't friends with the right people if they always tear you down, they don't understand your love for Christ, and they aren't interested when you try to show them Christ. People who don't know us will judge us based on who we befriend.

If you know your friends aren't the people that you want to be friends with, find new friends. It won't be easy, but it will be worth it. There's always someone out there facing the same problems you are no matter how old you are. When you find the people you need to be with, you will be amazed by the difference in your life.

"A friend loves at all times..." (Proverbs 17:17).

Claire Williams is the oldest daughter of Tony and Deanna Williams. She is a sophomore at Farragut High School. Claire is in the Color guard at FHS. She enjoys youth group activities and hanging out with friends.

Sigmund

My friend Gloria hatched a chicken egg in an incubator in her bedroom. She made it herself with no instructions. Gloria did not live on a farm. She lived in a two-bedroom house on my street with her family of eight. She bought nothing to make the incubator. She used what was around. I thought the whole project was a marvel. I admired the light bulb shining so diligently on the one lone egg and the clock beside it ticking as if it knew its value to the event. Gloria had her egg timed exactly. We checked him every day after school, but not to see if he hatched. Gloria named the day and time that he would hatch. He did. He hatched precisely when she said. We named him Sigmund and had a wonderful time with him. We wrote songs and poems about him.

The psalmist said, "My times are in Thy hand..." (Psalm 31:15) These words have infinite usefulness to us. They contain comfort and certainty. When Job was questioned by God in chapters 39 to 41, God said, "Do you know when the mountain goats give birth? Do you watch when the doe bears her fawn? Do you count the months till they bear? Do you know the time they give birth?" (Job 39:1-2). God wasn't just tossing out assorted nature facts. He was accenting that His care and His times are constant, wise and intentional. Greater than the timing God has made explicit in the natural world is what God does with spiritual matters and time.

We do best to leave our times in His hand.

Melea Nash Smith is married to Steve. They have four children, Jordan, Melea Jean, Bryan, and Sarah. Melea had her life saved by Gloria's mother after a bike wreck in Gloria's yard, according to Gloria. Melea doesn't know if it is so because she was unconscious.

Eat Your Dinner!

Do you remember being told as a child to, "Eat your dinner?" Well, our parents told us that for a reason. They wanted our bodies to be nourished and prepared for our futures. Foolishly sometimes we rebelled in eating our carrots, broccoli or even meat. Sometimes, we argued to not eat at all. Lo, some may have even pinched their nose to swallow those seemingly flavorless, brussel sprouts.

Hebrews 5:13-14, says, "For everyone who partakes only of milk is unskilled in the word of righteousness, for he is a babe. But solid food belongs to those who are of full age, that is, those who by reason of use have their senses exercised to discern both good and evil."

Proverbs 3:5-8, says, "Trust in the LORD with all your heart, and lean not on your own understanding; In all your ways acknowledge Him, and He shall direct your paths. Do not be wise in your own eyes; Fear the LORD and depart from evil. It will be health to your flesh, and strength to your bones."

As we grew more full of age, we began to recognize (discern) that our parents weren't some crazed group that had stock in the broccoli and brussel sprout farms, but wanted the best for us.

God's preparing us for our futures. With a little Bible reading each day, more trust and reverence... those "brussel sprouts, broccoli, carrots and meat," will actually get each of us closer to that healthful point of knowledge and understanding that our Heavenly Father wants and needs us to attain. Eat your dinner!

Steve Aragon is married to Susan and is the father of 2 boys, John and Joseph. Steve is originally from Sitka, Alaska. He works as a Project Manager for GE and is also an officer in the TN Air National Guard. He enjoys many outdoor activities, flying airplanes, and playing guitar. Steve and Susan have been members of the Karns church of Christ since 2007.

The Elements

Each concept in our spiritual life builds on earlier truths. The avenue of learning may be directed study or experience in daily life. God has spiritual building blocks that fit as exactly as Solomon's prepared stones for the temple (1 Kings 5:17). When we study the Beatitudes, one by one, we find their connectedness to each other and we usually begin and end with the whole. When we study the Fruit of the Spirit, we see individual qualities and an overall lifestyle. When we study the armor of Ephesians 6, we examine each piece but are encouraged to take the "whole armor." 2 Peter 1:5-8 lists seven attributes to add to our faith. We act on the known and wait for what we cannot yet see.

When Russian scientist Dmitri Mendeleev arranged the 63 known elements in a periodic table, it was 1869. He predicted the existence and properties of new elements to come while creating a chart based on the current knowledge. By order of atomic weight, he grouped what was certain, but provided for variance in atomic weight order which would be needed for the isotopes. He left space for new elements and predicted and accommodated the discovery of the rare gases. So there you have your helium, neon, argon, krypton, xenon, and radon! Though the French had a spiral element chart of 24 elements and the British had one with 57 regions, Mendeleev's left a place for future knowledge. The known was proof for the unknown. Our spiritual life is designed by God to accommodate future understanding. It is a living faith informed by the Living Word.

Melea Nash Smith is married to Steve. They have four children, Jordan, Melea Jean, Bryan, and Sarah. Melea likes Meitnerium, element 109, the best.

Dealing with People

As a Christian, several things can be classified as hard. For example, evangelizing a lost friend or neighbor, or finding time alone with God is tough. For me, one of the hardest parts of my Christian walk is dealing with difficult people. I find it hard to deal with people when it seems their sole purpose in life is to make my life difficult.

The good news is God's Word gives us insight into dealing with difficult people. Consider Paul's words: "If it is possible, as much as depends on you, live peaceably with all men." (Romans 12:18). Paul told the Christians at Rome to live peaceably with all people. Don't you suppose difficult people fall into this category as well? I do. Yet, even though they may be difficult, we are to strive to live in peace with them.

Jesus had to deal with difficult people too. Some people opposed His ministry (Mark 5:1-17), while others sought to kill Him (John 7:1-25). It doesn't get much more difficult than this. Yet, Jesus preached, "So whatever you wish that others would do to you, do also to them, for this is the Law and the Prophets" (Matthew 7:12). Notice Jesus said we are to treat people the way we want to be treated, not the way people treat us.

The next time you are annoyed by the difficult people in your life, remember how the Bible teaches us to deal with them. Strive for peace and treat them in the manner you want them to treat you. Situations with difficult people will always occur, but our actions should be pleasing to God - that's what's most important.

Justin Morton has been in student ministry for almost 10 years. He has been the student and family minister for the Karns church of Christ since 2010. Justin is married to Miranda and they have one son, Caden. Justin enjoys spending time with his family, studying, teaching, writing and is a fan of the Tennessee Volunteers.

The Beginning of the Church

"Repent: for the kingdom of heaven is at hand," (Matthew 3:2) began the announcement of Jesus Christ, in the wilderness of Judea. At that time, there had never been an announcement with more importance than this one. It foretold of the promise of Isaiah who said: "Prepare the way of the Lord; Make His paths straight" (Isaiah 40:3).

Jesus of Nazareth, the Son of God, began His ministry after He was baptized. At that time, the heavens opened, the angel of God descended upon Him, and a voice spoke out of the heavens, acknowledging the divinity of the Son of God (Matthew 3:16). Jesus began to preach and, from among his disciples, he chose the twelve apostles (Matthew 10:1-4). He gave us the Word through them by inspiration of the Holy Spirit. He gave them the commission to preach the gospel, but limited them to Judea (Matthew 10:5), as they were under the Law until He fulfilled it and broke down "the middle wall of partition" by His death.

He, then, gave Himself to die for His people, and rose again on the third day (Luke 24:46). After His resurrection, He appeared to the disciples and extended the commission to "all the world" and to "every creature," (Mark 16:15-16), but told them to tarry at Jerusalem until they were "endued with power from on high." This promised power was given on the day of Pentecost, when they were enabled to speak under the influence of the Holy Ghost (Acts 2). The church begun on that day, is the church that Christ established in its infancy.

Tony Williams is originally from Chattanooga and was baptized at the East Ridge congregation. He is married to Deanna, and they have three daughters, Claire, Maggie, and Ella. Tony has a Bachelor's and Master's Degree from UT. Tony and his family have been at Karns since 1999, and during that time he has served as a deacon, and currently as an elder.

Are We Hiding Behind a Mask?

There are times throughout a year when we put on masks, whether as part of Halloween or another occasion, but do we hide our true identity under masks more then we think?

Worldly people accuse others of being two-faced or masking their real selves. Do we do that as Christians? Do we mask our Christianity sometimes to be embraced by the world? Or...do we mask our worldly selves during a service on a Sunday morning?

It is important to set a good example to others and not hide behind a worldly mask at all times. Yes...we will be persecuted. We will be made fun of but just like Jesus did in the face of persecution, we are to love our enemies and that includes revealing who we really should be to all.

There will be times where we find ourselves accidentally hiding behind a mask but through repentance, we will be forgiven.

We are told in Romans that we are to not be conformed to the world but be transformed by the renewing of your mind (Romans 12:2).

A good example is the VBS song "This Little Light of Mine." The light is you and just like the song says, "Don't hide it under a bushel but let it shine all around the neighborhood."

So, as you get ready to head into the world this day, are you prepared to be who you need to be, and God knows you can be, or are you hiding under a mask to impress the world?

Wayne Begarly has been a member of the Karns Church of Christ since 2011. Wayne graduated from UT in 2007 with a Bachelors in Communications. Wayne is involved with the local United Way and American Cancer Society. He enjoys sports and the outdoors in his free time.

Let Freedom Ring

Martina McBride, a country music singer, released "Independence Day" in 1994. It is well-known song around the 4th of July, especially with its famous chorus line "let freedom ring."

As America declared independence in 1776, mankind, through Jesus declared independence from sin around 33 AD. For the Christian, freedom bells rang on that old rugged cross at the hill of Golgotha. Jesus, fulfilled his mission as Emmanuel or God in the flesh by, "...taking the form of a bondservant, and coming in the likeness of men. And being found in appearance as a man, He humbled Himself and became obedient to the point of death, even the death of the cross." (Philippians 2:7-8).

Romans 5:7-8 declares the love Jesus has for mankind in that, ". . .while we were yet sinners, Christ died for us." To understand what He endured, consider 2 Corinthians 5:21 which tells that Jesus became sin so that we might become the righteousness of God in Him. While it would be a tragedy to disregard the physical suffering He endured at the cross, something greater than His death happened. He was obedient in being separated from God, because He took on the sins of the world. Since sin separates mankind from God, Jesus was separated from God until His reconciliation.

Consider your blessing of freedom today in hearing the freedom bells which continue to ring because of His obedience to bear the sins of the world through His death.

Todd Monahan is the husband of Julie Monahan. Todd and Julie have two children, Anniston and Baker. Todd grew up in Lancaster, PA. Todd is a 2002 graduate of Freed-Hardeman University. He is a CPA and operates an accounting firm in Knoxville, TN.

Priorities

A professor stood before his class and had some items in front of him. When class began, he picked up a large empty mayonnaise jar and proceeded to fill it with rocks about 2 inches in diameter. He then asked the students if the jar was full.

They agreed that it was. So, the professor then picked up a box of pebbles and poured them into the jar. He shook the jar lightly. The pebbles rolled in the open areas between the rocks. He then asked if the jar was full. They agreed it was. The professor picked up a box of sand and poured it into the jar. Of course, the sand filled up everything else.

"Now," said the professor, "We need to recognize that this is our life. The rocks are the important things–God, family, health, etc. The pebbles are the other things that matter, like our job, our house, and our car. The sand is everything else–the small stuff."

If we put the sand into the jar first, there is no room for the pebbles or the rocks. The same goes for our life. If we spend all our energy and time on the small stuff, we will never have room for the things that are important to us. Take care of the rocks first–the things that really matter. Set your priorities. The rest is just sand.

Speaking of priorities, we frequently go to a restaurant in Rockwood called "Junior's." We usually have the same waitress, so when we sit down she brings my coconut pie. I'm a firm believer in eating dessert first, but not at every meal.

Andy and Geneva Higginbotham are both retired, Geneva from the Lockheed Martin Company and Andy from Office of Personnel Management and the Military. They have lived in the Karns community since May 1977. They enjoy family and good friends.

Apply Blood

As a diabetic, these are words that are displayed by my blood sugar meter when I use it. Every time I check my sugar, I have to poke my finger and squeeze out a drop of blood. The blood gets drawn into the test strip and the meter displays my sugar level.

This very tiny drop of blood can yield a lot of information. For example, if I had eaten a brownie, the level would likely be high. But if a low number is displayed, that tells me that I need to eat some form of carbohydrate to bring it up. Sometimes I try to guess what my sugar level might be and I can get pretty close to the number on the display. But the only way to accurately tell if I need medicine or food is to poke my finger and apply the blood to the test strip.

It's the same way with Jesus. Without him we would be sin-sick and destined for a difficult life. We must let Jesus apply his blood to us so that we can be cleansed of our sins. Just like taking care of diabetes involves applying a drop of blood to a test strip, we can only be sure that our salvation is taken care of after we have applied his blood to our lives. It is the only treatment for the life diseased with sin.

Who would have thought that taking care of my diabetes would remind me to let Jesus apply his blood to me so that I can be spiritually healthy?

 Jill Cheatham is a graduate of the University of Tennessee. She is married to Daniel and they have two sons, Jonah and Conner. Jill is an avid couponer, reader, and proud supporter of Powell High School Marching Band.

I Just Don't See It

I remember many years ago when I first saw a "Magic Eye" print. I was in an art gallery for only a few minutes, when a friend called me over, pointed at a picture of repetitive art patterns, and yelled, "Check it out... dinosaurs!" I responded, "Dude, there's nothing there but a bunch of mind-numbing swirls and squiggles!" My friend instructed me to look through the imaginary plane in the picture, somewhat cross my eyes, and stare. Finally, after 30 frustrating minutes, the dinosaurs slowly appeared from the background in 3D-like clarity! In the months ahead, the "Magic Eye" pictures became a craze for many to enjoy - if one could patiently and acutely tune their visual senses to find the artist's true work hidden just beneath the surface.

In similar fashion, how many "Bible seekers" open up the inspired Word, give it a moment's glance, yet cannot fully grasp or appreciate the living, breathing, guiding work of God? Perhaps one notices only the seemingly innumerable rules or mind-boggling names, places, and facts, but never finds God "hidden" just beneath the surface! With patience, persistence, and little instruction from Philip, even the Ethiopian Eunuch discovered and appreciated the living word that breeds salvation and brings joy ever-lasting (Acts 8).

Occasionally I'll stumble across a Magic eye poster and find myself intrigued by the picture that lies "hidden" within. However, it certainly pales in comparison to the love story and the amazing attributes of God that manifest themselves from within the 30,000 verses of His inspired work. Certainly God's beauty and wonder are made obvious to those who patiently seek them and search for them as for hidden treasure (Proverbs 2:4-5).

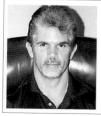

John Hoffarth has been a Christian for over 20 years and enjoys sharing the faith with friends or those seeking a stronger relationship with God. He also likes trying any new activity that challenges his fears or physical endurance. To relax, he enjoys the opportunity to travel abroad or spend quality time at home with his wife Karen and son Austin.

Make Wise Choices

Shortly after the construction began in the year 1174 the bell tower of Pisa began to tilt to one side and yet the tower was eventually completed 177 years later. The tilt gradually increased over the ensuing centuries until something had to be done to prevent the tower from toppling.

In 1964, the Italian government established a task force to determine ways to prevent the tower from toppling, but specified that it was important that the tower retain its current tilt because of the role the tower played in promoting tourism in Pisa. Aren't we sometimes reluctant to fully correct the deficiencies in our Christian lives? The reasons we sometimes fail to be all God would have us be may not be for financial reasons but may be for different reasons such as our personal time, limit on our recreational choices, and any number of other things.

The story of the rich young ruler in Mark 10 is an example of someone, when faced with a choice to be the person God would have him be, chose not to correct the deficiency in his life because of the cost. Jesus spoke about the cost of discipleship in Matthew 8:18-22. And on that occasion, one of his disciples said Lord, let me first go and bury my father (vs. 21). Typically, we also have "good reasons" for not fully following Jesus.

Perhaps the story of the Leaning Tower of Pisa can serve as a reminder to each of us to avoid making selfish choices today and be more diligent to making our calling and election sure (2 Peter 1:10a).

Don Denton serves as an elder of the Karns Church of Christ. He is married to Margaret Rymer and they have three children, Richard, Jeffrey and Leigh. They also have eight grandchildren, Clifton, Micah, Caitlin, Hunter, Sara, Denton, Joshua and Quincy. Don enjoys hiking, travel and Tennessee football and basketball.

Camp Rewards

We just finished up a week at Teenage Christian Camp. Our age group ranged from 11 to 14 year-olds and we had 63 campers. Watching these young people during Bible classes and chapel services was amazing. Their love for the Truth was humbling to observe. Their tender hearts brought tears to my eyes.

The young men were always more than willing to lead singing or prayers. And the same was true with the young ladies in the girls' classes and girls' devotionals. They want so much to serve and obey God to the best of their ability. We had 7 young people who decided to put on Christ in baptism and 10 that asked for prayers in rededicating their lives to Christ. Watching these 7 young people as they studied God's Word and asked questions was very special. It is actually hard to put into words the look in their eyes as they realized what they needed to do to be saved.

We made 4 different trips to the swimming pool (one at nearly 1 in the morning) to watch as they were baptized. All of the campers were excited to watch their friends as they became their brothers and sisters in Christ. As soon as the new Christian came out of the water, they were welcomed into God's Family by the campers with hugs, tears and love. Many times we actually sang "God's Family!" There were many times that I was brought to tears by our young people. They are not the church of tomorrow; they are the church of today!

Sherrye Woodall is married to Gregg. They have 4 children: Stephanie Harder, Tiffany Dresser, Benjamin Woodall and Jonathan Woodall. They have 4 grandchildren: Wrigley Harder, Walton Harder, Adalynn Dresser and Brooklynn Dresser. Sherrye has taught the 3 years old class at Karns for over 32 years.

When Two Elephants Fight

I have a friend whose name is Doka. He is a native of Nigeria and is now preaching in his home country. I met Doka when he came to the United States to be trained to preach at Freed-Hardeman University.

During his time in the States, Doka would come to our house and stay several weekends to get a break from his studies and some good home cooked meals. The week before he returned home to his family, we were talking about a number of things and he made the statement, "When two elephants fight, it's the grass that suffers."

While his imagery is not common to our culture, but I precisely understood the point he was making.

Think about this truth next time you are about to get into a scuffle with someone. You may be "big" enough to handle yourself quite well, but what impact will this scuffle have on those around you? What about your children? What do they see and hear in your house as you "have it out" with a brother or sister in Christ? What does that do to their faith and attitude?

Remember the next time you are tempted to get into a "fight," that while you may come out of the whole ordeal with only a few cuts and bruises, you may, in the process, crush and destroy innocent by-standers.

Yes, Doka was right. Although I don't think I would have ever thought to express it quite like he did, "When two elephants fight, it is the grass that suffers." Give it some thought.

Steve Higginbotham has been the pulpit minister for the Karns church of Christ since 2010. Steve is married to Kim and they have four children, Kelli, Michael, Matthew, and Anne Marie. Steve enjoys writing, playing golf, and is a fan of the Pittsburgh Steelers, the WVU Mountaineers, and the Andy Griffith Show.

The Golden Rule

Have you ever been out to a restaurant or a store and there was something not correct? Or maybe you think that someone mistreated you? How did you respond? Most of the time, people don't intend to mistreat you. Sometimes our response may not have been the best. When you arrived home, did you think to yourself, "I could have handled it better" or "I wonder if they know I am a Christian?" In James 1:19-21, the Bible states that we are to be quick to hear, slow to speak and slow to anger. When we make a mistake, we wish that others would treat us with patience and understanding. We should treat each other the way we want them to treat us (Luke 6:31).

The second greatest commandment is to love your neighbor as yourself (Mark 12:30-32). In John 13:33-35 Jesus tells us to love one another, "even as I have loved you, that you also love one another. By this all men will know that you are my disciples, if you have love for one another." Whatever we do, we should do it for the glory of God. If we want to positively affect non-Christians, we need to lead by example and treat them well.

So, the next time you get in one of those situations, pretend like you have a sign on you that states "Christian" before you respond. Show everyone that you are a Christian by your love and understanding. Let your Christian light shine that people may see your good works and glorify God (Matt 5:14-16). You may never know but your actions may save a soul.

Michael Albert is a deacon of the Karns Church of Christ. Michael is married to Terry and they have two children: Catherine and William. Michael is an engineer that works on environmental and process design projects. The Albert family has a small horse farm with 3 large horses and 7 miniature horses.

To Kill A Mockingbird

One of my favorite books is Harper Lee's classic "To Kill a Mockingbird." There are a number of reasons I hold the book in such high esteem, but Atticus Finch sums up my most valued attachment to the book. His character represents a challenge that continues to send chills through my soul!

In a culture whose social traditions held almost everyone in the cruel grip of racism, Atticus Finch uncompromisingly stood for justice. He towered over his cowardly peers as a man of rare courage. Atticus Finch is a hero to me; but he is a hero most especially because he reminds me of Jesus.

Jesus stood for righteousness as no man ever did or has. He stood for justice, righteousness, valor, and courage. His utter indignation for every false way was surpassed only by His singular devotion to truth.

We desperately need people today who will dare to shun the compromise of "political correctness" and stand for truth! In 1960 with the publication of "To Kill a Mockingbird," a nation torn by racial conflict paused to notice Harper Lee's portrayal of Atticus Finch. In a time when lesser men seemed to rule the day, Miss Lee gave us a much-needed hero. Today, though the triumph of unprincipled men may be less violent and often be disguised by hypocrisy, we still desperately need heroes.

We need Christ-like men and women who will dare to make the ever-unpopular decisions of the Christ. He was willing to live a life of principle regardless of the foes He faced (Mark 12:14). How about you?

Edwin Jones has been with Karns and the school of preaching for almost 27 years. Currently he is the Dean of Students with the school. Edwin and Sara have three children and four grandchildren as well as a variety of "adopted" family members they have incorporated into their mix over the years.

The Precious Present

The theme of the book entitled, "The Precious Present" is there is no better gift you can give, first to yourself and then to the people you love, than the "present." In this book Dr. Spencer tells a story of a young boy who searched to the tops of mountains, in cold damp caves, in dense, humid jungles, and underneath the sea for the precious present. But it was to no avail. His stressful search had exhausted him. Finally, it happened - he realized that the "precious present" was just that: the "present;" not the past and not the future, but "the precious present."

The young man found unhappiness in the past. When he returned to the present moment, he was happy again. When he started to worry about the future he would be unhappy again.

Today is the "Precious Present" God has given us. Today is a day that has never been opened. In Psalm 118:24 we read, "This is the day which the Lord has made; we will rejoice and be glad in it." In this Psalm, God had given victory to the Psalmist.

Christ's resurrection was a day of victory for Jesus. Our resurrection from the watery grave of baptism is a day of victory over our sin. Our resurrection when Jesus returns will be a victory over death. Today is a gracious opportunity and we should use this day to God's glory.

Today is the "Precious Present" God has given us. Let us rejoice and delight in this day. Let us give cheer to others and give them reason to be glad in God's "precious present!"

Jimmy Fox has been a member of the Karns congregation since 2007. Jimmy is heavily involved in the jail ministry and he also enjoys teaching the Bible to individuals and in classes.

Lost in Walmart

When I was little, I often went to WalMart with my grandparents. I had been taught to stay with them so I would be safe. I had also been taught what to do if I got lost. I was to go to the service desk and ask an employee to call whoever I was supposed to be with. As little boys sometimes do, I got interested in something in the aisles and wandered away from my grandfather. I looked around for him with no luck, so I did what I had been taught. I marched to the customer service desk and told them that my grandfather was lost and asked them call him to the desk so I would know where he was. It was obvious to me where I was, so he had to be the one who was lost. Everyone got a good laugh out of the incident and I never wandered away again.

As I reflect on this memory, I cannot help but notice the spiritual applications.

First, my grandfather was safety and I wandered away from him. He wasn't lost; I was. Yet, I told others that he was to blame. Sound familiar? Do we ever blame God and act as if He is the one who failed when we are really at fault?

Second, everyone is one of two people in the story—the lost boy or the store employee with the ability to help him. The lost need Jesus. He is the only way to eternal safety (John 14:6). Are you helping the lost find their way to safety?

Brad Alsup serves as a deacon at the Karns church of Christ. He is married to Jennifer, and they have two children, Evan and Allie. Brad is a hunter, a cyclist, and an avid reader.

Just Too Busy

Sherrye, Jonathan and I spent several days once just to clear out a large section of overgrown landscape beds at our house. There were several large creeping junipers that had literally crept along over the years and had overtaken and killed just about everything else trying to grow in the landscape beds. It took a lot of effort and became a monumental task just to get them out. We had to chain saw, chop, dig and prune and finally use Jonathan's truck to pull them out of the ground. If we had dealt with this problem much earlier, it would have been much easier to remove this plague from our otherwise beautiful and enjoyable flower beds.

So too, our spiritual growth can be hindered or choked out if we let things crowd out our spiritual life. Businessmen may become too busy to attend to God's business. A woman may be so occupied with housekeeping that she has little time for the house (family) of God. Parents and their kids may get so over-involved with sports and extracurricular activities that they leave precious little time for the Lord. Young people may be so busy with school activities that prayer, worship, good works and Bible study are neglected.

Jesus warned about the dangers of interference in Mark 4:18-19. If we desire to have healthy spiritual growth, we may need to "weed out" some things in our lives.

Have you allowed things to choke out and hinder your spiritual growth? If so, decide today that you are going to start weeding.

Gregg Woodall is an elder of the Karns Church of Christ. Gregg is married to Sherrye and they have four children, Stephanie, Tiffany, Benjamin, and Jonathan. They also have four grandchildren, Wrigley, Walton, Adalynn, and Brooklynn. Gregg enjoys golfing, dirt bike riding, spending time with family, and is a fan of the Tennessee Volunteers.

God Will Provide

During the Great Depression it was not uncommon for hobos to ride the trains that ran behind my grandmother's small farm house. Many times the men would find their way to Grandma's back porch and knock on the door. They were hungry and thirsty. Even though Grandma had very little food to feed her own hungry children, these men were never turned away. She always fed them and had kind words. She said they could be one of her boys stopping at someone else's home looking for a meal.

The word spread throughout the hobo community that Grandma would always have food for you if you were hungry. No one ever tried to harm her or the eight children she was raising alone as a young widow isolated out in the country. Times were tough and Grandma never had enough money to make ends meet. They had no electricity, no running water and no transportation off the farm. They cooked and heated the home with coal.

Mysteriously, as winter approached every year enough coal was found beside the railroad tracks to heat the little farm house for the winter. Those coal cars shook and out tumbled coal as they travelled down the tracks. God will provide for our needs. We need to trust him.

"God is our refuge and strength, an ever-present help in trouble" (Psalm 46:1).

Sharon Cawood is an Executive Sales Coordinator with N2 Publishing. She recruits for the State of Alabama and owns and manages two publications in the West Knoxville area. Both of Sharon's children are grown and gainfully employed. She has 3 grandchildren and 4 granddogs.

Hindered by Cockleburs

Back in the day, my great-grandfather tilled his fields with horse-driven plows. His horses were called Maw and Dixie. Every now and then when he began plowing, the horses would get feisty. They had gotten cockleburs stuck in their tails. Every time they swished their tails they felt the prickling barbs, and commenced kicking and prancing and whinnying. Pa Lyell knew that there was no use trying to plow until he pulled out all the cockleburs from Maw and Dixie's tails.

The same, I suppose, could be said of the church today. When Christians have cockleburs of sin, like selfishness, pride, jealousy, or. . . whatever, there is no use trying to get them to work together. There's just a lot of kicking and posturing and complaining.

Early Christians were hindered by cockleburs of sin. Paul said that all other types of sin had to be put away. "Let no corrupt word proceed out of your mouth, but what is good for necessary edification, that it may impart grace to the hearers. And do not grieve the Holy Spirit of God by whom you were sealed for the day of redemption. Let all bitterness, wrath, anger, clamor, and evil speaking be put away from you, with all malice. And be kind to one another, tenderhearted, forgiving one another, even as God in Christ forgave you" (Ephesians 4:29-32).

We have important things to do together. There is soil to till and the seed of God's word to plant. It's time to get rid of all the cockleburs.

Teresa Hampton, along with her husband, Gary, were members of the Karns congregation while he served as director of East Tennessee School of Preaching. Teresa has authored several ladies' books and currently writes a women's e-zine called Wellspring. Teresa and Gary recently moved to Jackson, MS where they labor with the Siwell Road church of Christ.

No Brakes!

As I reflect back on bad decisions I've made, this one quickly rises to the top. In ninth grade, a friend of mine left his bike at my house. I was heading his way and decided to return it. It was a 2 mile walk so a set of wheels made it easier. The only drawback was the bike did not have any brakes.

I made this trip many times as a youth, but this time I decided to take a different route to avoid riding up a big hill. In doing so I had to go down a hill which was only about 30 feet to get to his driveway. As I was going down, turning into his driveway I used my feet to slow down. In doing so, I managed to stop but only after flipping the bike and injuring my foot. I ended up having surgery and missed nearly half of the basketball season.

Sometimes we can do things which appear to be safe and normal to ourselves and the people around us; but if we lack the "brakes" to keep us in check and instead start to operate based on our will, relying on ourselves and our own merits, we can quickly flip our lives upside down.

Sin, like a disease, can quickly enter our lives. Sin comes dressed to impress, enticing the best of us. I only looked at the convenience and ease of traveling that day. As we consider succumbing to the pleasure, or the easy route, consider the consequences that may come, which at first seem very simple and easy to overcome.

Todd Monahan is the husband of Julie Monahan. Todd and Julie have two children, Anniston and Baker. Todd grew up in Lancaster, PA. Todd is a 2002 graduate of Freed-Hardeman University. He is a CPA and operates an accounting firm in Knoxville, TN.

Why Didn't He Just Fix the Hole?

I'm sure that most of you are old enough to remember the television show from the 1960's entitled, "Gilligan's Island." If you weren't old enough to remember it, I'm sure that at some point you may have seen reruns of it.

The show was about seven people who were shipwrecked on an uncharted island, and each storyline concerned itself with fumbled opportunities to be rescued.

As a boy growing up, I loved to watch the television show, but as much as I liked this show, one thing kept nagging at me and wouldn't allow me to fully enjoy it. I couldn't understand how the professor could make washing machines, generators, rather elaborate huts, batteries for their radio, and a host of other complex gadgets, but he couldn't fix that little hole in the S. S. Minnow and get off the island!

That just serves to remind me of how we sometimes readily agree to serve God in big ways, but when we have the daily opportunity to serve him, almost effortlessly, we fail to come through.

We may find ourselves sitting back, looking for and awaiting an occasion when we can make a huge "splash" for God. But while we wait for that earth shaking event, we leave undone small, daily, acts of service that could be done "in the name of the Lord."

Friends, don't overlook the small things that you can be doing every day in service to God while you await your "big chance!"

Steve Higginbotham has been the pulpit minister for the Karns church of Christ since 2010. Steve is married to Kim and they have four children, Kelli, Michael, Matthew, and Anne Marie. Steve enjoys writing, playing golf, and is a fan of the Pittsburgh Steelers, the WVU Mountaineers, and the Andy Griffith Show.

Love Your Enemies

Some of the ways to define an enemy are: one who hates you, curses you, abuses you, treats you badly, unfairly criticizes you, maliciously gossips about you, or undermines you. You get the picture. Your enemies are not the kind of folks you'd choose to be around and you might have to bite your tongue to avoid speaking ill of them. But guess what? In perhaps the greatest sermon in history, Jesus said you have to love your enemies (Matthew 5:44-48)!

This is a clearly inconvenient teaching, but it's also very clear. So, we have to deal with it if we want to do His will (Matthew 7:21). From Luke's account of the same teaching we find three ways to deal with those who are our enemies:

- Do good to them.
- Speak well/bless them.
- Pray for them.

Voila...there it is! Just start with #3! While loving our enemies is a difficult proposition from a purely human perspective, praying for them changes everything. Can we hate them back if we diligently pray for them? Can they curse and abuse us if we help meet their needs (Romans 12:20-21)?

Above all, the hidden message from Jesus is that He knows we can't handle this situation alone. Our strength isn't enough. We need God's too.

Don Scott was recruited to Knoxville from his home state of Virginia by his wife of 20 years, Amy, who is also responsible for bringing him to Christ. Don works from home as an engineer and Amy stays busy as a homeschooling mom. The children love to volunteer with various camps, little leagues, and scouting organizations.

Claim Your Verse

Do you have a verse in the Bible that always points you to God; that one defining verse you remember when things aren't going so great and you feel nothing will ever go right?

In the past I spent a lot of time saying, "why me," or "why can't I be as lucky as so and so," always wanting more and always thinking I need more than I had. When I was first introduced to Jeremiah 29:11, it was after spending 8 months looking for our first house. Shopping for a home is a very frustrating endeavor. After not winning the bid on three foreclosures, I was mad and upset to the point of tears. I couldn't understand why God didn't seem to be on my side. That is when I cried out to God. I put all my frustration at his feet. I prayed for a house that wasn't fancy or spectacular just a place where my kids would have their own rooms.

A week later we were having a house built. During this time I read this verse, Jeremiah 29:11, "For I know the plans I have for you, declares the Lord, plans to prosper you and not harm you, plans to give you hope and a future." It reminded me, and still reminds me, that God is only out for my best interests. I was amazed to read the following verses sometime later, "Then you will call on me and come and pray to me, and I will listen to you. You will seek me and find me when you seek me with all your heart."

Deanna Hudson became a member of the Karns church family in the Spring of 2011. She is the mother of two children, Zoe and Patrick.

Ready or Not

One day, there was a child who was playing Hide and Go Seek with his dad. It was the dad's turn to hide, and he was trying to find a hiding space he could actually fit into. Sooner or later the child called, "Ready or not here I come!"

The dad replied, "I'm not ready yet!" and looked around frantically for a place to hide. The son came into the room the dad was in before the dad had a chance to hide. The dad said, "I told you I wasn't ready!"

The child replied, "But the phrase is 'Ready or Not,' Dad. You aren't ready, and that's your fault not mine."

This story is like the return of Jesus, the game (Hide and Go Seek) is life, the 'Ready or Not' is when God calls us home, the dad is a sinner, and the child is Jesus. God will call us home whether we're ready or not.

The Bible says in Matthew 24:44, "Therefore you also be ready, for the Son of Man is coming at an hour you do not expect."

God will come someday. You never know when he will come, it could be today, or it could be tomorrow. It could be in this life-time or thirty lifetimes away. You never know.

God works in mysterious ways. One of His biggest mysteries is when is He coming? But my question to you is, when he does come, will you be "ready or not?"

Casey Jackson is 12 years old. She is the daughter of Gentry and Amy Jackson, and the older sister of Julie. She was baptized into Christ in 2012. She loves church youth activities, texting, hanging out with her friends, reading, writing, baby-sitting, and anything Paris. Most of all she loves God and her family.

Violator

I was rolling down the highway, not paying much attention to what was going on around me, when I saw the patrol car. There were several cars speeding along with me, but I just knew when the blue lights came on and the officer got closer that I would be the lucky one on the side of the road.

Great. Just great. How could I get out of this? By the time the man in blue tapped on my window, I had a dozen or so reasons for why he should let me off the hook, but when he asked if I had a reason for going so fast, nothing sounded good enough.

I had time to think while the officer took my license back to his car and ran my plate. Think! THINK! "What would Jesus do?" Then I realized, Jesus never would have been speeding, so I wondered, "What would Jesus want me to do?" Images of Bible stories flashed in my head. Oddly enough, the adulterous woman from John 8 was the prominent image as my license was returned to me along with a slip of paper with "VIOLATOR COPY" printed on the bottom. I was busted. And it was all my fault. And I knew it.

Now, I know that sin is sin and one is no better than another, but I like to think that speeding might be a little easier to forgive than adultery. Nevertheless, I've been branded. "VIOLATOR" sounds icky. My date in traffic court is this week and I will drive ever so carefully downtown to realize my fate (and the fate of my insurance rates). Regardless of what the judge has in store for me, the Judge has already instructed me. Fess up. Take your medicine. Go and sin no more.

Jill Green is used to seeing things differently. She grew up with brothers and is the only girl in her house with her husband, Craig, and two sons, Jake and Duncan. Her life is filled with blessings in her family, job and even in trials. She has an English/History degree from UT, but says she has yet to figure out what she wants to do with her life.

Peek-a-Boo

When we picture a cute little boy playing peek-a-boo with his daddy, he seems to think that just because his eyes are covered he cannot be seen. Every time he removes his hands from his eyes, he is surprised to see that Dad is still there.

We all know people who live a life full of sin and have this attitude. They seem to think "I cannot see God, so He must not see me." Sin has a way of snowballing! What started as a little thing can destroy church families, homes, and friendships.

1 Thessalonians 5:12–22 helps us to focus on the needs of others and not on self by being at peace, to warn, comfort, uphold, be patient, pursue, rejoice always, pray without ceasing, give thanks, hold fast to what is good, and to abstain from every form of evil.

Imagine how rewarding our lives would be if we follow this simple plan, fervently seek an eternal home in heaven, and make it our goal to take as many souls as possible with us. The sweet words of a familiar hymn entitled, "How Beautiful Heaven Must Be" help us to strive for this goal

Do not play with sin! Sometimes it is hard to focus on God because we cannot physically see Him, but let us not be fooled like a little child. God does see what we do! Seek Him and make a home in heaven your goal.

Jeremy Gillentine is married to Amber Gillentine (13 years) and has four children Sidney (11), Hutson (9), Raegen (7), Linden (4). He is currently a student at the Southeast Institute of Biblical Studies.

What Friends Are For

Say one day you met that friend. You know, the one you're going to spend all your school years with? Well, I met mine in first grade. She lives about a quarter of a mile from me. You know, Paul had a friend. He was even younger than me when he started evangelizing. His name was Timothy.

1 Timothy 1:2 says, "To Timothy, a true son in the faith: Grace, mercy, and peace from God our Father and Jesus Christ our Lord."

That is a greeting from the start of a letter Paul wrote Timothy. 1 Timothy 2:9-10 says, "women [should] adorn themselves in modest apparel, with propriety and moderation, not with braided hair or gold or pearls or costly clothing, but, which is proper for women professing godliness, with good works."

For you girls out there, you have your girlfriends you hang out with, right? I think a good, Christian friend should be one that says "Hey Maggie, that's not a good thing to wear. It's immodest." Romans 14:13 says, "Therefore let us stop passing judgment on one another. Instead, make up your mind not to put any stumbling block or obstacle in your brother's way." A good friend will help you if you are hurt, also. Proverbs 27:6 says, "Wounds from a friend can be trusted, but an enemy multiplies kisses." John 15:13-14 says, "Greater love has no other than this, that he lay his life down for his friends. You are my friends if you do what I command."

In conclusion, I think friends are for evangelism, modesty, and trust.

Maggie Williams is the 12 year old daughter of Tony and Deanna Williams. She is in 7th grade at Farragut Middle School. She loves chocolate, Asian food, and listening to Taylor Swift. Having fun with her friends and being in the youth group at Karns are her favorite things.

Grandma's "Slop Bucket"

One of the childhood memories I have of my grandma and granddad's house in Reader, West Virginia was the "slop bucket" they kept by the kitchen sink.

Now, for those of you who don't know what a slop bucket is, it was a bucket that contained all the scraps from previous meals. My grandma didn't have a garbage disposal, so following a meal, the "scraps" from dinner went into the slop bucket. When it filled up, my granddad would take it out back and bury the contents of the bucket.

Now this particular "slop bucket" had a lid - because it needed one! There was no use in exposing the decaying scraps from previous meals. Those meals were over, and those remaining scraps were sealed up and to be buried in the back yard by the garden.

If only we all had and used our own personal "slop buckets." What do I mean? Well, how often do you get into a little fuss with someone, and before you know it, you dump out the scraps from previous conflicts? Things that should be forgiven, resolved, and buried away, never to be mentioned again, often reappear when we find ourselves in confrontation.

Friends, when something finds its way into a "slop bucket," that's where it needs to stay. Put a lid on it and when it gets full, go bury it. Give it some thought!

Steve Higginbotham has been the pulpit minister for the Karns church of Christ since 2010. Steve is married to Kim and they have four children, Kelli, Michael, Matthew, and Anne Marie. Steve enjoys writing, playing golf, and is a fan of the Pittsburgh Steelers, the WVU Mountaineers, and the Andy Griffith Show.

Craig's List, Mayberry, & the Gospel

Strange title? Maybe, but let me explain...In 2011, I was looking to purchase a Mayberry squad car. I looked for several months with no success. I checked Ebay, Craig's List, asked collectors–but still no luck. Finally, one day on Craig's List, I found a beige 1964 Ford Galaxie. I contacted the owner, drove to Livingston, TN to test drive the car, and I bought it the following day. I then had it painted as a "black and white" squad car, put decals on it, installed a light and siren, and I was ready to go.

Steve Higginbotham, who is also a fan of the Andy Griffith show, saw my car and encouraged me to use it as a tool to evangelize. According to Steve, I possessed a car that would naturally attract people to me. What a great way to spread the gospel - having people come to me! Steve developed a "Mayberry brochure" that contains the plan of salvation in it, and since that time, I've been spending most of my Saturdays driving around neighborhoods, seeing kids of all ages, and passing out the brochures.

I estimate I will be giving out around 2,000 brochures this year to people who need the Gospel in their hands. My hobby has become a tool to reach people with the gospel. Allow me to encourage you to use what you have, and evangelize as you go. You'll find that the more you do it, the easier and easier it will be for you to do. Plus, you are doing your neighbors a BIG favor!

Mark Cawood has been attending the Karns Church of Christ since 1954. He was baptized in 1970. Mark's mother, Joyce Cawood, was one of the original members of the Karns congregation. Mark has served on the Knox County Commission from 1986-2008. He loves to travel in the USA and he's been to every state. He's also a fan of the Andy Griffith Show.

He Kneeled

"Now when Daniel knew that the writing was signed, he went home. And in his upper room, with his windows open toward Jerusalem, he knelt down on his knees three times that day, and prayed and gave thanks before his God, as was his custom since early days" (Daniel 6:10).

In 2nd grade Bible class, I remember two very clear moments. One was the day Mrs. Cox, stately with very white hair, said to us, "No one is ever, ever, ever too old to get on their knees to pray!" I had thought till then that kneeling in prayer was mostly for children. I am very grateful to Mrs. Cox for telling me this ahead of time before I missed many years of knowing it and perhaps had to relearn it at another stage in my life. As Mrs. Cox must have known, and as it comes to all Christians, there have been many, many times when that was the exact type of prayer my journey made necessary. The privilege, the comfort, the assurance of prayer is unchanged through history. I don't believe Daniel prayed in defiance, or to answer a challenge, or to set an example. I believe Daniel prayed because he had a God who listened, a God who loved him, a God whom Daniel loved and honored above all else.

Second, in visual impact, was the Sunday Johnny B. burst into class, pulled off his loafers and socks, and showed us how he could wiggle his pinky toe independently of the other toes. This seemed to me a must-have skill. It became a goal I worked toward whole-heartedly and achieved.

Melea Nash Smith is married to Steve. They have four children, Jordan, Melea Jean, Bryan, and Sarah. Her favorite Bible story as a kid was Jesus calming the storm. It still is.

Missed Opportunities

It looked like they were going to do it again! The United States Women's Soccer Team was only four minutes away from winning their record-setting third World Cup title. Eyes all across this country were glued to the television set, anticipating a celebration like no other in women's soccer history. What they saw instead may have been the most disappointing loss in the history of the U. S. women's soccer team.

On two separate occasions, the United States looked like they were going to be victorious. Unfortunately for the U. S. , their luck ran out. Japan beat the United States on penalty kicks securing a marvelous run to the World Cup title. Anyone who watched this match knows that the United States should have won. They completely dominated the majority of the match. Regrettably, they fell short because of missed opportunities.

I'm afraid many of us do exactly the same thing every day. We miss opportunities that could impact and change the outcome of something far more important than a soccer game. We miss opportunities that could change the outcome of people's lives. The apostle Paul said, "While we have opportunity, let us do good to all people" (Galatians 6:10).

Every morning we wake up and have multiple opportunities to do things for others. Maybe it is something small like being kind to them, or asking them how they are doing. Perhaps it's something bigger, like helping them through a difficult time, or teaching them the Gospel of Christ. Big or small doesn't matter. Just take the opportunities presented. You never know, you may have an opportunity to affect someone's eternal destiny.

Justin Morton has been in student ministry for almost 10 years. He has been the student and family minister for the Karns church of Christ since 2010. Justin is married to Miranda and they have one son, Caden. Justin enjoys spending time with his family, studying, teaching, writing and is a fan of the Tennessee Volunteers.

Your Christian 401K

Some of us are interested in 401k plans at our workplaces. We can invest in various funds and sometimes our employer will put something in our account for us. This is almost like free money to us, but you have to participate in the plan to receive these benefits. Is our Christian 401k different? I do not believe that it is.

We make a public declaration that we believe in Christ Jesus thus we belong to the plan. We must invest some of our money, time, and talents. We must set a good example in our daily lives. We must work in our own family to be a Christian example. Our children must see Christ in us seven days a week! When we invest in these things in our Christian 401k then we receive benefits. We receive the gift of being saved by God. "For by grace you have been saved through faith, and that not of yourselves; it is the gift of God," (Ephesians 2:8).

As we receive this gift of grace we must work to present the kingdom of God to others. God gave each of us spiritual gifts that we can and should use. Ephesians 2:10 says, "For we are His workmanship, created in Christ Jesus for good works, which God prepared beforehand that we should walk in them."

Today let us focus on the good works that God prepared for us to do. What can we do today to tell someone about the Good News of Jesus?

Ken Couch is a sales representative for Royal Brass and Hose, an industrial hose and fitting supplier in Knoxville Tn. He regularly travels in his job throughout East Tennessee, Eastern Kentucky and Southwestern Virginia. He enjoys High School football and following the Tennessee Volunteers.

Study

At eight or nine years of age my mother and I started reading the Bible, intending to read it completely. It wasn't long until I began to fade. The names, the details, the repetition all overwhelmed me. I didn't understand the importance of the details. I quit.

Even though His word instructs us to study, men have always struggled with the issue of studying His word. On one level, we know He is faithful and true and to be obeyed. On another level, we often pay lip service to obedience.

Struggling with studying the Bible as a 9 year-old is one thing; not wanting to read and study God's word as a maturing Christian is something altogether different. It isn't always convenient, it isn't always easy, it isn't always what we might want to do, but it's what God expects. It's self-centered and arrogant to think that it doesn't matter. It's self-serving to think that God is "flexible" about what He wants. In the Old Testament God was very specific about what he wanted: worship, marriage, sacrifices, feasts, priestly duties, and instructions for war were among the things about which God was very specific. Ignoring His instructions had serious consequences and obedience brought abundant blessings.

Let's accept Paul's admonition to Timothy to study. Enjoy the satisfaction and blessings of obedience to God by committing to the regular study of His word. Today let's strive for true obedience in all we do.

Conrad Slate graduated from Tennessee Tech, and was a member of the Air National Guard for 31 years, retiring as a Colonel. He holds a MS in Financial Services. Currently he is a principal in Slate, Disharoon, Parrish & Associates, a fee based financial planning firm. Married to Brenda for over 40 years, they have two children and three grandchildren.

Investment Determines Interest

Why is it that my parents, who used to never miss a Little League Baseball game rarely, if ever attend one anymore? Or why is it that my parents no longer attend PTA or PTO meetings any more? Well, the answer should be rather obvious, shouldn't it? The reason my parents don't do those things any more is because they no longer have an investment in those activities.

The principle of investment is clear. We exhibit an interest in matters in which we have made an investment. And the greater the investment, the greater the interest. While this principle holds true in worldly matters, it also is true in spiritual matters as well.

As we invest more and more of our time, talents, thoughts, prayers, dreams, and money into the work of the church, our interest in the same is bound to grow.

If you find yourself concerned about your spiritual condition because you can feel yourself drifting; if your interest in the church is waning, then maybe the solution is that you might need to invest more in it. When you do, your interest will surely follow.

I'm convinced that investment determines interest. Maybe that's why God is so interested in us, for he invested His Son in us (John 3:16).

Steve Higginbotham has been the pulpit minister for the Karns church of Christ since 2010. Steve is married to Kim and they have four children, Kelli, Michael, Matthew, and Anne Marie. Steve enjoys writing, playing golf, and is a fan of the Pittsburgh Steelers, the WVU Mountaineers, and the Andy Griffith Show.

The Right Church

One of the significant issues for Christians is the knowledge that you are in the church that Christ is ruling over. How do you know you are at Christ's church? I did not grow up in Christ's church. I was born into another religious group. My wife and a few visits to Christ's church opened my mind and I wondered why I went to the other church.

I started a journey with the help of several church members and studying God's word. My decision came down to several factors. It started with the basics. Do I believe in God? Do I believe that Jesus Christ is the son of God? The next question was "do I believe that the Bible is the inspired word of God?" Once you say "yes" to these 3 questions, then you can explore the Bible to learn about Christ's church.

Ephesians 1:22 states that Christ is the head of the church and Hebrews 8:1 states that Christ is in heaven. Man does not set the rules for the church. Only Christ can set the rules for the church and the Bible contains Christ's rules. The Bible contains all the answers to the church's organization (Ephesians 1), when we get together (Acts 20), what we do when we are together (Ephesians 5), how we pray (1 Timothy 2), and the qualifications for elders and deacons (Titus 1). These are just a few examples of Christ's church.

If your church is not organized according to Christ's rules, search for Christ's church. Becoming a part of Christ's church, not just any church, will lead you to eternal salvation.

Theophilus means "lover of God." It was the name of the man to whom Luke wrote the book of Acts. However for this article, it is the "pen name" of one of our members here at Karns.

Defense of the Righteous

Have you ever been at school or at your job when the conversation of religion comes up? I'm sure it has happened sometime in your life. And if the conversation switched to an attack on your Christian beliefs, did you want to reply back, but for one reason or another, you remained silent? We wanted to say something, but we didn't want to voice our feelings out of fear of judgment or ridicule.

1 Peter chapter 3:13-17 talks about this and the sufferings we will endure. It tells us not to be afraid of threats, or be discouraged by things people might say because of our belief. Moreover, it tells us to sanctify God in our hearts and be prepared to defend Him when someone asks why we have so much hope. We must know what God commands us and have our defenses ready to support what we say.

In today's world, people want to believe in those things they can see, touch, or fully understand. We might not be able to see God directly, but He has given us everything imaginable to trust in His existence; from the sky, to the sea. He has also left His word for us so that we can hear Him and know His will. People may understand what we believe, but still try to convince us otherwise. They may try to get us to follow them on the broad road of deception. Verse 17 says it is better to suffer for doing good, than for doing evil. We may suffer for our faith, but the result is so much better than following the spiritually blind down the broad road; which ultimately will lead to destruction.

Austin Hoffarth has lived in Tennessee all his life. He attends high school at Webb School of Knoxville. He likes to draw, play tennis, go camping and hiking. He became a Christian in 2011 and enjoys the activities within the youth group at Karns and area-wide churches.

Glorify God's Name

Shortly after the Lord's triumphal entry into Jerusalem, there were two Gentiles who wished to have a conference with him. Being in a place where Gentiles were not expected or welcomed, they asked one of his disciples if they could see him. We read of this in John chapter 12 beginning in verse 21, where they asked Philip, "Sir, we wish to see Jesus."

Perhaps they asked Philip because his name was Greek in origin. We only know that Philip took their request first to Andrew, and then the pair approached Jesus together. Both Philip and Andrew knew that Jesus' plan thus far was a mission to the lost sheep of Israel. However, they did not recognize that the Lord's reference to "other sheep" (John 10:16) was Gentiles. Verse 23 indicates Jesus answered them, but we are not sure who he answered. It is not possible to know if the two Greeks were granted access to the Lord.

This is one of the earliest indications of interest on the part of Gentiles in the teachings of Jesus. Jesus answered that the hour had come that the Son of Man should be glorified. He petitioned, "Father, glorify Your name." At this point, a voice came from the sky. The voice was that of the Father. Only two other times in the New Testament has the Father audibly spoken from heaven: in Matthew 3 when Jesus was baptized; and in Matthew 17 on the Mount of Transfiguration. The Father's voice was so robust that some by-standers thought it was thunder when He answered, "I have both glorified it, and will glorify it again."

Tony Williams is originally from Chattanooga and was baptized at the East Ridge congregation. He is married to Deanna, and they have three daughters, Claire, Maggie, and Ella. Tony has a Bachelor's and Master's Degree from UT. Tony and his family have been at Karns since 1999, and during that time he has served as a deacon, and currently as an elder.

God's Promises

I grew up on a farm with my parents and five brothers and four sisters. I still remember working in the fields as crops were planted and tended. Our livelihood depended on their maturing and producing the food we needed. Even when I was quite young I knew that even though we did all the work, our crops depended on God's blessings.

Sometimes we got too much rain and other times we had drought times. Either way was not good. I remember my parents having concerns about whether the crops would yield enough to keep our family fed. Even though I knew of their concerns, I also knew that they looked to God for taking care of us. They never complained and blamed Him during too much rain or drought times. Their faith in God helped me to have that faith also. And God did bless us. We always had enough to eat, thankfully, even though sometimes there was barely enough to go around!

Even though I'm "all grown up" now, as they say, there are times when I wonder if the rains will never stop, if the drought will never end, if winter will be too harsh, or if spring will never come so summer and fall may follow. At those times, I find such assurance of God's love and care when I turn to Genesis 8:22 and read His promise to Noah, and so also to all His children:

As long as the earth endures,
Seedtime and harvest,
Cold and heat,
Summer and winter,
Day and night
Will never cease!

Mattie Lou Robinson I've been married to Grover Cleveland (G. C.) Robinson, Jr. since June 27, 1954. We have four children: Timothy, Amy, Andy and Penny;and three grandchildren: Victoria, Quintin and Ransom. I'm a homemaker and also taught school for 15 years. I'll be 83 October 9th, 2012.

Are You Ready?

In the summer of 2012, I was on a mission trip to Honduras. I didn't stay in a hotel or even a solid building the first four days. Food, water and plenty of sunshine were provided. I had to bring everything else from home. As Dad and I were preparing for the trip, we packed items such as a tent, clothes, air mattresses, toiletries, etc. I also decided to pack my green rain jacket because of the heavy rains we had experienced the previous year during monsoon season. After we arrived at the Honduran airport, the clouds were dark and the air was heavy, so I got out my rain jacket and said, "Good thing I brought my rain jacket!"

This was my saying for the rest of the week. Every time I said this, I got mixed responses. Some people smiled and rolled their eyes, some were annoyed, and some kept saying they didn't think it would rain at all. On the next to last night, it started to get cloudy. I said, "Good thing I brought my. . . rain jacket!" Everyone gave their usual response and kept walking on. . . until it started to rain. I was prepared for the rain and stayed dry, while most of the others got very wet. Nobody was rolling their eyes anymore.

In the Bible, it talks about how no one knows when Jesus is returning except God. In 1 Thessalonians 5:2, Paul says that Jesus will come "as a thief in the night." If Jesus came back today would you return with Him to spend eternity in heaven? Are you prepared for His coming? Are you ready for the Lord?

Lindsey Seibel attends the Karns Church of Christ with her parents, John and Christy Seibel, and her three sisters. Lindsey is an active member of the Karns Youth Group and enjoys ballet, reading, writing, singing, being around family and friends in the mountains and in Florida, and eating Extreme Moose Tracks Ice Cream.

Potential

I inherited a trait from both of my parents; namely, believing that one can undertake about any task even if one has nothing with which to begin. At age 8, my Daddy and I tore down a house and used the material to build our house. He saw potential in the house we tore down even to the last nail which I straightened for reuse. One man's trash was our treasure.

We pulled firebrick out of a dump for our future chimney. My Daddy saw potential in nearly everything. We tore down standing chimneys from deserted home places to build our chimney, construct a brick wall, and make a front porch. Daddy would say, "There is a lot of potential in these old bricks. All we have to do is clean them. Just imagine what we can do with these." I tried but I am sure I did not see the things my parents did.

Everything has potential, especially that which is made in the very image of God. I taught my girls they could be anything they wanted to be in this life. I knew this because Mama and Daddy told me the same thing. Few of us are able or will ever be able to achieve like some notables among us, but we can amount to something great in the eyes of God. Each person has potential to be what he or she wants to be.

They say you can't make a silk purse out of a sow's ear but each of us can become something great in the Kingdom. God sees limitless possibilities for us.

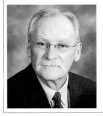

David Lipe was born in Charleston, MS and is married to his wife Linda (Wilson). They have three daughters and five grandchildren. David presently serves as the Director of the Southeast Institute of Biblical Studies.

Shopping with a Two-Year-Old

One day, as Paige and I were shopping, we just so happened to walk by the swim suits while wandering from one side of the store to the other. (Paige was just getting to the age at which she was becoming very aware of her surroundings.)

So as Paige and I are walking by the swim suits (which I had not even noticed were there) Paige said, "Look mama, bra!" I quickly looked around to see just what she is referring to as a "bra" and quickly saw that she is pointing to a bathing suit top. Just as I was about to explain to her how that what she saw was not a "bra," I suddenly stopped myself and quickly said, "Yes baby girl, a bra. You remember that!"

This was coincidently around the same time we had our ladies class on modesty at Karns and the verse 1 Timothy 2:9 quickly came to mind.

I thought, "If an almost 2 year-old can see that what the world views as a bathing suit top, resembles a bra, then why is it that so many "Christian women" can go to the beach or the pool wearing a bathing suit or "Christian men" wearing trunks without a shirt, that are no more covering than that of underwear?

We must always remember that God wants us to adorn ourselves with respectable apparel, with modesty and self control. If we are wearing something that shows what is meant only for our husbands or our wives to see then are we adorning ourselves respectably? Or with modesty? Are we posing a stumbling block for someone who might see us? Just a lesson from the innocence of a little child.

Amberly Champion graduated from the University of TN in 2006 and worked as a preschool teacher before she became a stay at home mommy in August of 2010. Amberly is married to Lance Champion and they have one daughter Paige Analyse, born in August of 2010. Amberly enjoys reading, cleaning, working out, and visiting with friends and family.

Lemons or Lemonade?

We were on a cruise with our family and it had rained every day of our vacation. As we woke the kids up to start the day, Tiffany asked "Is it raining?" Our answer was "Yes!" She sighed and was very upset. Gregg asked her, "You know what you do when you are given lemons? Her answer was "Yes, you make a sour face!" Gregg's response was "No, you make lemonade!"

It's all about our attitude! We all have days when we are given lemons! But we choose whether to make lemonade or a sour face. Life isn't always fair and we have to deal with the good and the bad. Christ wasn't treated fairly, and He was definitely given some lemons. But He always chose to make lemonade.

We decide how we are going to handle what comes our way every day. We have all known people that always have a positive attitude and we enjoy being with these people. But we have also known people that always have a negative attitude. It is harder being around negative people.

As Christians, we can look for opportunities to turn the bad into good or lemons into lemonade. As a side benefit, people who have better attitudes also enjoy better health. We have God on our side every day, every hour and every minute. There is nothing my God cannot do!!! Ask yourselves, "Am I a positive or negative thinking person?" "Let this mind be in you which was also in Christ Jesus" (Philippians 2:5).

Sherrye Woodall is married to Gregg. They have 4 children: Stephanie Harder, Tiffany Dresser, Benjamin Woodall and Jonathan Woodall. They have 4 grandchildren: Wrigley Harder, Walton Harder, Adalynn Dresser and Brooklynn Dresser. Sherrye has taught the 3 years old class at Karns for over 32 years.

Lessons Learned

When my son, Jake was 11 years-old, he was riding with me to visit my friend's son, Ethan, at East Tennessee Children's Hospital. Ethan was being treated for bone cancer.

For days leading up to our visit, Jake and I talked about how hard it would be to miss your friends at school and not have play days at home and how nice it would be to have someone to talk to or hang out with if we were in his situation. I detailed Ethan's process of getting through radiation, surgery and chemo before learning to walk again in rehab. I felt certain that Jake knew what he was doing as we headed out to spend time with Ethan, but in the car on the way to the hospital, Jake had one question that I could barely answer. He asked, "Is cancer contagious?"

A lump formed in my throat. I tried to swallow it and squeaked out, "No, baby, cancer is not contagious." In all of the talks we'd had about what cancer could do to your body and how it wasn't fair that Ethan was going through all of the pain and sickness, Jake knew he was going to be right there in the room with Ethan passing video game controllers back and forth and breathing the same air, yet he never hesitated to get in the car and go with me. Would I have been that brave? Who's teaching who a lesson here?! I finished the drive in silence to keep from crying.

In all my years of enlightenment in school, college and oddball seminars, I have never learned as much as when I have learned something from my boys. One thing I have learned is that I know absolutely nothing compared to the innocent wisdom of my two precious angels.

Jill Green is used to seeing things differently. She grew up with brothers and is the only girl in her house with her husband, Craig, and two sons, Jake and Duncan. Her life is filled with blessings in her family, job and even in trials. She has an English/History degree from UT, but says she has yet to figure out what she wants to do with her life.

First Grade

One day I was asked by my first grade teacher to read the day's lesson. Very proudly, I marched to the stage and read perfectly the two or three pages from my reader. The only problem was, I was not following the words nor turning the pages as I read. After a little questioning from my teacher I told her I took my book home with me at night and had my older sister read the lesson to me. I memorized it. I didn't know it was wrong, it was so easy.

Many years later I was teaching a young adult Bible class. We were discussing different sins, and I mentioned the fact that if we exceeded the speed limit we were breaking our state (or federal) law. One young man spoke up and asked, "Is that wrong? I do it all the time." Like me, in the first grade, he didn't realize what he was doing was wrong. I wonder how many of us do things without thinking if it is right or wrong? I wonder if we sometimes really care enough to check things out, to do a little research? Do we put just enough effort in to get by? Do we allow others to do our "reading" for us?

For me, no effort was involved in memorizing a few pages read to me, but to learn to read I had to put forth effort. As Christians we all need to heed Paul's advice, "That you may walk worthy of the Lord, fully pleasing Him, being fruitful in every good work and increasing in the knowledge of God" (Colossians 1:10). Also consider Luke 12:47,48.

Wendell Agee was born and raised in Pikeville, TN. He served 20 years in the USAF and was a successful business man for over 30 years. Wendell has served the Lord as a missionary to Cuba, Jamaica, Honduras and other countries. He's a member of the Karns Church of Christ.

Memories

Memories are what keep us going sometimes. I had a home, a wonderful husband and children. So what could be better? He had arthritis that hurt so bad, but that was part of his life for him. Then came the really bad news that he had cancer. The doctor gave him a year to live, but he lived two years. The Lord had work for him to do. During all this he never complained of pain.

Then three years later here came bad news again. Our oldest daughter had cancer. Both of them loved the church and the church family. I know that the Lord is there to help and love us, and I also know someday that there will be no more pain or cancer and no heartbreak.

We thank God for giving us all he has and hope we have used our time and money like he would have it used. I know the Lord will see me through, but it's hard.

I guess one of the good things about memories is they bring back the years. We asked one of our teenagers what they remembered from when they were younger. They said sitting in a circle on the living room floor reading Bible stories, and prayer, and going to the mountains as a family, and their granddaddy taking them for long walks in the park.

Martha Insell was a widow, and the mother of five children. Martha wrote this article just a week prior to her own death. Memories are indeed important to us, and our memories of Martha are of a quiet, Christian lady. Although she is gone, I'm glad to have her still speaking to us today through her devotional message.

Citizenship

I am a proud citizen of these United States: however, I was born and raised in the United Kingdom. Since I became a citizen in 1958 in Santa Fe, NM, I have made certain to vote in all elections. I consider it an honor and privilege to do so. In order to become a citizen one must obey all the laws of entry into this country, must learn the form of government and be able to read and write in English. Those were the rules then, and one was expected to obey all of them.

There is not supposed to be a sneaky entry into this beautiful country by becoming an overseas student in a university and then staying without ever obeying all the rules of entry, or perhaps crossing the border from Canada or Mexico and mingling in with the citizens.

I was struck by a similar entry into Christ's kingdom by a man, long gone from this world, who worshipped with us in a small church in Mississippi. He went forward one Sunday morning and said he was guilty of "insliding." I had never heard of that. Apparently he had been unfaithful for many years. He had come to the assemblies every time the doors were open, and everyone assumed he was a faithful member and had been for many years. At that time there were no elders, or I don't believe that would have happened. I am so grateful for our elders here at Karns. Entry into God's kingdom has entry rules also. We must hear, believe, confess Christ, repent, be immersed, and then live a righteous life. "Insliding" is sinful and that man repented and lived and died a true Christian man.

June Agee was born and raised in the UK and came to the United States when she married Wendell and became a U. S. citizen in Santa Fe, NM. June and Wendell have four living children and five grandchildren. June is a member of the Karns Church of Christ.

Spiritual Anorexia

"Behold, the days are coming," says the Lord GOD, "That I will send a famine on the land, Not a famine of bread, Nor a thirst for water, But of hearing the words of the LORD" (Amos 8:11).

A part of Amos's prophecy which was fulfilled concerned an unusual famine that would come upon the people: a famine for the Word of God (Amos 8:11). I am often made to wonder just how applicable this prophecy of Amos is even for us today. Can we truly say that we are receiving the daily nourishment that we need by feeding upon the Word of God? Or is it possible that we have become spiritually anorexic?

A simple practice of daily Bible reading will go a long way to ending this famine for the Word of God! A reasonable goal at first is to read a chapter a day. Once the habit of daily Bible reading has been established, reading three chapters a day will enable one to read through the entire Bible once a year. As you read, make it a time for meditation and prayer. Take the time to apply the things learned into your daily walk as a child of God. By God's grace we have so much more of God's revealed word to enjoy and yet some turn aside and refuse to partake of this spiritual feast! I challenge everyone to:

1. Make the commitment to not neglect the all-powerful Word of God!
2. Feast daily upon that Word which can save our souls!

Gregg Woodall is an elder of the Karns Church of Christ. Gregg is married to Sherrye and they have four children, Stephanie, Tiffany, Benjamin, and Jonathan. They also have four grandchildren, Wrigley, Walton, Adalynn, and Brooklynn. Gregg enjoys golfing, dirt bike riding, spending time with family, and is a fan of the Tennessee Volunteers.

The Sermon for Today

Yes...the title is also the name of a famous Andy Griffith Show episode but yet still applies here in the 21st century of Christian living. The preacher in this episode spoke about why we are rushing everywhere and that we all need to slow down. Fifty years later, it is even worse than in that fictional television setting.

In Jesus' ministry, He would always stop and offer help to those who needed it. He didn't worry about a time schedule even if His efforts were thwarted by different people.

Do you do that in your Christian walk? Do you stop and offer help even if it means that you will be late to an appointment? Chances are that answer is probably no. We still rush off after we skim the news, quickly eat a meal, and rush as quickly as possible to work, possibly putting others in danger because we are in a hurry.

Just as was shown in that episode with the bandstand, we just don't see sometimes how rushed we really are until someone says that we need to slow down.

Whether it is as simple as helping someone to their car with groceries or being able to assist a distressed driver on the side of the road, we all need to be mindful to slow down and see what opportunities to show God's love to others.

Unlike the end of that episode, failure is not an option. We need to slow down, just like Jesus, and be ready to help at a moment's notice because the next need could be right in front of us.

Wayne Begarly has been a member of the Karns Church of Christ since 2011. Wayne graduated from UT in 2007 with a Bachelors in Communications. Wayne is involved with the local United Way and American Cancer Society. He enjoys sports and the outdoors in his free time.

To Him, They are Perfect!

Have you ever wondered why God would allow a child to be born with birth defects? Why He would allow a baby to be born without the ability to walk or speak or see? Why would a child have an intellectual disability where they will never live a normal or independent life?

I think I know part of the answer to that question. I teach those children every day. I see their struggles. I look into their eyes. While most of the world sees these children as "throw away" children who should not even be allowed to be born, I believe that God sees these children as opportunities for the rest of us who truly are imperfect. While they look imperfect to us, God sees their hearts and their souls. He knows just how perfect they are and sees us as the imperfect ones. These "perfect ones" give the rest of us "imperfect ones" the opportunity to develop Christ-likeness through our response to them.

When we turn toward a person with a disability rather than turning away from them; when we find ways to minister to them rather than ignoring them, we develop the mind of Christ. Jesus was all about loving, healing, and caring for the outcasts. He values them so how can we do any less?

I look forward to the day when I get to meet all my children in heaven. I want to see my little ones run, have sight restored, and be able to have a conversation with me. I hope that they will be able to tell me that they knew from my actions and attitudes that I loved them. I hope that they are able to now see Jesus in me, just as I see Jesus in them.

Kim Higginbotham grew up in Poplar Bluff, MO. She is married to Steve and has four children: Kelli, Michael, Matthew, and Anne Marie. Kim teaches children with multiple disabilities for Knox County, a ladies' class at SEIBS, conducts teacher training seminars, and maintains two blogs, "Teaching Help," and "Relative Taste." She enjoys teaching and cooking.

God's Point of View

Have you ever wondered what God is thinking when he looks at this world? I often try to look at this life from God's perspective. That is the journey we as Christians are all on, to become Christ-like and to think more like Him. In my simple mind, I imagine Him shaking His head and thinking that we have really missed the whole point!

Our eternal destiny is on the line and most people don't take the decision to seek out truth very seriously. All around the world people believe what their culture tells them to believe, what their family believed, or what is convenient for them to believe. I know people who have put more effort into researching their next car purchase than into what they believe about God. We're busy, we're distracted and Satan's plan has been effective for far too many in this world.

1 Peter 5:8 says, "Be sober, be vigilant; because your adversary the devil walks about like a roaring lion, seeking whom he may devour."

For followers of Christ, it is our duty to shed light on the darkness. It's far too easy for us to fall into the trap of being "respectful" of other people's beliefs - by this I mean being politically correct and not lovingly engaging in the difficult conversations that we need to have with those whom we know and come in contact with. If you really love in the way that God loves, you will resist Satan's trap and talk to everyone that you can about the Good News of the Gospel. Make it your priority to seek and save the lost in your life.

Gerri Nath has been a member at Karns since 2009 and has been a Christian since 1977. Gerri is married to Michael and they have a daughter, Elliana Grace. She is the Vice President of Accounting Services at Marriott International, Inc. , and enjoys spending time with Ellie, watching her play softball, photography, traveling, scrap booking, reading, and writing.

Who is Watching You?

Sometimes we can learn lessons from children that are otherwise difficult to teach in a classroom setting. One such lesson was vividly illustrated while two families, consisting of four adults and seven young children, were vacationing at Disney World.

While going from one activity to another our eight-year-old grandson was lost. During the parents' frantic search of the crowded park his mom received a call from him on a cell phone she did not recognize telling her he was lost and where he was. Later, I asked him why he asked that particular man to use his cell phone. His explanation was very simple and to the point. "The man's wife was in a wheel chair eating an ice cream cone. When the man wiped his wife's face, I thought he is a good man and I told him I was lost and asked him if I could borrow his cell phone to call my mom."

The lesson is heart-warming and frightening. The frightening part is that someone is usually observing our everyday activities and many times we are unaware of people watching us. Does our demeanor and the way we go about our daily activities portray that of a good person, or are we so focused and busy we are oblivious to the world around us?

The positive side is that people are watching us and we can influence those around us by simply being Christians in every way, every day. By being a kind and gentle person, we can help rescue lost souls and bring joy to those looking for answers.

Margaret Denton is married to Don Denton and they have three children, Richard, Jeffrey and Leigh. They have eight grandchildren Clifton, Micah, Caitlin, Hunter, Sara, Denton, Joshua and Quincy. Margaret enjoys travel, reading, summer vacation trips with the children and grandchildren, and watching grand-children's sports, and Tennessee sports.

Oh, No!

We have probably all done something we were told not to do. As a child I can remember doing this on a few occasions. I knew, as soon as I did it, I was going to be in trouble. Immediately, I would have one of those, "Oh, no!" moments. You know, the moment you realize you did something you were not supposed to do. At that moment, I knew I was in trouble for my disobedience.

Imagine how Adam and Eve must have felt. They were living the good life in the Garden of Eden until one day Satan appeared and helped change that. After giving in and breaking the one commandment God had given them, the Bible says, "The man and his wife hid themselves from the presence of the Lord God among the trees of the garden" (Genesis 3:8). Why did they hide? I imagine they hid because they had one of those "Oh, no!" moments. They knew they had disobeyed God.

Satan tricked them and he continues to trick Christians today. Just like Eve, Satan deceives Christians into believing that sin will bring them great joy and pleasure. His desire is for Christians to see only the fun that comes with sin. Unfortunately, sin always results in consequences.

Friends, remember...sin is not all it's cracked up to be. Sure it looks, feels, tastes and appears good; however, with sin come consequences, and those consequences often have a far higher price than we want to pay. Let's fight to keep from being deceived by sin. We don't want to have one of those "Oh, no" moments with God!

Justin Morton has been in student ministry for almost 10 years. He has been the student and family minister for the Karns church of Christ since 2010. Justin is married to Miranda and they have one son, Caden. Justin enjoys spending time with his family, studying, teaching, writing and is a fan of the Tennessee Volunteers.

Lord, I Believe. . . Really

Reading Hebrews 11, we are inspired by the "cloud of witnesses" (Hebrews 12:1). When we reflect on the lives and faith of Noah, Abraham, Sarah, Moses, Joseph, Rahab, David, Samuel, and unnamed others, we are encouraged to remain faithful in our daily walk with God.

Who best describes you? Who best describes me? I would like to think I have the persistence of Noah, the faith of Abraham, the leadership abilities of Moses, the courage of David, or any other characteristics of these faithful people. No, honest evaluation takes me from Hebrews 11 to Mark 9:24. Here I find the words of a concerned father, "Lord, I believe; help my unbelief!"

Each day is a challenge to believe what I believe; do you find yourself there too?

When our faith is tested, how do we respond? We could throw in the towel and just give up, but what good would that do? We would be no better off than those who do not know God. It is on those days, we need to review the history behind Hebrews 11. Simply stated, God is the constant throughout the lives of faith's heroes. Regardless of the circumstances around them or around us, we can build an unshakable faith on the fact that God is faithful! He proved that in the lives of these individuals and He can do it in our lives too!

May my unbelief in the circumstances around me, never diminish my belief in the One who is faithful! May my daily prayer be, "Lord, I believe; help my unbelief!"

Jeff Smith is married to Sherry and they have two children, Lauren and Hannah. Jeff and his family have been members at Karns since 2001. Jeff has served the congregation as an elder and is often referred to as "The Bible Bowl Man." He enjoys reading, writing, congregational singing, and passionate gospel preaching.

I've Lectured. . . Now What?

"I've lectured until I'm blue in the face! Now what do I do?" This question, and others just like it are sometimes asked by parents of adult children who have chosen to turn their backs on Jesus and his church. Just what should parents do when their adult children spiritually disappoint them? Here are some suggestions. . .

- First, respect your child's decision. Now that doesn't mean you have to like it or agree with it, but you must come to grips with the fact that your child is now an adult and able to make decisions on his/her own. Disagree with them. Attempt to convince them otherwise. Plead with them. But when all is said and done, accept their right to make their own choices and realize you can't make them do right.

- Second, don't rescue them. Don't fall into the "good parent" trap and rescue your children when they are faced with the consequences of poor decisions. As tempting as it may be to step in and take over, a "responsible parent" allows an adult child to learn from his/her mistakes. Be there for them, but don't bail them out.

- Third, wait for them to return. Expect it. Pray for it.

- Fourth, don't give up hope. Understand that the final chapter in your child's life has not yet been written.

- And fifth, if and when your adult child returns, welcome him/her back without any "I told you so's."

And remember this: just because your children have strayed does not necessarily mean that you have failed as a parent. God has given us all, even our children, the freedom of choice.

Steve Higginbotham has been the pulpit minister for the Karns church of Christ since 2010. Steve is married to Kim and they have four children, Kelli, Michael, Matthew, and Anne Marie. Steve enjoys writing, playing golf, and is a fan of the Pittsburgh Steelers, the WVU Mountaineers, and the Andy Griffith Show.

Vanity

Ecclesiastes 1:2 says, "Vanity of vanities," says the Preacher; "Vanity of vanities, all is vanity." Day in and day out we get up in the morning, get ready for the day, and go to work or school. Then, the day is over and we go to sleep to do the same thing the next day. What motivates you to get through the day? Is it your own personal abilities? Or Jesus?

There are many people who try to live their life by getting their happiness by accumulating wealth. They measure their success by what type of career they have because money and worldly acceptance are what many people live for. "All is vanity."

By the end of Ecclesiastes, Solomon tells us the conclusion of *everything*! We should fear God and keep His commandments (Ecclesiastes 12:13). With God in our lives we do not need to measure our success by the world's standards. We should be thankful for what we have been blessed with. Every day is an opportunity to shine our Christian lights and be examples of Jesus to our co-workers, friends, and family. Don't get bogged down by the earthly vain things that will only last a little while. Let your focus be on God and His abounding love. Spend time enjoying all that He has done for you.

"As you therefore have received Christ Jesus the Lord, so walk in him, rooted and built up in Him and established in the faith, as you have been taught, abounding in it with thanksgiving" (Colossians 2:6-7).

"In everything give thanks; for this is the will of God in Christ Jesus for you" (1 Thessalonians 5:18).

Daniel Tanner is a graduate of University of Tennessee with a degree in finance. Daniel is a native of Knoxville. He is married to Jessie Tanner. Daniel likes hiking, fishing, and cooking.

Time Out

Sometimes one of the hardest words in the English language for Christians to master is the little two letter word "no." We often feel guilty about saying "no" when faced with choices of multiple good things needing to be done. Always saying "yes" to every good choice, however, can result in burnout, fatigue, and stress. God wants us to exercise balance and order in our lives.

Even Jesus sometimes had to say "no." Jesus had only three short years to accomplish his mission for the Father and had to make choices and set priorities. In Mark 1:31-35 we see Jesus making a choice to leave Capernaum on a particularly busy day of healing the sick and demon possessed while others needing his help were still lined up at the door. Jesus left and went off to a solitary place to pray. When he was found and told "everyone is looking for you," he answered "Let's go to the nearby villages so I can preach there as well, since that is why I have come." It could not have been easy for Jesus to say "no" when faced with so many needing his help, but he knew that he could not put all his eggs in one basket and still accomplish all that was expected of him.

Like Jesus, we do not have to feel guilty when we can't say "yes" to everything good there is to do as long as we are not making excuses, or avoiding our responsibilities. We don't have to live overscheduled, frazzled lives, but should strive for reasonable balance and limits in our service to God.

"He who considers too much will accomplish little." - Friedrich von Shiller.

Sara Jones was born in Camden, AL and became a Christian in 1969. She received her education at Alabama Christian College where she met and married Edwin S. Jones. They have three children and four grandchildren. Sara is the manager of Evangelist Bookstore and teaches women's classes at SEIBS. Her hobbies are interior decorating and gardening.

The Ride is Worth the Wait

A few years ago, some friends told me stories about the craziest roller coaster of its time, the Millennium Force at Cedar Point Amusement Park. As they told me about its extreme speed and height, the eight hour drive from Knoxville didn't bother me at all! From the moment we arrived at the park, it seemed every force imaginable was keeping me from the adrenaline rush I had so eagerly anticipated, but I was not distracted in the least. The long walk from the parking lot, standing at the gate with thousands of other guests, and waiting in the ride's long line actually gave me more time to anticipate the ride as I continually stared at the twisted and rolling metal track rising 310 feet above my head! And you know what? The ride was definitely worth the wait.

In 2 Corinthians 4:17, Paul states, "For our light affliction, which is but for a moment, works for us a far more exceeding and eternal weight of glory."

Yes, we will have to endure the trials of life that might tempt us to the core. We will, most likely, have to face moments of frustration that challenge our faith and test our character. But these setbacks are reduced to "light afflictions" as our attention is steadfastly focused on loftier things... the promises of God and the eternal home with Him. Yeah, the distractions we face may be somewhat bothersome for a moment, but oh how they pale in comparison to the joy that awaits us in heavenly places!

Certainly, this "Ride" will definitely be worth the wait!

John Hoffarth has been a Christian for over 20 years and enjoys sharing the faith with friends or those seeking a stronger relationship with God. He also likes trying any new activity that challenges his fears or physical endurance. To relax, he enjoys the opportunity to travel abroad or spend quality time at home with his wife Karen and son Austin.

You Can Do It!

I am always amazed at what people are capable of doing. It never fails, regardless of how many outstanding athletes have competed in previous Olympic games, new world and Olympic records are set each time the games are held. As much as I enjoy the games themselves, I really like to hear the stories of how the athletes became Olympic champions. The story of Olympic champion diver David Boudia is simply amazing to me. Here are a few quotes from David after his recent Olympic victory:

- "To think 10 years ago I was petrified to jump off a 10-meter platform, and now I'm Olympic champion, it's crazy."

- "Diving is 60 percent or 70 percent mental and the rest is physical. If you can get your brain in line, it will be fine."

How many times have you been paralyzed by fear? I have been more times than I care to admit. While we like to make excuses about our lack of abilities, talents or opportunities, many times we don't excel because we become paralyzed by fear of failure. When the apostles Peter and John were arrested, I'm sure they felt a great deal of fear. However, they prayed for and received boldness so they could continue teaching the truth in the midst of those who wanted nothing more than to destroy the Christian way (Acts 4:1-31).

Almost 2,000 years later, we are still enjoying the fruits of their labor - the spreading of the gospel to every nation. Next time you are fearful, remember that you can do all things through Christ who strengthens you (Philippians 4:13), and then go out and get it done!

Chris Cox serves as a deacon at the Karns congregation. He is also a computer programmer and small business owner. Chris is married to Hannah, and they have two children, Samuel and Rachel. Chris enjoys gardening, reading non-fiction, learning new things, teaching others, and spending time with his family.

GPS

Recently, I had to find a sister's home in order to transport her to an eye appointment. She gave me verbal directions to her house and added that I would not find her small street on any maps.

Luckily, I have a GPS (Global Positioning System) as part of my phone service. I simply typed in her address and the GPS gave me precise instructions to get to her house. I got there on time and we proceeded to her appointment.

Using the GPS reminded me of the Bible. I sometimes think of it as mankind's EPS (Eternity Positioning System). One cannot simply take any of life's paths and end up in Heaven. The Lord tells us in Matthew 7:14, "narrow is the gate and difficult is the way which leads to life, and there are few who find it." How can one find the narrow gate and the way to eternal life? Determine that Heaven is your final destination, then follow the gospel.

A very useful feature of the GPS is that it will tell you when you are off-route and advise you how to get back on track. The Bible also does this for you. Daily review and study of your Bible or EPS will tell you if you are on the right track. If you have problems understanding your EPS or discover you have strayed from the way, your brethren will help you. All of us, at times, have taken a side road and needed to get back on the right way.

Let us all thank God for His love and mercy that we can be counted among His children through His son Jesus.

Dave Benner is married to Sue and they have three children. Dave retired after 40 years with USDA. He and his wife, Sue moved back to TN in 2012. He enjoys hunting, fishing, and is a fan of the Pittsburgh Steelers.

The Crucifixion of Jesus

I am thankful that Jesus died on the cross. The Bible says that the enemies of Jesus killed him because he did good things like healing people. Here are some reasons why the crucifixion was important.

- He did it for us.
- He did it to forgive our sins.
- He did it so that we could go to heaven.
- He did it so that we won't go to hell.

I am grateful that he did this for the entire world and that after three days, he rose up from the dead.

(S. H. - I agree with Raegen. I too am glad that Jesus made this great sacrifice for the entire world. If Jesus wouldn't have been willing to die on the cross, we would be denied access to heaven because of our sins. There is no greater way to express one's love for another than to lay down one's life for another, and that is what Jesus did for us.

The cross of Christ is a great paradox. It was the darkest day in human history, yet it was also the finest hour for man. It was a shameful display of hatred that put him on the cross, yet it was an amazing display of love. It demonstrated God's hatred of sin, but his love for the sinner. On the cross, Jesus won by losing and he gained the victory by surrendering. For these reasons, and the reasons Raegen set forth, we should always glory in the cross!)

Raegen Gillentine is 7 years-old and is the child of Amber and Jeremy Gillentine. She is currently home schooled and is in the second grade. She is very involved in the Lads-to-Leaders program, loves to play softball, and dress-up as a little princess.

Be Careful Little Eyes

We teach the song to our little children. We protect their innocence by being careful what they see, hear and say, but do we make scars and calluses on our own hearts when we aren't careful about what we see, hear and say?

Our hearts can become scarred and callused from repeated exposure to the world's culture. We do, little by little, what we would not do in full (i. e. a little bit of foul language, a little pornography in a movie or TV show, lyrics in music, books with very un-Christlike topics and language). We say, "a little bit isn't bad" or "I skip over the bad bits." Once it's in your mind, you have put another scar or callus on your heart. The next time, it will be easier to justify what you see, hear or say.

We would never intentionally watch a pornographic movie or read a book full of expletives or descriptions of activity not conducive to Christian growth, nor fill our heads with songs whose lyrics are detrimental to our Christian living, but, little by little, we accept what we put in front of our eyes, into our ears, or what comes out of our mouth. We need God's word to help us heal the scars on our hearts. Psalm 51:10 says, "Create in me a clean heart, Oh God. . ."

My favorite barriers to fighting off the scars and calluses are found in Philippians 4:6-9, James 4:7, and Psalm 119:105.

This is a daily battle that can be won, but only with God's help (Jeremiah 10:23).

Chris Kelsey has been married to Gary Kelsey for the past 57 years. They have four children, 10 grandchildren, and 7 great-grandchildren.

The Sands of Time

Eventually your life will end. Like my title, "The Sands of Time," we need to get on the right track (to Heaven) before our hourglass runs out. Recently, at Teenage Christian Camp I witnessed a few of my friends being baptized and now they are on the right track. For example, there are two houses. One is all beautiful and whitewashed clean on the outside. The other is all dirty and rusty on the outside. All of us would want to pick the whitewashed one, but don't always judge a book by its cover. Well, the whitewashed house on the inside is all rotted, torn up and moldy. But the dirty and rusty house is clean, organized and very elegant. Since you now know this about the insides, now you want to pick the rusty house.

That is like heaven and hell. There are two paths. The dirty one represents the path to heaven; the clean one hell. You would want the clean one because it is easier and being a Christian isn't always easy. We need to be on the right path to Heaven. So, let's all join together as one in Christ and get on the right path before our hourglass is empty.

Eventually, if you live your life like a Christian, your hourglass will remain full in heaven. "Enter by the narrow gate; for wide is the gate and broad is the way that leads to destruction, and there are many who go in by it. Because narrow is the gate and difficult is the way which leads life and few there be who find it" (Matthew 7:13-14).

Daniel Guthrie is the 13 year-old son of Todd and Yvette Guthrie and is the younger brother to Ethan. Daniel likes to read the Bible, play soccer and watch the Volunteers.

Where Could I Go But to the Lord?

When we lost our son and his family, it took us to our knees. The pain seemed unbearable. The grief surrounded us. We learned the true meaning of Romans 12:15, "Rejoice with them that do rejoice, and weep with them that weep." Our brothers and sisters in Christ wept with us, fed us when we were hungry, and prayed for us to come to terms with our loss. I went to the Lord and His word for comfort. James 4:10, "Humble yourselves in the sight of the Lord, and he shall lift you up."

Someone once said, "to realize the worth of the anchor, we must first feel the storm." Every hardship is to make us a stronger Christian. 1 Corinthians 10:13 says, "No temptation has overtaken you except such as is common to man; but God is faithful, who will not allow you to be tempted beyond what you are able, but with the temptation will also make the way of escape, that you may be able to bear it."

Jason left behind Bibles in all three cars, and one at work. His employer asked if they could keep the one he left at work in his memory. His employer also donated Bibles in his memory. Psalm 116:15 reminds us, "Precious in the sight of the Lord is the death of His saints."

The moral of the story is to keep moving forward, and not get stuck in the valley. Psalm 23:4 says, "Yea, though I walk through the valley of the shadow of death, I will fear no evil for thou art with me; thy rod and thy staff they comfort me."

Marlene Monroe is married to Allen Monroe and they have two children, Jason (in heaven) and Jill. They also have six grandchildren, Dalton, Mikayla (in heaven) Haley, Tyler, Austin and Bryce. Marlene and Allen moved to Karns in November 2009. Marlene enjoys spending time with family, reading, and traveling.

A Watch Tower

"I will stand my watch And set myself on the rampart, And watch to see what He will say to me, And what I will answer when I am corrected" (Habakkuk 2:1).

When Habakkuk purposed to stand and watch and wait for God's answer, he received this: "Then the LORD answered me and said: 'Write the vision And make it plain on tablets, That he may run who reads it" (Habakkuk 2:2).

For Habakkuk to stop, stand, wait, and watch for God's direction, the result would be words plain and direct which could be transmitted to others. To stand and watch would lead to momentum.

On summer days, Gloria and I sat on the top of a wooden fort built by an Eagle Scout for the playground of the Fellowship church. We were keeping watch. We regularly visited the Norris Post Office and studied to memorization the FBI poster of the Ten Most Wanted. Gloria and I would be ready. We knew Norris was the likely place to hide for a top-notch bad guy seeking a small, quiet town. Our town needed us to anticipate and foil such a plan with our sharp look-out. Our plan, for one, required that the criminal would turn on West Norris and choose to come down Dogwood Road or turn on Crescent and come up Dogwood Road. If he were the 11th Most Wanted, he would slip past us. You may see flaws in our strategy, but do recognize our sense of civic duty.

I recommend Habakkuk 2:1. To stand and watch to see what God is doing brings blessings into plain view.

Melea Nash Smith is married to Steve. They have four children, Jordan, Melea Jean, Bryan, and Sarah. Melea is semi-retired from surveillance work.

Sisters in Christ

I believe in the special bond shared by sisters. I believe in having a friendship that lasts a lifetime, a constant supporter, and a bond that cannot be shared with any other person. Sisters are more than just relatives; they are best friends, role models, advisors, and everything else imaginable. This eternal love between two sisters is immeasurable and is what makes the joy of sisterhood something I cherish daily. This bond that physical sisters have is the same type of connection that sisters in Christ should share.

Being members of the Lord's church, we are called to edify one another and to be encouragers to our fellow brothers and sisters. 1 Thessalonians 5:11 says, "Therefore comfort each other and edify one another, just as you also are doing."

Sisters in Christ should encourage one another and be there to lift one another up during trials, and rejoice with them in times of happiness. Having a loving church family is the closest thing to how life in heaven will be that we can experience together on this earth. When Paul said, "I have fought the good fight, I have finished the race, I have kept the faith" in 2 Timothy 4:7, I cannot help but think it would have a lot harder for him to do that, had he not had support from his Christian family.

As sisters in the Lord's church, we need to love and edify each other daily to help us all reach our eternal goal of Heaven.

Hannah Smith is the daughter of Jeff and Sherry Smith. She has been attending Karns since 2001. She currently attends Freed-Hardeman University and is studying to be an Occupational Therapist.

A New Beginning

"Brethren, I do not count myself to have apprehended; but one thing I do, forgetting those things which are behind and reaching forward to those things which are ahead, I press toward the goal for the prize of the upward call of God in Christ Jesus" (Philippians 3:13-14).

One must learn to forget the past. You can't go back. The scars may remain but the sins have been forgiven when one obeys the Lord. Learn from your past mistakes.

A Russian Proverb says, "If one lives in the past he loses one eye, but if one forgets the past he loses both eyes." Overcome old habits and quit living in the past.

Set yourself a goal. Paul said, "I press toward the goal for the prize of the upward call of God in Christ Jesus" (Philippians 3:14).

When Earl Nightingale was eighteen years of age he resolved to retire when he was thirty-five years of age with an income of fifty-thousand dollars a year. From that time on every decision he made and every friendship he developed helped him toward that goal. Learn to live in the present. "whereas you do not know what will happen tomorrow..." (James 4:14).

James Meadows was born March 10, 1930. He graduated from high school in 1949, and Freed-Hardeman College in 1955. He later attended Union University and Harding Graduate School. He has done local work in Tennessee, Kentucky, and South Carolina. He served as Director of ETSPM from 1996 to 2006, and presently serves as Dean of Students.

God's Plan

Joseph, a man of true commitment, is one of the most respected and admired characters we read about in the Bible. In Matthew 1:18-25 it is told that Joseph and Mary were betrothed (engaged), which during Biblical times, was as legally binding as being married, though the ceremony had not taken place. The betrothal could only be broken by a formal divorce.

When Joseph found out that Mary was with child he planned on putting her away secretly, because he was a righteous man and did not want this to be a disgrace upon her (Matthew 1:20). While trying to decide what his plan of action would be, he was visited by an angel who explained to him that Mary had conceived through the Holy Spirit and that she would bear a son who would save people from their sins (Matthew 1:22).

Once he was told of the situation, Joseph became fully committed to God's plan. He stayed with Mary, even though this was looked down upon. He did not come to know her intimately until after Jesus was born (Matthew 1:25). This courageous action shows true commitment to the Lord.

Have you ever had a situation that you knew would make you look bad, but you stuck it out because you believed it was the Lord's plan? We do not have the privilege of an angel coming to let us know directly what God's plan is in a specific situation, but we do have the plan book: the BIBLE. We need to study and do our best to comply with the way God would have us to live.

Amber Gillentine is married to Jeremy Gillentine (13 years) and has four children Sidney (11), Hutson (9), Raegen (7), Linden (4). She is currently a student at the Southeast Institute of Biblical Studies. She also home schools her four children and maintains a very organized home.

Look for the Good

When I was a boy I lived at my grandmother's for a time. We did not have much by way of material things—no running water, no inside bathroom, etc. We had clothes to wear, had a good place to sleep, and always had plenty to eat. A staple was chicken. Chickens were not hard to find. We simply went outside and got one for supper.

One day when I went to get a chicken for supper I witnessed a most interesting site. One chicken had a sore on it and another chicken was pecking at the sore. After a while another chicken would peck at it. And, later still, another would peck at it as well. Eventually, the poor chicken died from being pecked to death. It just broke my heart to watch the scene. Despite all my efforts, it seemed inevitable that the chicken would die. What was so sad was that besides the sore, the chicken seemed to be in good health. Were it not for the pecking, it might have survived.

The more I think about this the more I realize how, too many times, we do the very same thing. We all have faults. Sooner or later we find out what those faults are. The question remains: "How are we going to treat one another once we discover the fault?" We can try to see the good which is characteristic of a person, or we can focus on that one thing that is amiss in one's life. In doing so, we can tear a person down to the extent that they fail to realize their potential.

Look for the good—not the bad.

David Lipe was born in Charleston, MS and is married to his wife Linda (Wilson). They have three daughters and five grandchildren. David presently serves as the Director of the Southeast Institute of Biblical Studies.

Junk? Not so Fast

When I was preaching in Kentucky, we underwent a major expansion and renovation to our church building. What a mess it was for the better part of a year. Much of what took place was demolition. Before new construction could begin, much of the old building had to be torn down. The facilities that once served us well, were soon reduced to rubble.

Ah, but for talent. Charles, one of our preachers and one of our elders saw potential in the demolition. As the workers tore down the old stairs, Charles salvaged wood that at one time served as steps leading to our classrooms. From that pile of rubble, Charles was able to make a beautiful oak bookcase with glass doors.

For several years, every time I went into his office and saw that bookcase, I was reminded that something that was at worst, a pile of rubble, and at best, nothing more than steps that we walked on, had been transformed into something beautiful.

Doesn't that sound a lot like what God does every day? He takes people who at worst were rebellious sinners, and who at best were unprofitable servants, and transforms them by his power into something beautiful and valuable.

Before you throw your hands up in the air and give up on yourself; before you get discouraged with the way your life has turned out, remember that you possess the potential, in the hands of God, to be shaped and molded into something of great beauty and value.

Steve Higginbotham has been the pulpit minister for the Karns church of Christ since 2010. Steve is married to Kim and they have four children, Kelli, Michael, Matthew, and Anne Marie. Steve enjoys writing, playing golf, and is a fan of the Pittsburgh Steelers, the WVU Mountaineers, and the Andy Griffith Show.

Why Obey?

Have you ever wondered why people obey the Gospel? I grew up in a very traditional family that followed their denominational beliefs very sincerely. While growing up I was not allowed to even walk across the lawn surrounding the church; I had to use the sidewalk or I'd be in sin. I knew little else until I met Christians.

At first, I was very resistant; it's easier to believe a lie that you've heard over and over, especially one that is seared into your brain. When I began dating a Christian, we had some very interesting conversations early in our relationship about the true nature of God and Christianity. I remember our discussion on heaven and my challenging this young man who said only true believers are going to heaven. I asked him if he was telling me that I was going to hell and he shook his head and said softly, "it doesn't matter what I think, what matters is what the Bible says." That took the wind out of my sails but it made me wonder what else the Bible was saying.

I began to study and the more I learned the more one message kept coming back to me: you are either in Christ or you are outside of Christ. Especially haunting were the images in Matthew 24:36-44. I simply did not want to be left behind.

That young man I dated? He is now my husband. I credit his love for God and his love for me for making me want to study. We experienced one of our greatest joys the day he baptized me into new life.

Mary Lindner has been a member of the Karns congregation since 2011. She is married to Kyle and they have one child, Kathryn. Mary likes traveling, reading and knitting; often managing to do the last two at the same time. A recent transplant from Minnesota, Mary is enjoying the lush scenery and temperate weather of her new home.

A Verse Upon Which to Reflect

The importance of God's Word in our lives is clearly summed up in this familiar verse, "All Scripture is given by inspiration of God, and is profitable for doctrine, for reproof, for correction, for instruction in righteousness" (2 Timothy 3:16). Yet, there are some verses that stand out, in that, they cause the reader to pause and do a self-evaluation. John 8:47 is such a verse.

The Jews and Pharisees, who claimed to be Abraham's descendants, were critical of Jesus almost from the beginning of His ministry. They questioned who He said He was, and on one occasion said Jesus had a demon. Following a long running discourse between Jesus and the Jews and Pharisees, Jesus simply said, "He who is of God hears God's words" (John 8:47a). And He added: "you [those that were questioning Him] do not hear because you are not of God" (John 8:47b).

This verse should cause us to reflect on our desire and commitment to fully adhere to the teachings in the Bible. Do we in our daily activities thoughtfully act and speak in ways that reflect God's teachings? Or do we put our lives on "cruise control" and go about our day without thinking that we are God's children? Like many moms and dads have said to their children as they leave home, "remember who you are," we should remember daily whose we are.

Dear God, help me today to remember to reflect upon your word, and conduct myself as one who is of God.

Don Denton serves as an elder of the Karns Church of Christ. He is married to Margaret Rymer and they have three children, Richard, Jeffrey and Leigh. They also have eight grandchildren, Clifton, Micah, Caitlin, Hunter, Sara, Denton, Joshua and Quincy. Don enjoys hiking, travel and Tennessee football and basketball.

The Fixed Game

In 1919, the infamous Black Sox scandal took shape during the World Series. The scandal involved eight players from the Chicago White Sox, the most notable of whom was "Shoeless Joe Jackson." The eight men were involved in throwing, or "fixing" the series so the White Sox would lose to benefit the gambling world. As a result, the men involved were banned from baseball for life.

Unfortunately, fixing sporting events is a part of sports. Where big money is, corruption is soon to follow. In considering a fixed game, I often think of eternal life as a fixed game. It is fixed in that the Christian team has already won. Through the plan of salvation, the victor has already been decided. I have often questioned why the people in the time of Noah did not heed the warning and prepare for the flood. It is understandable though, in that they did not have the information we have today.

We face the same issue today. The flood we face is not an actual flood, but either our death or the return of the Lord. We have been given the instructions and know what is ahead of us, similar to the information received by the people Noah interacted with. Let us rejoice in being a part of the winning team, which is more than just the outcome of a sporting event, but an outcome of the events in our life through the blessings of our Lord.

Todd Monahan is the husband of Julie Monahan. Todd and Julie have two children, Anniston and Baker. Todd grew up in Lancaster, PA. Todd is a 2002 graduate of Freed-Hardeman University. He is a CPA and operates an accounting firm in Knoxville, TN.

Be a Barnabas

If you have ever attended one of the graduations from Southeast Institute of Biblical Studies (formerly known as East Tennessee School of Preaching and Missions), then you know that every year they award a Barnabas Award. This award goes to the student who exemplifies the traits of Barnabas. He is an encourager to his fellow students and always has a good attitude. Every year when this award is given out I try to guess who will receive the award before it is announced. Most of the time I am correct, but I have missed it a few times. Then I wonder, would I be considered a Barnabas? Do I encourage or do I discourage people?

We need encouragers in the church. Every one of us has times when we are down and discouraged. If we have an encourager near us, these times don't seem to last as long. We all like to hear words of encouragement or receive notes of encouragement.

Who needs encouragement or a pat on the back for a job well done? Our ministers and elders, who spend many hours visiting the physically and spiritually sick, and get calls at all hours of the day and the night. Our deacons, they spend many hours in service to God and this congregation. The secretaries, who work to make sure the office runs smoothly. Our Bible class teachers, who spend time preparing for and teaching our Bible classes. The person sitting next to you in the pew - you may not know what they are going through right now.

A word of encouragement can go a long way. "...Beloved Barnabas..." (Acts 15:25).

Sherrye Woodall is married to Gregg. They have 4 children: Stephanie Harder, Tiffany Dresser, Benjamin Woodall and Jonathan Woodall. They have 4 grandchildren: Wrigley Harder, Walton Harder, Adalynn Dresser and Brooklynn Dresser. Sherrye has taught the 3 years old class at Karns for over 32 years.

How to Respond to Warnings

During my preschool years a sweet, kindly old black lady made daily treks through the white folks' section of town to look for any cast-off food or clothing to help her to survive deep poverty. In addition to this she was a buttress to harried mothers' worries about keeping their children out of mischief. In spite of her kindly nature, this lady adopted the character of a villain whose name children dreaded to hear, "Soap Sally." Every child knew that if they were caught in mischief Soap Sally would make soap out of it.

One day my older sister pulled me in a little wagon for an adventure jaunt. We made a secret trip into an abandoned house. Oh, it was so thrilling! Then, all of sudden, Soap Sally seemed to appear from nowhere. We escaped screaming and crying, desperately headed for home. Soap Sally slowly followed us. Mother was waiting on the sidewalk in front of the house. Then Soap Sally proceeded with her verbal scolding. I believe Mother was nodding her approval of the message. This experience was life-long in value!

I have often since mused on how poorly we respond to wonderfully presented lessons and sermons in our Sunday worship. Yes, we have a real Devil at work on us every day presenting temptations that too often enslave us in this life and permanently bar us from heaven.

G. C. (Grover Cleveland) Robinson, Jr. has been married to Mattie Lou Geer since June 27, 1954. They have four children: Timothy, Amy, Andy, and Penny; and three grandchildren: Victoria, Quintin and Ransom. G. C. is a retired mechanical engineer. He turned 86 December 1st, 2012.

Be Still and Know that I Am God

If we adopt the thinking of Psalm 46, should we expect a miraculous deliverance from trouble? God does not need to work a miracle to help us in times of trouble. The miracles of the past continue to teach us (John 20:30-31). Their repetition is unnecessary for the accomplishment of His will. Trust in Him, believe in Him, for the Lord has said, "I will never leave you nor forsake you" (Hebrews 13:5). Do you believe Him?

Isn't it comforting to know that if the world falls apart, if the unthinkable happens, in the end we'll be saved? The apostle Paul says also, "What then shall we say to these things? If God is for us, who can be against us? He who did not spare His own Son but gave him up for us all, how will He not also with Him graciously give us all things?" (Romans 8:31-32). Both the psalmist and Paul invite us to accept God's love and presence in our lives based on what God has done in the past.

God's past provides calm for our future. He is the ruler of kingdoms of this earth and the all-powerful Creator of the universe. We may be pressed, perplexed, and pursued, but not unto despair (cf. 2 Corinthians 4:8-9). If you are the last man or woman standing, be still, stand fast, and be strong. "Therefore we will not fear, though the earth should change and though the mountains slip into the heart of the sea" (Psalm 46:2).

Gregg Woodall is an elder of the Karns Church of Christ. Gregg is married to Sherrye and they have four children, Stephanie, Tiffany, Benjamin, and Jonathan. They also have four grandchildren, Wrigley, Walton, Adalynn, and Brooklynn. Gregg enjoys golfing, dirt bike riding, spending time with family, and is a fan of the Tennessee Volunteers.

Mother Nature

When my sons, Michael and Matthew were small boys, we were in the van one day when Matthew, 6 years-old at the time, asked, "Dad, why do people give Mother Nature credit for all the beautiful things God does?" To say the least, I was taken back by the question. I didn't even know that he had ever heard the expression, "Mother Nature."

But how insightful? I never cease to be amazed at what children say. I didn't know quite how to answer his question. Why do we refer to the works of "Mother Nature" rather than the works of God? Is it an effort to avoid offending someone? Is it intended to disguise our faith in God? Or is it just a phrase we've picked up that has not theological significance intended?

Whatever the case may be, don't you think more glory and honor would be directed to God if instead of talking about what "Mother Nature" does, we talked about what God does?

Instead of talking about how Mother Nature takes care of the animals during the cold winter months, wouldn't it be more honoring to God to talk about how God takes care of the animals during the winter?

Instead of talking about the beautiful sunset Mother Nature gave us, wouldn't it be more honoring to God if we talked about the beautiful sunset God gave us?

You get the idea. By changing our verbiage, not only can we honor God more, but we might also open doors to further discussion about God with others.

Steve Higginbotham has been the pulpit minister for the Karns church of Christ since 2010. Steve is married to Kim and they have four children, Kelli, Michael, Matthew, and Anne Marie. Steve enjoys writing, playing golf, and is a fan of the Pittsburgh Steelers, the WVU Mountaineers, and the Andy Griffith Show.

I Almost Missed It

I was baptized at the age of 12 by Larry Haslip. I also had the benefit of the teaching of Tony Ash and Joe Goodspeed. Joe was our preacher, neighbor and my senior English teacher. Both Tony and Joe spent much time in our home. I was surrounded by Christian teaching and example. My mother's family were Christians since the early 1800's. I went to church three times a week, but somewhere along the way I missed out on how Grace works. I thought that as soon as you sinned, you were lost until you prayed and asked for forgiveness. Sin-Lost-Confess-Pray-Forgiven. Sin-Lost-Confess-Pray-Forgiven. I knew I could not live that way, no one could! One would need to die with a "prayer on his lips" to have any security.

After about 10 years of being lost, I decided I wanted what my parents and grandparents had. I returned to Jesus and His church. About a year later, I heard a lesson about the assurance of Salvation, including Romans 8:35-39 and 1 John 1:7 & 5:13. I learned that as I walked in the light (which doesn't mean perfection, but has reference to a way of life), God would continually forgive my sins. All my sins, past, present, and future are forgiven as long as I walk in the light! What good news! What peace!

Not long after I found my way back, God rewarded me with my life partner, my wife, Bobbie. Had it not been for the Christian examples of my teachers and family I would have missed this life with my Christian family and worst of all I would have missed God's amazing grace.

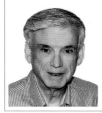

Vascoe Stephen "Steve" Martin is married to Bobbie Lynch Martin. Steve and Bobbie have three children, Gabe (Sarah), Leah (David), and Cory, (Rose Anne); 8 grandchildren; and In-laws are Red & Helen Lynch. All 4 generations attend church at Karns. Steve is a Navy veteran. He enjoys woodworking, reading, sports & grandchildren.

The Meaning of Life

"Let us hear the conclusion of the whole matter: Fear God and keep His commandments, For this is man's all" (Ecclesiastes 12:13).

Why am I here? What am I supposed to do in life? What is the purpose of everything?

Throughout history, men have wanted to know the meaning of life. Countless philosophers have put forth their ideas. Men have sought greatness through conquests of various sorts. Solomon himself, the wisest man who ever lived, sought the meaning of life in everything under the sun. After all of his experimentation and self-indulgence, Solomon reached a very simple conclusion: the meaning of life is reverence of and service to God.

Why is it that men seek meaning in anything other than God? Why do we strive so hard to establish something lasting and important when the history of man is replete with examples of our failures to do this very thing? Civilizations crumble, works of art are destroyed, memories of fun fade away, and great accomplishments are reduced to the few words recorded in history books. Everything man seeks to establish as truly important fails to last and therefore loses its meaning.

If we want to grasp something of importance, something that will last, we must turn to God. Through Solomon's example, we know what gives meaning and purpose to our lives. Living for God may not bring about the fame and fortune the world finds important, but it will result in an eternal dwelling place with God. That result gives life the ultimate meaning.

Brad Alsup serves as a deacon at the Karns church of Christ. He is married to Jennifer, and they have two children, Evan and Allie. Brad is a hunter, a cyclist, and an avid reader.

Sweeter as the Years Pass

I really don't know how to start this, but God has been so good to me, I feel like I have to.

I was raised in a denominational church, but as I became older I could not go along with a lot of their teachings. My dad was a preacher in a denominational church. He knew a lot about the Word, but he sure didn't live it, but that was long ago.

I remember when I was very young, in my Sunday School Class, my teacher told us anyone who could learn the fourteenth chapter of John and recite it in a week, would receive a dollar. We did not have a lot, so that sounded great to me. I learned it, got up, recited it, and got a whole dollar.

Since then we searched and searched and finally came upon the church of Christ. We were baptized by Jim Waldron. God has been so good to us. We don't have riches here on earth, but we have a home in Heaven and that's what it is all about.

I have so many scriptures in the Bible, except all the names I can't pronounce. I read every day, and as I get older they seem to be so much sweeter to me. Just to think that God would send His Son to die on the cross for me makes me think how much I owe Him. I will never pay Him enough!

I still have family members who are not yet Christians, as many of you may have as well. Let us diligently pray for each other, and our family members whom we love so much, so that they too can come to know the joy and peace of being a child of God.

LaVerne Maddox is marred to Bob Maddox and she has three boys, Danny, Mike, and Tony. She has been a member at Karns since 1982. She and her husband have been the custodians of the church building since 1996.

Honesty is the Best Policy

There was a time in my life when I left a major company with excellent benefits to work for a small company that had just started. At the time, I had a wife and three small children for which I needed to provide.

Almost immediately, I was tested in my new job. I discovered a problem, discussed it with my boss, and explained how the company was in the wrong. I realized that if this problem was not resolved successfully, I could lose my account with a customer, but I also saw that my company would not do what the customer wanted.

After several attempts to solve the problem, I asked my boss what I should do. I will never forget his response, "Well Ken, this is one of those times when you need to tell a little white lie." I was taken back by this response. My boss was telling me to lie about a business transaction. What was I to do? This was my boss at a new job. What could I do?

Gathering all my strength, and with God's help, I told my boss that I would not lie about it. I said I would tell the customer the truth and if we lost his business then we would deal with it. I explained to the customer what had happened and that my company was not going to change. I will never forget his response, "Ken, I know that but I wanted somebody from your company to tell me that. I will continue to do business with you and thanks for your honesty." That was a reminder to me that honesty is the best policy (Exodus 20:16).

Ken Couch is a sales representative for Royal Brass and Hose, an industrial hose and fitting supplier in Knoxville Tn. He regularly travels in his job throughout East Tennessee, Eastern Kentucky and Southwestern Virginia. He enjoys High School football and following the Tennessee Volunteers.

Real Love

He was tall and handsome with a smile that would light up a room. We met one day, by chance, when I was working as a cashier at a big box store. We chatted and flirted and said our good-byes. I thought, "What a nice guy. Wish I had someone like that in my life." Months later, I saw Mr. Smiles again at another store (guess we both like stores) and we actually exchanged numbers this time. We played phone tag for several months and I had practically given up on going out with him. As faith would have it, I started working a new job and found out he was moonlighting there. We saw each other every day and eventually had that first date, which was at Burger King!!!

The weeks turned into months, which led to a wedding. I eventually started attending Karns with my new husband, but I also wanted him to attend my Baptist church with me, which soon led to a Bible study. We would read, and I would argue, then we would read some more. I had to admit that I could not find anything about my precious Baptist church in the Bible. One Sunday at Karns, I listened to what the minister was saying and I knew God was speaking to me. I was baptized by David Lipe that very day. I knew I loved God, but now I had an even stronger love for Him and I believed that His Son had died on the cross for my sins. I'm looking forward to heaven and all the great things that the Bible speaks about heaven.

I know that my husband (Bennie Williams) of now 29 years really does love me, because he shared the best gift ever when he opened the Bible and showed me God's gift of everlasting life. That is what I call "Real Love!" If you ever see my husband, ask him about his blue light special!

Jacquie Williams has been married to Bennie Williams for 29 years! They have one son, Jerrell Williams. Two grandchildren, Levi and Avani. Jacquie has worked for ORNL for 28 years. She loves to read, shop, cook and laugh! She has been attending Karns Church of Christ since 1984, and her favorite scripture is Philippians 4:13.

A Moving Experience

One in six Americans move each year, with the average citizen of the United States moving 11. 7 times over his lifetime. Since my dad preached, I have helped make up for some of you that have lived in the same house since birth. Teresa and I lived in: Jackson, TN; Henderson, TN; North Little Rock, AR; Mobile, AL; Valdosta, GA; Cookeville, TN; Knoxville, TN; and Jackson, MS.

Our current move presented us with a most unusual opportunity. Thanks to the gracious hospitality of Drew and Morgan Dulaney, we were able to settle into our work in Jackson before our house sold in Knoxville, with most of our "stuff" remaining there. The couple buying our house has an almost newborn baby. Three days after signing a contract to sell our house to them, our real estate agent asked if they could move in early. Teresa and I discussed it and decided it was what we would want someone to do for us, so we said yes.

This has resulted in the formation of an unusual friendship. They and their real estate agent have repeatedly thanked us. Several of our good sisters in Christ, who are helping pack everything up, have gotten to know the couple and their baby well. They and their agent have no church home. Their impression of us and our many brethren has resulted in the real estate agent and the couple expressing an interest in attending the Karns church of Christ.

Live the life of a Christian. Pray for open doors. Then keep your eyes open (1 Corinthians 16:8-9; Colossians 4:2-4).

Gary Hampton is the former director of the East Tennessee School of Preaching and Missions. He has preached for more than 30 years in AR, AL, GA, and TN, He and his wife, Teresa are currently living in Jackson, MS where Gary is preaching.

Miracles in the Bible

In Psalm 119:160 David says, "The entirety of Thy Word is true." Over and over again David will use the phrase "Word of God," but particularly in verse 160 he is saying "thy Word is true from the beginning or in its entirety."

Verse 160 establishes that if one accepts Genesis 1, they will also accept the text through Revelation 22. The text in Genesis 1 states, "In the beginning God created the heavens and the earth." The fact of creation is established.

When someone reads Genesis 1:1-2 and accepts these at face value, they have solved any difficulties in believing any miracle in the Bible. Establishing the existence of God solves the problem of all miracles of the Bible.

If God exists, then the miracles are so. If this is God's Book, then the account of the miracles is factual and accurate and reliable.

Therefore, how someone views the first part of the Bible determines what they can do with the remainder of the Bible. When one rejects the first part of the Bible, they have no real reason to say they believe anything else. On what basis could a man say he rejects one part of the Bible and then accepts another part of the Bible?

Conversely though, if we accept the first part of the Bible as God's Will and God's Word–factual, reliable, and inspired–then we can turn each page with confidence.

Tony Williams is originally from Chattanooga and was baptized at the East Ridge congregation. He is married to Deanna, and they have three daughters, Claire, Maggie, and Ella. Tony has a Bachelor's and Master's Degree from UT. Tony and his family have been at Karns since 1999, and during that time he has served as a deacon, and currently as an elder.

Called to be Holy

God has called to us, "Be holy, because I am holy" (1 Peter 1:16). God called for this from his people in Leviticus 11: 44,45. This is a request God repeatedly makes of us in scripture.

What does being holy mean to you? What does being holy mean to God? It should mean the same thing, right? Davis Bible Dictionary says that the word for holy is "Agios" in the Greek language. It is used to indicate being set apart from common use to a sacred use.

No doubt God has a sacred use for us and has separated us from the uncleanness of our sins. We have been raised from the water of baptism as "new creations" (2 Corinthians 5:17), but, it appears we have to put additional effort into being useful to God going forward. Peter admonishes us in verses 13 and 14 of 1 Peter chapter one to prepare our minds and be like obedient children.

We prepare our minds for success in other things we do. When we need to focus we control our attention. That's how we learn. It's how we get things done in a timely manner. God is asking that we do just that for his purposes. God wants obedient children. Obedience takes self-control. As a grandmother I've watched my grandchildren when they exercised obedience and when they didn't. I observed that they were happiest when they pleased their daddy. Obedient children make happy daddies, as well.

God defines holy by who he is and asks the same of us. Let's make him happy.

Sara Terlecki is married to her husband Bill. They moved to Knoxville from Ohio. Sara has worked in the church office since 2010. They have two grown children. Gerri married Michael Nath and blessed them with granddaughter, Ellie. Bill Jr. married Hope Whittington and blessed them with two grandsons, Allen and Evan.

A Mustard Seed

You may have met Jason when he visits us at the Karns church. He will usually be with his very good friend, Paul, who drives the pick-up truck that gets the two of them and Jason's wheelchair to outings. They are from the Clinton Church of Christ. As best I can tell, Jason and Paul are two people who love a good sermon and love good gospel singing! Jason was a greeter at Walmart for years, which was a job he had the friendliness and smile to nail down perfectly.

When Garry Jones, also from the Clinton church, made trips with Don Iverson and Jim Waldron, he changed to full-time mission work for India. Robbie Lee Goolsby, a retired schoolteacher, spent her life supporting missions and specified money in her will for children's work. Garry, among other works, began the Mustard Seed Village for children in India to further Robbie Lee's wishes. Garry began listing orphans in his newsletters and seeking sponsors for their monthly care, food, and school uniforms.

Jason did not sponsor an orphan. Jason sponsored an entire cottage. Today children from many far-flung villages and different languages have a bed, a trunk, and a mosquito net in a bamboo house where they run back and forth beside a sign that says Jason's Cottage. They have a Christian housemother, meals, chores, Bible classes, school, devotionals, and what is valued universally, family and home. They have a friend named Jason who shared his blessings from a grateful and generous heart.

"Assuredly, I say to you, if you have faith as a mustard seed. . ." (Matthew 17:20).

Melea Nash Smith is married to Steve. They have four children, Jordan, Melea Jean, Bryan, and Sarah. Melea grew up at the Clinton Church of Christ under the preaching of Clifford Reel, M. H. Tucker, Mike Kirk, Tommy Irons, Richard Powlus, Gary Kelsey, Waymon Summers, and Arthur Pigman.

One Another

Sometimes we don't know how to act or react in a situation or a relationship. We have choices to make. The Bible tells us exactly how to treat one another. Notice in the following verses there are no qualifiers for when it is OK to not follow the instruction. So even when we are mad, sad, offended, jealous, hurt, confused or whatever weakness we are experiencing, we are not excused from treating one another as we are instructed.

"A new commandment I give to you, that you love one another; as I have loved you, that you also love one another. By this all will know that you are My disciples, if you have love for one another" (John 13:34-35).

"Be of the same mind toward one another. . . " (Romans 12:16).

"Therefore let us not judge one another anymore, but rather resolve this, not to put a stumbling block or a cause to fall in our brother's way" (Romans 14:13).

"And be kind to one another, tenderhearted, forgiving one another, even as God in Christ forgave you" (Ephesians 4:32).

"Therefore comfort each other and edify one another, just as you also are doing. . ." (1 Thessalonians 5:11).

"And let us consider one another in order to stir up love and good works" (Hebrews 10:24).

"And above all things have fervent love for one another, for 'love will cover a multitude of sins'" (1 Peter 4:8).

Pam McCoy and her husband Darren have worshipped at Karns since 1997. Pam was the church secretary from 1998-2001. She is now working part-time for an architecture and design firm doing interior design for commercial projects. She enjoys her full time job as a homemaker, traveling, and spending time with family and friends.

Renovating Your Life

A great deal of renovation has taken place around our building recently. For instance, the bathrooms, the library and various other parts of the building have been renovated. Renovations are an important part of improving things. Just as we look for things in our homes to renovate, we should be looking for things in our lives that need renovation as well.

Paul was a man who understood the importance of renovation in one's life. When we are first introduced to Saul, he is standing by in support of the stoning of Stephen (Acts 7:58). From that point forward, Saul went about "ravaging the church" (Acts 8:3). When he gave his defense before Agrippa, Paul told of how he was hostile toward Christians (Acts 26:9-11). If there was ever a person who needed to renovate his life, it was Saul.

The wonderful thing about Saul is he took the time to renovate his life. He was convicted while on the road to Damascus, and was later baptized for the forgiveness of his sins (Acts 9:18). Saul's name was later changed to Paul, and he would go on to become one of the greatest preachers the world has ever known.

Friends, what about us? Are there things in our lives we need to renovate? Are we the kind of people God would have us to be? Do we let our lights shine for others to see? Are we fornicators, idolaters, adulterers, thieves, coveters, liars, drunkards, revilers, gluttons or prideful? Have we given our full hearts to God?

Why not begin renovating your life today to resemble a disciple of Jesus Christ?

Justin Morton has been in student ministry for almost 10 years. He has been the student and family minister for the Karns church of Christ since 2010. Justin is married to Miranda and they have one son, Caden. Justin enjoys spending time with his family, studying, teaching, writing and is a fan of the Tennessee Volunteers.

The Beginning of the Church

"Repent: for the kingdom of heaven is at hand," (Matthew 3:2) began the announcement of Jesus Christ, in the wilderness of Judea. At that time, there had never been an announcement with more importance than this one. It foretold of the promise of Isaiah who said: "Prepare the way of the Lord; Make His paths straight" (Isaiah 40:3).

Jesus of Nazareth, the Son of God, began His ministry after He was baptized. At that time, the heavens opened, the angel of God descended upon Him, and a voice spoke out of the heavens, acknowledging the divinity of the Son of God (Matthew 3:16). Jesus began to preach and, from among his disciples, he chose the twelve apostles (Matthew 10:1-4). He gave us the Word through them by inspiration of the Holy Spirit. He gave them the commission to preach the gospel, but limited them to Judea (Matthew 10:5), as they were under the Law until He fulfilled it and broke down "the middle wall of partition" by His death.

He, then, gave Himself to die for His people, and rose again on the third day (Luke 24:46). After His resurrection, He appeared to the disciples and extended the commission to "all the world" and to "every creature," (Mark 16:15-16), but told them to tarry at Jerusalem until they were "endued with power from on high." This promised power was given on the day of Pentecost, when they were enabled to speak under the influence of the Holy Ghost (Acts 2). The church began on that day, and it is that church that still exists today, and is the church of which we must be a part.

Tony Williams is originally from Chattanooga and was baptized at the East Ridge congregation. He is married to Deanna, and they have three daughters, Claire, Maggie, and Ella. Tony has a Bachelor's and Master's Degree from UT. Tony and his family have been at Karns since 1999, and during that time he has served as a deacon, and currently as an elder.

Adam and Eve

God protected mankind from knowing evil and experiencing the suffering that follows the practice of evil by telling Adam and Eve not to eat from the tree of knowledge of good and evil.

In fact, God told Adam that the day he ate of that tree, he would surely die (spiritually, not physically). However, Satan told Eve that they would not die, but would become as wise as God. They had to make a decision. Whose voice would they listen to? Well, Adam and Eve chose to disobey God and listen to Satan, and sin overtook them.

Immediately following their disobedience, they felt ashamed of themselves and tried to hide themselves from God. However, God knew what they had done, and he knew that they were hiding. So God confronted them, and they had to pay the price for their disobedience.

Although the setting is different today, we don't live in the Garden of Eden like Adam and Eve did, and we are not tempted to eat fruit from a forbidden tree, but we are still faced with the same temptation that Adam and Eve were faced with. We have to decide whose voice we're going to listen to.

Are we going to listen to the voice of God, or the voice of Satan? If we listen to Satan, we will suffer just like Adam and Eve did. However, if we listen to God, we'll learn that he always wants the best for us.

Sidney Gillentine is 11 years-old. She is the daughter of Amber and Jeremy Gillentine. She is currently home schooled and is in the sixth grade. She is heavily involved with the Lads-to-Leaders/Leaderettes program and also loves playing softball.

Stuck in the Mud

When I was in the sand and gravel business, I once was required to build a dam, the location of which was very muddy. In the process of building this dam, I sank the excavator, which is a 75,000 lb. machine. I was only going to build up a small portion and then let the dirt dry for a couple of days; but, before I realized what was happening I had "gone too far" and was stuck in the mud. If you have ever had your shoe stuck in the mud and tried to remove it then you can only imagine how difficult it would be to pull out a 75,000 lb. shoe!

Sometimes we do not count the cost of sin as "going too far." We often start something that really does not seem to be that big of a deal; but, once we get involved, we tend to go just a little farther and think, "well, that did not hurt me" or "no one caught me," then we go just a little farther. You have probably guessed the result - we get stuck in the mud of sin.

Whether your mud hole is private or public, you need to be on guard at all times (Mark 13:32-37). Sin is a tricky thing and if we do not decide ahead of time where the crossing line is, it steadily creeps further away. Let us not allow Satan to lure us into the "mud" out of ignorance. We need to always study to show ourselves approved before God (2 Timothy 2:15).

Jeremy Gillentine is married to Amber Gillentine (13 years) and has four children Sidney (11), Hutson (9), Raegen (7), Linden (4). He is currently a student at the Southeast Institute of Biblical Studies.

Forerunner and High Priest

One of the most unique descriptions of Jesus in the Bible is when he is called a "forerunner" (Hebrews 6:20). The concept of "forerunner" would have been new to the Jewish Christians whom the writer addressed. Under the old covenant the high priest entered the Holy Place as a representative of the people to offer sacrifice for sins, but the people could not follow. Jesus, as a high priest under the new covenant, entered the veil and made atonement for the people through the sacrifice of Himself. However, through His death He granted all people access to God the Father.

Our forerunner, Jesus, shows us how to enter the presence of God, namely, by faith. With the examples of Hebrews 11 in mind, Christians are admonished to "run with patience the race that is set before us" (Hebrews 12:1). He then described Jesus as the preeminent and supreme example of faith (Hebrews 12:2).

Christians look by faith to Jesus, the forerunner, who has run the race and now stands at the finish line cheering his followers on. He has illuminated the path and now urges Christians to endure in order to obtain the promise of heaven. As such the Hebrew writer admonishes Christians to "lift up the hands which hang down, and the feeble knees; and make straight paths for your feet, lest that which is lame be turned out of the way; but let it rather be healed" (Hebrews 12:12-13). Yet, if our knees do become feeble during the race, we may enter the presence of God our Father through Christ Jesus. Our forerunner makes intercession for us and thus perfects our faith.

Matthew Menarchek has been a member of the Church of Christ since 2006. He was born in Huntsville, Alabama, and lived there until he moved to Knoxville, Tennessee, in August 2012. He attended the East Huntsville Church of Christ in Alabama and now worships at Karns. He studies history at the University of Tennessee.

A Picture's Worth

We have heard many times that if we hear something long enough we will begin to believe it. This hit home recently on my husband's birthday. My daughter said, "I know that Dad is in his 50's and that sounds old but Dad doesn't seem old to me." I had the bright idea to ask if I seem old to her (I'm one year older than Dad). She hesitatingly said, "yes." When asked why I seem old and Dad doesn't she said, "I guess because you talk about being old."

She's right. I have always been able to do 10 things at once and now do well to concentrate on one, my memory doesn't work the same, and some days I just can't seem to move very fast. I have verbalized these things and although I have always planned on being a "spry old lady" I have presented just the opposite picture. I wondered why she thinks everyone we meet is younger than I am.

What about our "Christian" picture? Do others see a picture of "Christ-likeness?" Is Christ in our daily interactions with people? Do we focus on the good in others or the not so good? What kind of music are we listening to? Do we use words of encouragement or are we quick to criticize?

How others see us depends on what we give them to see. Let's make sure the picture we present is the one we intend.

By the way, I'm changing my picture. I only verbalize the good days now. When the time comes, I'll be that "spry old lady" yet.

Terry Albert is a home-school mom of two teenagers and a 4-H volunteer leader with a BS in Animal Science and MS in Rehabilitation Counseling. Her hobbies include reading and sharing the family's many animals through a variety of 4-H, school, and community activities.

Why Go to Church?

Several years ago, I baptized a young man who played on a local high school football team. As I walked into the water, I could feel through my rubber wader that the water was really cold! So I apologized to the young man and said I was sorry to tell him the water heater had apparently stopped functioning and the water was really cold.

In a macho sort of way this young man said, "Ah, no problem, that doesn't matter to me." Then he put his first foot in the water.

To say it took his breath would be an understatement. He stood there a long time before he ever attempted to put his second foot in, and for about the next 10 minutes, he inched his way into the baptistery. (So much for macho!)

I share that story because I think it illustrates how some people try to serve God. Instead of just giving themselves fully to him, they try to "inch" their way into following him. However, God is not looking for "toe testers" to test the waters of discipleship, he's looking for "cannonballers" who are wholly sold out to Jesus and his cause.

If you were to describe yourself, which would you be more like, a "toe-tester" or a "canonballer?" Friends, if you're trying to test the waters of discipleship, you'll find more than enough reasons to give up and get out. But if you really want to serve the Lord, forget about testing the waters and jump in!

Steve Higginbotham has been the pulpit minister for the Karns church of Christ since 2010. Steve is married to Kim and they have four children, Kelli, Michael, Matthew, and Anne Marie. Steve enjoys writing, playing golf, and is a fan of the Pittsburgh Steelers, the WVU Mountaineers, and the Andy Griffith Show.

Live for Jesus

This summer I was fortunate enough to go to Honduras on a mission trip. I didn't know much about what we would be doing, just that we would have a free medical clinic and preach about the Bible. Once we got there, I learned I was part of a group that would go out into the village and preach. Throughout the week we knocked on doors, and it was surprising to me how many people wanted to have Bible studies.

After we got back home, I began to think about the trip. Then the questions came to my mind. Why aren't we like that? How many of us back home wouldn't answer the door if an evangelist knocked? If we supposedly are Christians, why don't we accept the Word of God and live it like the people in Honduras do? We are all greatly blessed, yet sometimes we say we don't have the time for God.

Galatians 2:20 says that Christ lives in us. If this is true, why don't we live like it? Hebrews 12:1 reads, "Therefore we also, since we are surrounded by so great a cloud of witnesses, let us lay aside every weight, and the sin which so easily ensnares us, and let us run with endurance the race that is set before us."

All of our sin, doubt, worries, guilt and anything else holding us back - we need to let it go and live our lives for Jesus. No matter where you are or what you are doing, you can be an influence to people around you and bring them to Christ. So, are you living your life for Jesus?

Joel Turner is a freshman at Oak Ridge High School in Oak Ridge, TN and has been a member of Karns Church of Christ since May, 2011. He enjoys participating in Karns youth group activities and has attended Hillsboro Christian Camp for several years. He has also been on a mission trip to Honduras. He enjoys playing basketball and officiating soccer matches.

The Power of Words

Words. How often do you think about them? Try to recall the conversations you had yesterday. Did you criticize someone because they didn't do something the way you would have? Unfortunately, I am guilty of this. How can we expect others to know we are Christians if we are constantly being negative about things that really do not matter?

James says this about the tongue, "With it we bless our God and Father, and with it we curse men, who have been made in the similitude of God. Out of the same mouth proceed blessing and cursing. My brethren, these things ought not to be so" (James 3:9-10). What can we do with our words instead of using them to tear someone down? We can let others know we are Christians by having a positive attitude and lift them up with loving words. Try these:

- Always start your day in prayer.
- Encourage a child who is struggling.
- Let someone know you are praying for them.
- Tell a friend they are appreciated.
- Thank an older person for being a good example.

Today, try listening more and remember to ask yourself if what you are about to say to someone is necessary and would please God. We will fail some days, but we must keep trying and encourage each other! I am so blessed to have friends in my life that lift me up even when I am being negative. Let's all try to be that kind of friend today!

Deanna Williams is a native of Chattanooga, TN. She has lived in Knoxville, TN since 1999. She is the wife of Tony, and stay at home mother to their 3 beautiful daughters, Claire, Maggie, and Ella. Deanna loves being active with her church family at Karns.

The Flywheel Effect

The flywheel effect is a commonly used business term referring to the idea that once forward progress is being made it is the best time to keep things going and increasing. It is also related to the idea that consistent steady work is the key to success, not some sudden great big thing. Old tractors used to operate under the same principle; they ran better when you kept them steadily going along.

We all have witnessed many good steady things that keep happening within our church family and we should all work at keeping that going. Did you participate in VBS or help with Wednesday meals, or correspondence courses and Bible studies? Have you personally begun a daily devotional of prayer, Bible reading and a commitment to live for Jesus in your daily actions? Start now and keep it growing.

Let's all resolve to start and keep good things happening by committing to do our individual parts. We still have a lot to do in better serving God and with daily steady progress we will be pleasing to Him. As Paul was always "pressing on" we would do well to do likewise. We will not be done until we rest with our Lord in heaven.

"But, speaking the truth in love, may grow up in all things into Him who is the head - Christ - from whom the whole body, joined and knit together by what every joint supplies, according to the effective working by which every part does its share, causes growth of the body for the edifying of itself in love" (Ephesians 4:15-16).

Gregg Woodall is an elder of the Karns Church of Christ. Gregg is married to Sherrye and they have four children, Stephanie, Tiffany, Benjamin, and Jonathan. They also have four grandchildren, Wrigley, Walton, Adalynn, and Brooklynn. Gregg enjoys golfing, dirt bike riding, spending time with family, and is a fan of the Tennessee Volunteers.

Don't Fence Me In

Shortly after Kim and I married, we bought a dog. We had a fenced in backyard where she could run and chase birds and squirrels to her heart's content. She was living a "dog's life." Pampered, petted, well fed, and loved. However, one day she escaped the confines of our yard, ran into the street, and was killed by a passing truck. It was a sad day for our family.

But now, this article isn't really about our dog, but about the purpose of fences. The fence we had in the backyard was not an effort to punish or unnecessarily restrict our dog from "enjoying the good things of life." It was there for protection. It was there for safety. Placed within the confines of the fence were all the things a dog needed for happiness. The fence wasn't there to torment our dog, but to keep her safe.

Can you not see the application? God loves us dearly, and has "fenced us in," not as a punishment, but as protection. God is not a killjoy. The boundaries he sets, which restrict our conduct, are given with the intent of protecting us from harm. Within the confines of the Christian lifestyle are all the things a person needs to be happy, satisfied, and fulfilled. But what do we do? We escape, and eventually, we get hurt. How it must break God's heart to witness his children "break free" from his constraints only to be hurt from the dangers he knew were just outside his "fence."

Remember, the commandments of God are for our good. They are given because God loves us and wants the best for us. Learn to be content and satisfy yourself with the good God has fenced you in with.

Steve Higginbotham has been the pulpit minister for the Karns church of Christ since 2010. Steve is married to Kim and they have four children, Kelli, Michael, Matthew, and Anne Marie. Steve enjoys writing, playing golf, and is a fan of the Pittsburgh Steelers, the WVU Mountaineers, and the Andy Griffith Show.

The Nature of Christians

As a Christian, we take up the name and banner of Christ in the world. We subject ourselves to discrimination, hatred, and possibly persecution before men. Yet, 1 Peter 2:4–5, 9 offers some reassurance. We share a bond with Christ that goes beyond our pursuit of Christlikeness. We, in God's eyes, share in the nature of Christ and his role in the world.

Christ (v. 4)	Christian (v. 5,9)
Chief Cornerstone	Royal Priesthood
Living Stone	Living Stones
Chosen	Chosen Race
Precious	Special
Rejected	Rejected

God values our bearing of the name of His Son. God values when we devote ourselves to Him. He values that we are living stones building up His Kingdom. He has chosen us to be special, just as Christ was precious. Just like Him, we have also been rejected from the world.

While we ourselves are not Christ, we can have joy, knowing that Christ shares in our struggles. He is our comforter in times of need. He is the captain of the mighty ship and we are but lowly scrubbers on the darkest deck. He understands each and every grind we make against the wood of the ship. He understands every time we go to the bucket to refill. He understands when we run out of water and must seek more, because He is beside us, scrubbing the deck with us; sharing in our struggles and, eventually, in the joy of finishing the work.

Spencer Clark is the son of Terry and Teresa Clark. He was born and raised in the Karns Congregation. As of December 2012, Spencer will have graduated from Freed-Hardeman University with a degree in Bible. He plans to continue onto graduate studies and begin work in the ministry.

The "Insert-Name-Here" Show

Television has gone in many different directions with the evolution of reality TV. Those shows can't hold a candle to what your show might be like.

I have had thoughts in the past on what judgment day will be like when our lives are evaluated by the Lord and how that will be done. Since I work in the business, I think of it as a TV show or even a movie with all the other inhabitants of the earth watching. I imagine our lives on some kind of media and it is being recorded every day for evaluation. When we respond to an invitation to repent and confess our sins, the media is erased and a new one begins. What will that show be like? Would you be embarrassed at some point and want to explain your actions? Do we live our lives that way each day?

As Christians, we should be prepared for that show to air at any time. As is taught in the Bible, no one knows the time the Lord shall come so we are to be ready at any time and when that time comes, that show could be aired for the entire world to see

We should be cautious what activities we do in our daily lives because God is watching, 24 hours a day, 7 days a week, 365 days a year until the day where the media is stopped, whether through the second coming or our time to pass on.

So, while going through your day, always ask before doing an activity, "Would you want this to be seen by God?"

Wayne Begarly has been a member of the Karns Church of Christ since 2011. Wayne graduated from UT in 2007 with a Bachelors in Communications. Wayne is involved with the local United Way and American Cancer Society. He enjoys sports and the outdoors in his free time.

Just Like Medicine

God is amazing because:
He healed a man who could not walk.
He raised Jesus from the dead after he died on the cross.
He can heal us.

God is like taking medicine. He's able to make you better when you are sick.

(S. H. - Linden is our youngest contributor to this devotional book, and above are his thoughts, and what good thoughts they are! Twice in the Old Testament, Bible writers asked the following question in astonishment, "Who is a God like you?" That's precisely the impact God should have upon us.

Children especially love to sing the song, "Jesus Loves Me." As you know, the first part of the song goes like this:

"Jesus loves me this I know, for the Bible tells me so. . ."

Well if we changed the words to that line just a bit, we are reminded of another amazing truth about God. Consider this truth as well:

"Jesus knows me this I love, for the Bible tells me so. . ."

Not only does God love us, he also knows us! Like Linden, Moses, and Micah, I too am amazed by our God! And I am thankful that just as Linden said, "God is like medicine. He's able to make us better when we are sick."

Linden Gillentine is 4 years-old and is the child of Amber and Jeremy Gillentine. He is currently home schooled and is in kindergarten. He is involved in the Lads-to-Leaders program and is a rough, tough little man who loves his family.

Adoption

Adoption has a special place in my family. I have two wonderful sisters who my parents adopted from China. They are as dear to me as any other family member. When I first saw them, they were scared about these strange foreigners who were taking them away from their orphanage and the only comfort they knew. As the bus took us back to our hotel in China, I held my little sister and felt a surprisingly strong connection. Just one month earlier, I'd never seen this little girl and had no duty to care for her as family, but she was now my little sister and her life was about to get so much better.

Adoption was also a common occurrence within the Roman Empire. Christians would immediately have understood Paul when he wrote, "And because you are sons, God has sent forth the Spirit of His Son into your hearts, crying out, 'Abba, Father!' Therefore you are no longer a slave but a son, and if a son, then an heir of God through Christ" (Galatians 4:6-7).

Sometimes we can be so lost that we don't even know it. We hang on to the only comforts we know, like the comfort of an orphanage that provides so very little for our emotional well-being–and yet, God is there, arms outstretched, ready not just to save us, but to adopt us as His very own sons and daughters.

As Christians, let's let go of any fear we may possess. Our former lives as slaves to sin have been replaced by an adoption that is so intensely personal that we may refer to the Maker of this universe as our own dear Father.

Justin Boitnott is a second year law student at the University of Tennessee. He enjoys watching football, soccer, basketball, baseball, NASCAR, Formula 1, Indy car racing, golf, hockey, cycling, cricket, lacrosse, rugby, tennis, and curling. He also plays piano and enjoys cooking with his wife, Kelli.

What Will You Do Today?

"This is the day the LORD has made; We will rejoice and be glad in it" (Psalm 118:24).

There are so many things that require our time! What will I do with the day the Lord has given me? I could clean the house until it is spotless and be known for having a spotless house or I could make a hospital visit or encourage a shut-in. I could sit and watch TV or I could make phone calls or send cards to those who are widowed. I could go shopping or I could spend time with some of our young people, letting them know how much I appreciate them. I could read a book by my favorite author or I could spend time in Bible study and prayer. I could fix dinner for my family or I could make a little extra for a new mom who is getting very little sleep and needs to know that this will soon pass. I could take a nap or I could grade a Bible correspondence course. I could talk to my friend about UT football or a recent movie or I could talk to them about Christ.

We all make choices every day! None of these things are bad and most of them we need to take care of and do. But do we allow these things to dominate our lives? If you are reading this, then God has given you a gift, another day in His service. Use your gift wisely!

Sherrye Woodall is married to Gregg. They have 4 children: Stephanie Harder, Tiffany Dresser, Benjamin Woodall and Jonathan Woodall. They have 4 grandchildren: Wrigley Harder, Walton Harder, Adalynn Dresser and Brooklynn Dresser. Sherrye has taught the 3 years old class at Karns for over 32 years.

Surviving Stress

In today's world we tend to live a lifestyle that is far too hectic and fast paced to be healthy. In this day of hurry-sickness and overscheduled lives, stress has become a common problem. The ongoing state of anxiety and tension that can result from continuous exposure to the stressors that seem to be all around us can cause one's emotional state to become likened to a rubber band that has been stretched to the max and kept that way for a period of time, causing it to lose its elasticity, crack, and eventually snap.

There is no better solution for stress management than the principles for living found in God's Word. The scripture is a powerful prescription for coping with stress and avoiding the negative physical and mental consequences that it can bring.

Jesus is our perfect example of dealing successfully with stress. We can see Jesus' attitude and advice about stress in the words he spoke to his disciples when faced with the storm on the sea in Mark 4:38, as well as those spoken to Martha when she was seemingly stressed by making preparations for her visitor in Luke 10:38-42.

By having faith in God, planning our lives around his value system, and utilizing the principles for living set forth for us in his Word, it is possible for Christians to successfully live lives that are peaceful and in harmony with God's purposes in spite of the stressful 21st century world we live in.

"and the peace of God, which surpasses all understanding, will guard your hearts and minds through Christ Jesus" (Phil 4:7).

Sara Jones was born in Camden, AL and became a Christian in 1969. She received her education at Alabama Christian College where she met and married Edwin S. Jones. They have three children and four grandchildren. Sara is the manager of Evangelist Bookstore and teaches women's classes at SEIBS. Her hobbies are interior decorating and gardening.

Rejoice in Suffering

"And not only that, but we also glory in tribulations. . ." (Romans 5:3).

Can we really rejoice in our suffering? It seems counter-intuitive, to say the least. If asked, most people would argue that suffering comes about in our lives as punishment for wrong-doing, or as the consequence for someone else's actions. However, have you ever stopped to think that sometimes suffering is provided to us as a blessing?

Romans 5:3 tells us that we rejoice in our suffering. Why? Because, "suffering produces endurance, and endurance produces character and character produces hope." Sometimes we confront suffering in our lives not as punishment, but as preparation. Have you ever had a bad day at work? Have those bad days ever prepared you to handle new challenges? Have you experienced loss? Did that loss make you more appreciative of what you had? Did it bring you closer to others who have experienced loss?

Ultimately there is a goal. We see this even in the example of Jesus. Hebrews 5:8-9 states, "although He was a son, He learned obedience through what He suffered. And being made perfect, He became the source of eternal salvation to all who obey Him."

We, too, can learn obedience through our suffering, and we can be prepared for better things.

C. John Chavis has been a member of the Karns Church of Christ since 1997. John is a graduate of University of Tennessee College of Law, and practices law with Hagood, Tarpy, and Cox, PLLC. John enjoys softball and following the LSU Tigers and Atlanta Braves.

So What?

Christians read and study their Bibles. They attend Bible classes and listen to sermons. Over a period of time they assimilate a large body of Biblical facts and truths. So what?

Don't misunderstand me. We need knowledge. God's people can be destroyed for lack of knowledge (Hosea 4:6). Peter urged Christians to "grow in the grace and knowledge of our Lord and Savior Jesus Christ" (2 Peter 3:18). But knowledge simply for the sake of knowledge is woefully inadequate.

As we read the Bible, study it in class, and hear sermons, we need to ask, "What am I going to do with what I have learned? How am I going to incorporate this into my life? How is this information going to change my attitudes and my actions?"

James says that we are to be doers of the Word and not hearers only. To hear and to know but not do, James goes on to say, is like a person looking at herself/himself in a mirror, then immediately forgetting what she/he saw (James 1:22-26). Jesus asked, "But why do you call Me 'Lord, Lord,' and not do the things which I say" (Luke 6:46)? We must take action with reference to what we learn from the Word of God.

So, when you read the Bible, study it in a class, or hear it preached, don't forget to ask, "So what?" Give serious thought, perhaps even to writing down a step-by-step action plan, as to how you intend to put into practice the things you have learned.

Hugh Fulford has been a gospel preacher for almost sixty years. He was the first full-time minister of the Karns church (1959-1962). He and his wife Jan make their home in Gallatin, TN. Hugh continues to preach, lecture, and write.

Eat Your Lunch
and Be Strong in the Lord

Chicken makes us strong because it has protein in it. We eat good food to be healthy and strong. We also need to get exercise and use our muscles for them to be strong.

Samson was strong because God gave him strength. He continued to be strong as long as he obeyed God and didn't let his hair be cut. Then he told his secret to a pretty girl named Delilah. She was pretty on the outside but not on the inside! His hair got cut, he lost his strength, and he was hurt by the Philistines. He prayed to God to please let him have his strength back just one more time to push the pillars down and kill the Philistines. God gave him strength one more time (Judges 16).

God wants us to be strong too. He wants us to be strong on the inside. The Bible says: "Be strong in the Lord and in the strength of His might." It says we need to put on the armor of God so we can stand strong against the devil. (Ephesians 6:10-11) We get strong by reading the Bible and by trying to do what's right every day. We fill ourselves up with God's Word, which is like our protein. When we are tempted to do something bad, if we run away from temptation and don't do it, we will get stronger. It's like our exercise. That is how we build our spiritual muscles (I Timothy 6:11-12).

So eat healthy and exercise. Eat your lunch, and be STRONG IN THE LORD!

John Aragon is the 8 year-old son of Steve and Susan Aragon. He is a third grader at Hardin Valley Elementary School. He has one 5 year old brother, and best friend, Joe. John runs cross country, plays football, basketball and soccer. His hobbies include reading, singing and playing with Joe. He loves learning about and exploring God's amazing world.

Between a Rock and a Hard Place

There are times that we all succumb to pressure or stress just from the events in our daily lives. Stress can also occur at times when we are trying to do good things but are unduly criticized or feel inadequate because we have not accomplished our goals. Often in these situations, we find ourselves making wrong choices. But we are not the first to fall prey to such tactics from Satan.

Moses was under a ton of pressure from the children of Israel as they were constantly complaining and bemoaning their circumstances. He did quite well at dealing with all their problems until he found himself between a rock and a hard place. You know well the scene where they were in the desert of Zin and they were all very thirsty and were giving Moses no small amount of grief.

"And the LORD spoke to Moses, saying ... speak to the rock before their eyes, that it may yield its water. ... Then Moses lifted up his hand and struck the rock twice with his rod; ... But the LORD said to Moses and Aaron, Because you have not believed Me, to treat Me as holy in the sight of the sons of Israel, therefore you shall not bring this assembly into the land which I have given them" (Numbers 20:7-12).

When you find yourself between a rock and a hard place, remember to consider what the Lord would have you to do and then do it His way. God means what He says and expects us to believe him and do his will.

Gregg Woodall is an elder of the Karns Church of Christ. Gregg is married to Sherrye and they have four children, Stephanie, Tiffany, Benjamin, and Jonathan. They also have four grandchildren, Wrigley, Walton, Adalynn, and Brooklynn. Gregg enjoys golfing, dirt bike riding, spending time with family, and is a fan of the Tennessee Volunteers.

Today

Hebrews presents us with a host of "by faith" statements showing that following God made the seemingly impossible possible. Paul told the Corinthian Christians that the wisdom of men was foolishness to God. Jesus said that whoever seeks to save his life will lose it and he who loses his life will save it. Scripture after scripture makes statements and paints contrasts that don't make (human) sense to the casual reader.

We are told to study to show ourselves approved before Him, not men. God didn't direct us to become wealthy business people, climb to the top of the career ladder, or be a marvel in the sports world. He did encourage us to be good husbands and wives, parents, children, and neighbors. Isn't it interesting that the things of the world are not what He told us to excel in doing? It was in the simple, everyday person-to-person relationships in which He encouraged us to excel.

Each of us can be kind, but we all can't be sports stars. Each of us can be faithful in our relationships, but we all can't be president of a company. Each of us can glorify God through our lives. Each of us can be cheerful and speak a good word. Today, let's make an effort to be good neighbors, friends, and family members by going beyond what is expected in our relationships. Today let's let God's light shine through our lives.

Conrad Slate graduated from Tennessee Tech, and was a member of the Air National Guard for 31 years, retiring as a Colonel. He holds a MS in Financial Services. Currently he is a principal in Slate, Disharoon, Parrish & Associates, a fee based financial planning firm. Married to Brenda for over 40 years, they have two children and three grandchildren.

Encouragement

"But exhorting one another, and so much the more as you see the Day approaching" (Hebrews 10:25).

These are the things that encourage me: Family members sitting together on a pew. The single mother bringing her children to worship services. Couples married to one another fifty plus years. One spouse tirelessly and faithfully caring for their mate. The energy of Vacation Bible School. The anticipation of campaigns followed by the good feeling of exhaustion. The sounds of conversation during a fellowship meal. A birthday card with ice cream money in it. Smiling faces during singing, it's just natural when singing joyfully from the heart. Harmony of all of God's singers! Sermons and lessons that are well prepared. Large crowds, especially on Sunday and Wednesday nights. Baptisms and the shuffle (people moving to see better) that goes with them. Dads bringing their children to service when mom works (been there and done it). Being known as the "Bible Bowl Man." Bright smiles, tender voices, sincere words. The reunions at lectureship time, along with the great lessons, and great singing! Not sure which is better, great singing or great preaching! The faith of those around me. Battles my brothers and sisters have overcome. A firm handshake, a gentle touch on the shoulder. Weddings and their new beginnings. Funerals, and their new beginning for the faithful Christian. The hope and confidence to stand before the creator of the universe pure and sinless because of the blood of Jesus Christ. The promise of Jesus' second coming!

I have listed the things that encourage me. Now it's time to make your list!

Jeff Smith is married to Sherry and they have two children, Lauren and Hannah. Jeff and his family have been members at Karns since 2001. Jeff has served the congregation as an elder and is often referred to as "The Bible Bowl Man." He enjoys reading, writing, congregational singing, and passionate gospel preaching.

Learning to Share

I started learning to share at a very young age. In a Bible cradle roll class we learned the Bible and learned about sharing toys with others in the class. Then at home we have to learn to share many different things such as toys and food. One lesson I learned while sitting on my Grand Paw's lap was sharing chips while watching a fishing show in the afternoon. A short while later I had to share toys with a cousin.

In John 6:1-14 a large crowd of people followed Jesus to a place where there was no food. The disciples did not have enough money to buy bread for such a large number. One disciple said, "There is a lad here with five barley loaves and two fish." There were about five thousand men here. Jesus gave thanks for the food and all ate their fill. When gathering the scraps there were twelve baskets full left over. Jesus did not want any food to be wasted.

There is another example of sharing in the Bible that I think is great. In 1 Kings 17:8-16, Elijah asked this widow to share her food and water with him. At this time she only had enough for her and her son, after this they would starve to death. The widow shared her food with Elijah. After this she miraculously had plenty of flour and oil.

The greatest thing that I like to share with others now is the gospel. When I share the gospel with my peers, I feel like I am giving them an opportunity for eternal life.

Sasha Russell is the daughter of Steve and Becky Russell. Sasha is a 14 year-old Freshman in high school. She enjoys band and is currently in the color guard.

God Has a Purpose

At first it might seem like Exodus 13:17-18 are just unimportant facts about the geography of the land or the direction of the Israelites' travel, but when we take time to consider what God is telling us, we learn something incredible: God could have led his people by the easier path. After all, His reason for saving the Israelites was because he had heard their cries for rescue (Exodus 2:23-25). The people were tired and beaten down. I'm sure they would have wanted to take the route that was closer. Instead, God took them the way that was farther. Not only that, but it was a trek through the wilderness towards the sea! Can you imagine how the Israelites must have felt?

God didn't lead them by this route without a purpose. The purpose was to keep the Israelites from becoming so discouraged by war that they would want to turn back. God didn't want his people to suffer as slaves in Egypt, but wanted them to be free and to live in a good land. So, he took them another, harder way that would help them in the end.

When we deal with difficulties and feel like God has forsaken us, we need to remember these verses. God acts in our lives for our own good. Sometimes this means taking us a way that is longer or perhaps more difficult, but God does it according to His wisdom to protect us from something that we may not even know about. He has a purpose. Let's trust God every day to lead us down the best path.

Julia Apple is originally from Pennsylvania and moved to Knoxville in 2009. She has a B. A. in Spanish from Freed-Hardeman University and is currently a nursing student at Tennessee Wesleyan. Julia has been involved in short-term campaigns in Peru since 2006 and hopes to continue her involvement in medical missions in the future.

God Always Has a Plan

When I graduated from college at Western Kentucky University with a teaching degree, a college friend and I decided to try and get jobs in the big city of Atlanta, GA. As we had both been raised as pretty sheltered gals in small hometowns, it seemed like it would be such a great adventure. I had been a Christian since I was 16, but had never really had any hardships or problems up to that point.

Well, we did indeed get jobs and moved to a suburb of Atlanta. I missed my hometown, but began to love my job teaching 6th graders and my new church family as well. Then came Labor Day weekend. My friend (and roommate) decided that she didn't like it and was homesick. And so, she moved back to Kentucky. I was shocked, and I had a decision to make. Did I stay in Atlanta or go back home? I did a lot of praying during that time, and ultimately decided to stay. I had a job I loved, a church family I was growing to love, and the only thing missing was a roommate. I know lots of people were praying on my behalf because a couple of short weeks later, God did send a wonderful girl (also from KY) to a school near mine, and she was looking for a place to live. My prayers were answered.

I met a lot of wonderful people while living in Atlanta, including my husband. I also learned to trust in God. He always has a plan for us, even when we may not realize it.

Kathy Turner has been a member of Karns Church of Christ since May 2011. She is married to Tony and has three children: Richard, age 17; Joel, age 15; and Brigitte, age 9. She grew up in Franklin, KY and currently resides in Oak Ridge, TN.

The Blame Game

Perry Noble said, "The person who always has to blame is always lame." This quote got me to thinking about my life. "Am I a person who spends a lot of my time and energy blaming others?"

Many people seem somewhat incapable of taking the blame for their mistakes. Instead, they want to pass their mistakes off on others. Unfortunately, this is nothing new. The Blame Game has been going on since the beginning of time. Remember Adam and Eve? After having disobeyed God by eating of the forbidden fruit, neither one of them was willing to take responsibility for their sin. In fact, when God asked Adam about what he had done, Adam immediately blamed his disobedience on Eve (Genesis 3:12). As if that weren't bad enough, Adam seemed to push the blame even further away from himself when he described Eve as "the woman whom you gave to be with me." Not only is Adam blaming Eve for his actions, but it appears he had the audacity to blame God.

Eve didn't do any better. When God asked her what she had done, she said, "The serpent deceived me, and I ate" (Genesis 3:13). Eve followed in the steps of Adam and placed the blame on someone else. Both took the easy way out; blaming others!

Friends, that's just lame! If we are guilty we need to take responsibility for what has happened. Paul wrote, "For each one shall bear his own load" (Galatians 6:5). Each of us is responsible before God for our actions, mistakes and struggles. Don't be lame; accept the blame and make things right!

Justin Morton has been in student ministry for almost 10 years. He has been the student and family minister for the Karns church of Christ since 2010. Justin is married to Miranda and they have one son, Caden. Justin enjoys spending time with his family, studying, teaching, writing and is a fan of the Tennessee Volunteers.

My Daddy

My daddy almost died from spinal meningitis when he was 5 years old, but he survived, and grew up to live a full life as a faithful Christian until his death from a work-related train accident when he was 59.

I have many good memories of him and of Mama as she was always there right beside him. I remember his love and care for all ten of us children, even though we were sharecroppers and very poor. I remember his faithfulness to the church, and leading us all into becoming faithful Christians. I also remember him leading singing many years, and helping in other ways to promote the growth of the church.

I have lots of other dear memories but one of the most special ones involves our lack of ready cash for buying seeds to plant the crops in the spring when I was 8 or so years old. I can still "hear and see" him as he told about his going to the local bank to borrow money. He had no collateral whatsoever. He told them he had to borrow money or we wouldn't be able to buy the necessary seeds for planting. The bank president said, "Mr. Geer, we know you and how you live. We know if your crops succeed we'll get our share. Your good name is your collateral." I'm not sure the bank president really quite understood what their trust in him meant to him. But he understood and Mama and all of us children understood and were thankful for God's great blessings!

No doubt: A good name is more desired than great riches!

Mattie Lou Robinson has been married to Grover Cleveland (G. C.) Robinson, Jr. since June 27, 1954. They have four children: Timothy, Amy, Andy and Penny; and three grandchildren: Victoria, Quintin and Ransom. Mattie Lou is a homemaker and also taught school for 15 years. Mattie Lou turned 83 on October 9th, 2012.

The Pearl Necklace

The little girl's most prized possession was a pearl necklace. It was the dollar-store variety. Certainly not worth much, but she was unaware of the value. In her mind, it was priceless. She never took it off, even at bath time, and soon it began to turn green from constant wear.

One night, when her daddy put her to bed, he asked her to give him the necklace. She said, "I love you, Daddy, but I really need my necklace." Each night the scene was repeated. Finally, after he had once again asked for her necklace, she removed the pearl treasure. With tears in her eyes, she placed it in her father's hand. He reached into his pocket, retrieved a small velvet pouch, and placed it in the girl's hand. She quickly discovered a beautiful strand of pearls inside. Real pearls!

Jesus talked about a merchant who sought beautiful pearls. When he found a pearl of great price, he sold everything and bought the pearl (Matthew 13:45-46). He realized the worthlessness of his possessions in light of a priceless pearl.

I wonder. Do we love material things more than we love God? Do we cling to things we think we need? They will, after all, turn green with constant use. In other words: they will not last.

If we are willing to give up the cheap, worthless things in order to get something valuable, and if we are willing to surrender everything–body, mind, heart, and possessions–to our Father, we'll find we have a worthy, valuable, and enduring treasure, a pearl of great price!

Teresa Hampton, along with her husband, Gary, were members of the Karns congregation while he served as director of East Tennessee School of Preaching. Teresa has authored several ladies' books and currently writes a women's e-zine called Wellspring. Teresa and Gary recently moved to Jackson, MS where they labor with the Siwell Road church of Christ.

Life Isn't Easy

1 John 4: 8 & 16 – God is Love
Psalm 116:5 – God is Merciful
John 3:33 – God is True

Life isn't always easy. Sometimes it is actually tough and other times we make it tougher on ourselves than it needs to be. Either way, life is tough and rough and we need a source of comfort to extinguish the difficulty - especially as we get overwhelmed and weak. Psalm 46:1 says, "God is our refuge and strength, a very present help in trouble." The God of all creation is there for you when you need to hide underneath the shelter of his wing and when you need encouragement or strength to overcome obstacles along the way. Also, in I Corinthians 10:13 (my favorite verse) the Bible states, "God is faithful." Paul explains to the Corinthians that all mankind will face temptations and we are subject to those challenges. We all know Satan will, at times, use the little temptations to lure us into bigger temptations. Other times, he flat out dangles the biggest temptations in front of our faces, making it extremely hard to resist, BUT our God is faithful!

Although we encounter temptation, we are not tempted beyond what we are able, and with that temptation a way of escape is always provided (I Corinthians 10:13). God's almighty hand places a barrier between Satan's works and what God knows we can and can't handle. So, you mean all those times I gave into sin I could have overcome it or escaped the temptation? YES! God is faithful, merciful, love, true, our strength when we are weak, and a refuge when we need to escape.

Corey Moore is from Knoxville,TN. Corey enjoys studying the Bible, debating, working out, traveling, good food, working with teens and playing video games.

Temptation

Tobacco was a foreign element in my earliest years. Neither my parents, nor my maternal grandparents used it. But my introduction to my paternal extended family stirred me with wide-eyed wonder. Tobacco in every conceivable form: cigarettes, cigars, pipes, snuff and chewing wads, were seen in use by teenagers to aged men and women. Old men would sit in cane-bottom chairs on the country house front porch spitting gobs while free-range chickens mingled freely in the crowd. Was I astounded? Yes!

I later learned from my school history lessons that Sir Walter Raleigh observed Native American Indians using native herbal species of tobacco. He and his underlings were convinced that tobacco was superbly suited to provide comfort, health and wealth and introduced it to European countries. The aftermath of this foul deed has not been yet corrected. A little poem titled, "Tobacco Is a Dirty Weed; I Like It," more honestly evaluates it.

I helped my maternal "grandpap" to care for his small tobacco patch, his only money crop. My jobs were to jab a little hole near the tobacco plant and fill it with sodium nitrate and to sling a solution of arsenic on the bottom of the leaves taking care not to be stung by any sidesaddle worms. I have in late years wondered if my efforts contributed significantly to the countless misery millions have suffered.

Tobacco is just another example of the unlimited temptations of the "I like it" type which Satan uses to express His hatred of mankind. We are gullible beyond explanation. Satan's hatred and God's love for mankind are beyond comprehension!

G. C. (Grover Cleveland) Robinson, Jr. has been married to Mattie Lou Geer since June 27, 1954. They have four children: Timothy, Amy, Andy, and Penny; and three grandchildren: Victoria, Quintin and Ransom. G. C. is a retired mechanical engineer. He turned 86 December 1st, 2012.

The Tulip Poplar

The day was a scorcher; my hometown isn't called "Hot-lanta" without reason. Rickey Jones, no relation, was wedged a few branches up in a large tulip poplar. "Edwin," he said groggily, "I don't ever want to grow up." "What are you talking about?" I said in my own midday stupor.

Then Rickey said one of the most profound things I've ever heard. "Because when people grow up they act stupid." I carefully collected myself in the face of such weighty thinking. It hit me for the first time with the full force of the reality. The grown-ups I knew had evidently gone through some sort of change when they stopped being children.

My peers in the just-before-teen range were different. It wasn't just about our not knowing as much or how we lacked in life skills, there was something more significant. We were still holding on to something special.

This was one of those life-changing moments! I made a promise to myself in classic Peter Pan style, "I'm not going to grow up."

I know some of you who know me are snickering and thinking, "That's one promise he kept." I'll admit, adult ways are sometimes not my favorite things. I still think Rickey made good sense.

Hopefully, I have advanced in knowledge and mastered at least a few life skills. I haven't, however, forgotten that long-ago moment of insight. In fact, I wish I did a better job with my promise (Matthew 18:1-3).

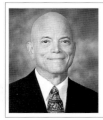

Edwin Jones has been with Karns and the school of preaching for almost 27 years. Currently he is the Dean of Students with the school. Edwin and Sara have three children and four grandchildren as well as a variety of "adopted" family members they have incorporated into their mix over the years.

Go Into All the World

Matthew 28:19 says, "Go therefore and make disciples of all the nations, baptizing them in the name of the Father and of the Son and of the Holy Spirit."

These words of Jesus made me think, "Just how can I do this?" During my life I have taught Bible classes to all age groups from babies to senior citizens. I also have enjoyed going from house to house door knocking and setting up in-home Bible studies.

In the early 1970's, Jimmy Lovell had a wonderful idea to advertise Bible Correspondence Courses free to people in foreign countries. I ordered these and also sent Bibles to my students in foreign lands. Through this method I have been able to teach hundreds of people. It is wonderful to hear that World Bible School has students in every country in the world.

Many people here at Karns have gone to foreign countries, as well as locally, to teach the Bible. We have four excellent preachers who teach in our School of Preaching, and also preach and teach classes for our congregation. The church helps support preachers all over the world.

Each person, working with whatever their talents are, certainly makes up a busy, happy and loving group of people all trying to serve and please our Lord in all we do!

Read Matthew 25:31-46 and James 1:27.

Joyce T. Cawood was born on October 14, 1920. She was married to Clarence Cawood, who passed away in 1995. She has three children, Gil, Chris, and Mark. Joyce was one of the original members of the Karns congregation when it was established, and Joyce was also part of the first women's program at ETSPM.

Let Them Know

One evening when our son, Michael was about four years old, I went in to say good night. It was my habit to tuck him into bed and say prayers before going to sleep. I have a very distinct memory of this particular evening. I went in to say good night and pull the covers up. That evening when I prayed with Michael, I specifically remember telling God thank you for giving Michael to us, for blessing us with such a precious little boy that brought so much joy to us. As I prayed, I opened my eyes for just a moment to see the biggest grin I'd ever seen on Michael's face. He was soaking up every word that I was saying as I thanked God for him.

I learned something from that evening. We need to not only thank God for the people that are blessings in our life, but we also should let those people know that we appreciate them and are thanking God for them.

It's easy to become discouraged in our life when we go through difficult times. I know for me, it is so encouraging when someone tells me that they are praying for me. Not just a rote, generic kind of prayer, but the kind of prayer that is very personal and specific. We all need to know that someone is taking a personal interest in us, enough to talk to the Father on our behalf.

I Timothy 2:1 says, "First of all, then, I urge that supplications, prayers, intercessions, and thanksgivings be made for all people."

Kim Higginbotham grew up in Poplar Bluff, MO. She is married to Steve and has four children: Kelli, Michael, Matthew, and Anne Marie. Kim teaches children with multiple disabilities for Knox County, a ladies' class at SEIBS, conducts teacher training seminars, and maintains two blogs, "Teaching Help," and "Relative Taste." She enjoys teaching and cooking.

Imagine

Imagine for a moment that you don't believe in God. Now, try to explain where the idea of forgiveness originated.

From an evolutionary perspective, isn't forgiving someone who has hurt you just silly or even dangerous? You could argue that forgiveness is simply a tool, a practical strategy we use to avoid the inconvenience of having to create new relationships, new families, or new circles of friends every time we are offended. But we realize the total inadequacy of this explanation when we notice how deeply true, heartfelt forgiveness can move the human heart.

Consider Peter's tragic, shameful denial of Jesus (Luke 22:54-62). Then, read Jesus' words to Peter only a few weeks later: "Simon, son of John, do you love me more than these?...Feed my lambs...Tend my sheep...Follow me" (John 21:13-19). In spite of Peter's past, the Lord made it clear that Peter would be a faithful, reliable worker in the kingdom of God. Can we read these words—or see Peter's total devotion to Christ in his first and second epistles—without being touched by the beauty of Christ's forgiveness? If the capacity to forgive is merely an evolved trait, why do we regard it as one of the very noblest of virtues?

The existence of forgiveness points to the reality of a supreme holy Being, whose very nature is forgiving. When we truly forgive, we are imitating Him. When we appreciate the magnificence of forgiveness, we are admiring a quality that flows from Him. The very concept of forgiveness could only come from God.

Evelyn Apple is married to Jody Apple, and they lived in Pennsylvania before moving to Knoxville in 2009. They have three grown children whom Evelyn home schooled. She enjoys yearly mission trips to Perú.

Ever Been Really Hungry?

Many years ago, my soon to be wife and I drove to Murfreesboro, Tennessee so that I could meet her grandfather, Pappy Cherry. We had just started dating, but were already in love. I walked into his kitchen as he was frying chicken. His wife, Elizabeth, was in the living room and came to join us and meet Debbie's friend.

His first words to me after the introductions were, "Rick, have you ever been so hungry you thought you might starve to death?" I told him that yes, I had gone a week before without food because I was in college and just didn't have the money until pay day. We had a common bond and he told stories about how poor they had been while his parents tried to feed the children and pay the bills. As he fried the huge pan of fried chicken and poured melted butter over the mashed potatoes he talked about never taking food for granted because he had known what it was like to be so hungry and yet have nothing to eat. As he led the prayer for the food, the gratitude to God came through clearly.

About two months later I was asked to give a Wednesday night devotional. It would be my first time speaking at such a large congregation. I was nervous but my wife was excited to hear what I would say since I had not told her my subject. I started out with Pappy Cherry's question, but I talked about how I had longed for spiritual food and how hungry I was for my spirit to be fed and satisfied. I spoke from the heart about my search to find the peace of God. I looked out at the congregation and saw tears fall as they listened to my search. I can still see Della Duncan wiping away tears. I had found my home.

Rick Slagle came from a diverse religious background. He began attending Karns Church of Christ in 1981 with a woman soon to become his wife, Debbie Insell. They were married almost 30 years before her death from brain cancer. Rick and Debbie both taught Bible classes and worked with young people through their lives together.

I Was Wrong

When I was a teenager I knew everything and by the time I graduated high school I knew even more. After high school I thought, "I don't need my parents or God." Being the "grown up" that I was, I started rebelling against everything I had ever been taught. I didn't care who I hurt in the process of my carelessness.

Now that I am in my mid-thirties, I realize one thing: I knew nothing about anything. I was not grown up like I thought I was. I was far from it! Even though I turned my back on family, good friends and God, they never gave up on me. I am thankful for that every day!

I believe God wanted me to get as close to rock-bottom as possible to teach me a lesson. When He saw that I was there and in trouble, He kept putting my husband in my way. I hated him for the longest time but he kept showing up every time I turned the corner. It never failed; he was always there. Then one day it hit me like a ton of bricks: God put him there. He knew what I needed even when I didn't. We have now been together for 13 years and married 10 and a half of it.

To me, he is a gift from God and I shouldn't be so lucky to have such a wonderful husband. I thank God for him every day, because my life would probably not be where it is today if it weren't for him. God has truly blessed me with a wonderful life and I don't deserve any of it.

Dana Brooks is married to Kevin, and they have three children, Jayde, Heidi, Lily, and Mya. She is also the daughter of Lloyd and Jean Thomas. Dana grew up here at Karns, but now is a member at the Morristown Church of Christ.

Urgency

I was a toddler when our family had the German measles. I don't remember having the measles but I do remember that weekend. My brother, Marvin had complications with the measles and was admitted to the hospital to try to determine what was wrong.

Marvin had been in the hospital about a week and was getting ready to go home the next day. The doctors could not find anything wrong with him or a reason for why the measles spots had turned black. Marvin had talked with his high school guidance counselor assuring her he would see her at school on Monday morning. Everyone was happy that Marvin was finally coming home.

That evening, Marvin's dinner arrived and was set on a tray in front of him while he lay in the hospital bed. He never ate a bite of it. As he pushed the tray away, Marvin, my 16 year-old brother, had a massive brain hemorrhage and died instantly.

You never know when you will take your last breath. Know your destiny. Be prepared. The story of Paul and the Ethiopian Eunuch is a wonderful example of how we should not waste time once we know what we need to do to obey the Gospel.

"Now as they went down the road, they came to some water. And the eunuch said, 'See, here is water. What hinders me from being baptized'" (Acts 8:25-40)?

Sharon Cawood is an Executive Sales Coordinator with N2 Publishing. She recruits for the State of Alabama and owns and manages two publications in the West Knoxville area. Both of Sharon's children are grown and gainfully employed. She has 3 grandchildren and 4 granddogs.

I'd Like to Ride with my Dad

Have you heard the story about the family who was moving from the East coast to the West coast? It seems that they were going to have to drive in two vehicles. The father was driving one vehicle, and his brother was driving the other. When it came time for the children to choose who to ride with, they chose their fun-loving uncle, to the uncle's great delight. He was flattered that they had chosen him over their own dad.

However, before they left town, the little boy asked his uncle, "What happens if we get separated from mom and dad as we're driving across the country?" To which the uncle said, "Don't worry, we won't get separated." But the boy persisted, "Well, what if we do?" The uncle jokingly remarked, "Well, if we get separated, I guess we'll just never see them again."

After a moment of silence, the little boy said, "I think I'm going to ride with my mom and dad."

This world contains many things that are flashy, fun, and exciting which capture our attention, but when it comes right down to it, we wouldn't want any of these things if it meant that we would be separated from our heavenly Father forever.

Maybe we ought to take a moment and think about the one with whom we have been riding. We surely wouldn't want to be separated from our Heavenly Father.

Steve Higginbotham has been the pulpit minister for the Karns church of Christ since 2010. Steve is married to Kim and they have four children, Kelli, Michael, Matthew, and Anne Marie. Steve enjoys writing, playing golf, and is a fan of the Pittsburgh Steelers, the WVU Mountaineers, and the Andy Griffith Show.

I Think

It will happen, could even happen today, might not happen till next month, but it is unavoidable. What do you do when you get asked that question you don't have an answer to? Or what if you are teaching a lesson in Sunday school and there is no avoiding it, you have to say it... "Well, I think."

I have many times in my short life tasted the leather of my boot when I find myself in a bind and don't really know how to answer the question asked. Instead of being humble and admitting that I'm not all-knowing on every Bible topic, I would go ahead and answer on what I thought would be best. Most times, after I had more time to study on the matter, I found out that what I thought best did not really line up with what God's Word said.

In most circumstances like these, it is tempting and easy just to go ahead and say what we think would be the best answer without really knowing what God has said on the matter. We should always strive to take that extra time, even if it means telling someone you don't have an answer right now, and study more on that topic so we can be sure we are making a sound Godly decision on the matter.

Let us strive to be like those of Berea (Acts 17:11) and search the scripture daily and not just when we are asked that tough question. For if we are in the Bible daily, When the time comes to answer Bible questions or questions about Christian living, we will find ourselves far more prepared if we are in the Bible daily.

Rodge Rives is from Wetumpka, AL and moved to Knoxville in 2011 to attend the Southeast Institute of Biblical Studies. Rodge has an infectious laugh (to put it nicely), and he enjoys listening to and making the sound of crickets.

Beyond the Call of Duty

We socialize with people every day. We see people at work, in school, and everywhere else we go. Unfortunately, in certain situations people may become upset, angry, or confused enough that they might get angry with you. When something like that happens, we may want to retaliate or fire right back at them. Knowing and appreciating God's word, we realize that God wants us to do the opposite.

In Matthew 5:38-42, we are told not to resist an evil person. In fact, we are told if we are slapped on the right cheek, we must turn the left cheek to the person. This means we should not "fight fire with fire," but respond with Christ-like maturity.

This passage not only speaks against retaliation, but also tells us to help others and "go the extra mile." As Christians, we have an obligation to go beyond the expected average. When we do things for people unasked, we glorify Christ by our actions. By showing compassion, we also encourage others to have that same compassion for one another.

We should be role models for everyone everywhere, because we live in a world where people are often too quick to defend their pride or ego by any means possible. Let's not fight "fire with fire" but tame the anger of others with godly action and helpful recourse.

Austin Hoffarth has lived in Tennessee all his life. He attends high school at Webb School of Knoxville. He likes to draw, play tennis, go camping and hiking. He became a Christian in 2011 and enjoys the activities within the youth group at Karns and area-wide churches.

Don't Wait Until It's Too Late

One day, I was playing chess with Mr. Steve Higginbotham in his office. As the game went on, he threatened to put me in checkmate. I saw what he was doing, but ignored it while I planned my own attack. But I waited too long. He had me in check. I looked and I wondered what I could do. However, it was too late. He checkmated me and we shook hands.

[*S. H.* - The above article is all that remains from an article that Ellie Nath began writing for this devotional book. The rest of it was inadvertently shredded by a grandmother who will remain nameless. But this much was salvaged, and I believe I know where Ellie was going with this article.

What I believe Ellie was getting at is that we can wait too late to make needed corrections to our lives. It's not that we don't know we need to make corrections and get our lives in order, we just put it off. We delay. We procrastinate. We wait for a more convenient time (Acts 24:25).

Some of us may get away with this risky way of life. We may be spared enough time to make corrections, but think of how many people will be lost on the day of judgment, who knew what to do to be saved, but just waited until it was too late.

Ellie and I were just playing a game of chess. The stakes weren't high. But someday, it won't be a game, and the stakes are our eternal destiny. Listen to the wisdom from this 8 year-old young lady, "Don't wait until it's too late!" (By the way, Ellie whipped me in the first game we played that day.)]

Ellie Nath is the daughter of Michael and Gerri Nath and the granddaughter to Bill and Sara Terlecki. Ellie is 8 years-old and attends CAK. She enjoys fast-pitch softball (playing second base), archery, crafts, and is quite the "chess master," playing in various chess tournaments.

Type-Casting

On February 24, 2006, in Beverly Hills, California, a well known actor passed away at the age of 81. He starred in such TV shows and movies as "In Search For Tomorrow," "The Last Time I Saw Archie," "Move Over, Darling," and "The Prize Fighter." Ring a bell yet?

Well, if you still don't know who I'm talking about, allow me to give you a few more hints. . .

- Deputy Sheriff
- Bullet in a shirt pocket
- Nip it in the bud
- Mayberry

Now I'm sure everyone knows who I'm talking about: Don Knotts. Don Knotts, who played the bumbling deputy on the Andy Griffith Show, will forever be known and identified as "Deputy Barney Fife." One will never be able to think of Don Knotts without thinking of his role as Barney Fife.

In Hollywood, that's called "type-casting." In Christianity, it's called discipleship. Would it not be wonderful to live in such a fashion that when someone thinks of us, they think of Jesus? What a noble goal!

May we so live that when it comes time for us to leave this world, we will be remembered, first and foremost, as a disciple of Jesus.

Steve Higginbotham has been the pulpit minister for the Karns church of Christ since 2010. Steve is married to Kim and they have four children, Kelli, Michael, Matthew, and Anne Marie. Steve enjoys writing, playing golf, and is a fan of the Pittsburgh Steelers, the WVU Mountaineers, and the Andy Griffith Show.

Setting an Example

My mother, Margaret Cagle, always had a tight budget having to feed and clothe six children. One day we went on an exciting trip to Almart, a new department store on Clinton Highway, so Mom could buy some necessities for the house. Mom carefully chose what she needed to purchase while Cathy and I looked for pennies on the floor. (We always found pennies on the floor in K-Mart.) Mom paid cash for her merchandise, loaded her purchases and children into the car, and drove home. After getting back to the house and unloading everything, Mom realized that the cashier at Almart had given her too much change. She immediately loaded us all back into the car, drove back to Almart, and returned the extra money. By the time we made it back home the manager of Almart was standing on the front porch with a bouquet of flowers for my mother. He said he had never had a customer come back to the store to return money.

WOW!! What a great example our mother was (and still is) for us! I have always remembered what my mother did that day and I have followed her example whenever I have been in similar situations. She must have read Proverbs 22:6, "Train up a child in the way he should go: and when he is old, he will not depart from it." My mother's actions also showed me how the example you set can impact others in your everyday life. Remember Matthew 5:16, "Let your light so shine before men, that they may see your good works, and glorify your Father which is in heaven."

Becky Cagle was born in Oak Ridge Hospital in 1960 and grew up in Karns. She is the youngest of six children (Cathy, my identical twin, is four minutes older than me). She has a degree in Nuclear Engineering and currently work in Oak Ridge.

The Greatest Commandment

"Teacher, which is the greatest commandment in the Law?" Jesus replied: 'Love the Lord your God with all your heart and with all your soul and with all your mind. This is the first and greatest commandment. And the second is like it: Love your neighbor as yourself'" (Matthew 22:36-39).

Jesus said that love is the greatest commandment. Sadly, this is the main one we fail to keep. One of the main reasons is because people have the wrong idea about what love is.

Read 1 Corinthians 13:4-7.

These verses tell us that if we have love, we will be patient with each other. We will be kind to one another. We will not envy each other. We will not boast and we will not be proud. We will not dishonor others. We will not be self-seeking. We will not get easily angered. We will keep no record of wrongs. We will not delight in evil, but will rejoice with the truth. We will always protect, trust, hope, and persevere.

In these verses, it's not just talking about having love toward your friends; it's also talking about enemies. Matthew 5:43-44 says, "You have heard that it was said, 'Love your neighbor and hate your enemy. ' But I tell you, love your enemies and pray for those who persecute you." In order to truly love each other, we must follow the golden rule: "Do to others as you would have them do to you" (Luke 6:31).

If you know what it means to love, then it will be a LOT easier to keep the greatest commandment.

Rachel Cox is the daughter of Chris and Hannah Cox. Rachel is in the 6th grade and enjoys ice skating, writing, reading and singing.

David and Goliath

The story of David and Goliath is one of my favorite Bible stories. It's about a Philistine giant by the name of Goliath. He was a soldier and he stood over 9 feet tall! He challenged the men in the army of Israel to come out and fight him. None of the soldiers would accept his challenge. However, a young man by the name of David heard his challenge and he accepted it. David was very brave to accept this challenge because he wasn't a soldier, he was just a shepherd. But David trusted God to take care of him.

When they met to fight, David didn't have a sword or a spear. He only had his sling shot with five stones. Goliath made fun of him for this. But David didn't quit. He put a stone in his sling and threw it at Goliath and it embedded in his forehead. Goliath fell to the ground and David went over to him, took Goliath's sword away from him, and cut off his head.

Even though Goliath was so much bigger than David, David won because God gave him the victory. The lesson that I learn from this Bible story is that even if you are small, if you have God helping you, you can do great things.

Hutson Gillentine is 9 years-old and is the child of Amber and Jeremy Gillentine. He is currently home schooled and is in the sixth grade. He is heavily involved in the Lads-to-Leaders program and works very hard at accomplishing the goal of being a valuable servant in the Church through his work with this program.

Gentleness

As happens occasionally, I received a question from one of my Bible Correspondence students last week. It was one that we, as mature Christians, sometimes view as inane and silly. As hard as I try to answer these questions with regard to the student's knowledge of the Bible and his self-esteem, I sometimes feel that I may be too harsh or too direct. It is hard to follow Paul's advice to Timothy in 1 Timothy 1:4, "nor give heed to fables and endless genealogies, which cause disputes rather than godly edification which is in faith." and 2 Timothy 2:23, "But avoid foolish and ignorant disputes, knowing that they generate strife."

I am reminded of a question I asked my older brother when I was just a little boy. It was hog-killing time at our farm. The hogs were butchered, meat was prepared for curing, etc. and rendering of lard began. When that was finished, the hot liquid was poured into a 6-8 gallon can to within an inch or so of the top. The next day, the liquid had become a solid. My brother and I were in the pantry. I saw this can of lard and asked my brother, "Is that can full of lard?"

His answer was a scathing, "Dummy, can't you see it's full?"

My reply was, "Well, I can see it's full at the top, but is it full in the bottom?" That is why I often ask June (my wife) to read my reply to the student, and on occasion, she will remind me to "tone it down a little."

Wendell Agee was born and raised in Pikeville, TN. He served 20 years in the USAF and was a successful business man for over 30 years. Wendell has served the Lord as a missionary to Cuba, Jamaica, Honduras and other countries. He's a member of the Karns Church of Christ.

Through God's Eyes

While traveling this past winter, my family and I visited a church out-of-state. The children had a lovely Bible class and shared with us what they learned: sometimes we treat people poorly because of how they look, but God doesn't want us to do that, because He cares about what's inside. Great lesson! Then we went into the auditorium for worship. When we stood to sing, we noticed certain people throughout the audience using microphones. We were told it was because they were the "good singers." After the first song, a lady in front of us complemented my husband on his voice then said, "They don't let me sing." Obviously she wasn't one of the "chosen" and it discouraged her. That made me so sad! The children had it right. The adults in the auditorium had it wrong.

As humans, we tend to think prettier is better. I Samuel 16:7 says: "For man looks at the outward appearance, but the Lord looks at the heart." We need to remember that, and try to look at things more the way God would. The Bible says we are ALL to "sing and make melody in our hearts" (Ephesians 5:19). It doesn't matter if we are "good" singers or not, in human terms. When we are singing out, making melody in our hearts, it is BEAUTIFUL to the Lord. It is, after all about HIS ears, not ours.

"For My thoughts are not your thoughts, nor are your ways My ways," says the Lord. "For as the heavens are higher than the earth, so are My ways higher than your ways, and My thoughts than your thoughts" (Isaiah 55:8-9).

Susan Aragon is married to Steve and they have two children, John and Joseph. She retired in 2005 from a career in professional sales to be a stay-at-home mom/homemaker. She loves spending time with her family. She also enjoys hiking, singing, cooking, traveling, meeting people, and exercise. Each day is a gift from God. Her goal is to live each day for God.

One Generation from Extinction

When I was a teenager, I heard someone make the statement that the Church is only one generation away from extinction. Now that I am an adult, I realize how that statement is oh, so true.

I was fortunate to be raised in a Christian home and to have a godly heritage given to me by my great-grandparents, grandparents, and parents. My great-grandfather was a song leader at the Buffalo Valley Church of Christ, and was a founding member of the Highland View Church of Christ in Oak Ridge, TN. It was there that I was baptized by Garland Elkins when I was 13 years-old.

Now, as an adult, I can see and appreciate even more, just how important it is for families to share their faith in Jesus with their children. When that faith isn't instilled in our children, and there is a "break in the chain," it has devastating consequences. Unfortunately, we've probably all seen it happen.

One of the reasons we came to be a part of the Karns congregation is that our children were approaching their teen years, and we wanted them to have the best spiritual training we could give them. We realized that there were many "voices" in the world whispering in their ears, so we wanted to place them in an environment where by word and example, they were taught the word of God and their faith could grow.

I thank God for my Christian heritage, and the help that the Karns congregation has been to me, helping me continue that heritage by instilling faith in my children and grandchildren.

Barbara "Bobbie" Lynch Martin is married to Vascoe Stephen Martin, Jr. Bobbie and Steve have three children, Gabe (Sarah), Leah (David), and Cory, (Rose Anne); 8 grandchildren; and her parents are Red & Helen Lynch. All 4 generations attend church at Karns. She enjoys arts, the beach, antiques, grandkids plus Oak Ridge History & WWII.

What's Your Bowl of Stew?

Have you ever been hungry? I mean, really hungry - to the point of feeling sick and weak. Have you ever felt like that? Esau did, and it cost him dearly.

In Genesis 25:29-34, we read about Esau coming in from the field hungry. Jacob, seeing this as a prime opportunity, told Esau he could have a bowl of stew if he was willing to part with his birthright. What happened next was one of the biggest mistakes of Esau's life. Esau, thinking he was going to die of hunger, traded his birthright for a small bowl of stew.

Esau was willing to give up his birthright for something as insignificant as a bowl of stew. Friends, the same thing happens today. Many people are willing to sacrifice something special for something trivial.

Pornography! How many men and women have traded in their happy families in order to fulfill a moment of lust?

Adultery! How many people have traded in a long, mature marriage in order to fulfill the fleeting desires of the flesh?

Cheating! How many people are willing to trade in honesty and integrity in order to move up in the corporate world?

You see, Esau gave up something that should have been special to him to fulfill a desire of the flesh, and we do the same thing. People today are willing to trade in their marriages, families and integrity for something as worthless as a bowl of stew.

What about you? Are you willing to trade something special for something of no value? What's your bowl of stew?

Justin Morton has been in student ministry for almost 10 years. He has been the student and family minister for the Karns church of Christ since 2010. Justin is married to Miranda and they have one son, Caden. Justin enjoys spending time with his family, studying, teaching, writing and is a fan of the Tennessee Volunteers.

A Special Team

Growing up I played fast pitch softball. Every summer was fun and, in its own way, rewarding. However, my favorite summer of all was my last one playing as an 18 year-old. Our team was a misfit team. We each had different levels of talent and people didn't have much hope that we would be very successful. We surprised everyone by making it to the state tournament. We didn't win the tournament that summer, but we played and beat some of the top teams.

What made that so special?

- First, we had a passion for the game. We each loved it and that love was visible when we played.
- Second, we encouraged each other. We genuinely loved each other and cheered for each teammate to do well.
- Third, we used our talents to the best of our ability. We worked hard to make the right decisions on the field and to ensure our team functioned properly. I look back and realize what wonderful lessons I learned that summer.

What if we in the church started with having a passion for God's word? What if we put aside differences and truly encouraged one another in our daily lives and struggles? What if we used our talents to further the kingdom of God and bring others to Him? If we approached our Christian lives like that misfit softball team did that summer, we would see the church flourish and someday we will be able to look back and say that we had the best Christian life we could on this earth.

Katie Pruett has been a member at Karns Church of Christ for 14 years. She has a passion to teach and is heavily involved in the Bible School Program. Her interests include spending time with family, watching the UT Volunteers and Green Bay Packers, and reading.

The Great Physician

It was just another flight for Dr. Tim Delgado, an emergency helicopter physician. He received a call that a young woman, who was riding a bike, needed to be transported to a trauma unit after being hit by a car. Upon his arrival, the young woman was obviously in critical condition. As Dr. Delgado began examining the patient, he noticed that she was wearing his cycling team's uniform. At that moment, Dr. Delgado's ordinary day became very abnormal. The patient that he was transporting to University Hospital in Cincinnati was his wife, Allison.

Tim Delgado immediately had a decision to make. He could step back and wait while another unit was called in to help his wife or he could try to contain his emotions and be the physician that he was. He chose to be a physician and helped to save his wife's life.

There is another physician who can do more than save your physical life. He can save your soul. Jesus said, "Those who are well have no need of a physician, but those who are sick." (Matthew 9:12). Those who are sick are those who are spiritually sick, those whose lives have been infected by sin. Paul said, "For the wages of sin is death, but the gift of God is eternal life in Christ Jesus our Lord" (Romans 6:23). Friends, sin has a price... death. But thanks be to God, who sent His son, Jesus - the Great Physician - to save us from our sins.

Is your life infected with sin? Come to Jesus and allow Him the opportunity to save you!

Justin Morton has been in student ministry for almost 10 years. He has been the student and family minister for the Karns church of Christ since 2010. Justin is married to Miranda and they have one son, Caden. Justin enjoys spending time with his family, studying, teaching, writing and is a fan of the Tennessee Volunteers.

You Have a Song

Mary had a song. Hannah had a song. Moses had a song. Miriam had a song. Zechariah had a song. David had many. David shares with us, "He has put a new song in my mouth --- Praise to our God; Many will see it and fear, And will trust in the LORD" (Psalm 40:3).

What were their songs about? God! They sang to God. They sang about God. They sang about what He had done, what He was doing and what He would do.

I don't have the musical talent to compose, but I do have a song. I have a story to tell, a heart message to share about the one who, "set my feet on a rock and gave me a firm place to stand" (Psalm 40:2).

Having a bad day? Don't really feel like singing today? Songs of praise have come out of people's hearts in good times and bad. I wonder what Paul and Silas were singing?

In the darkest hour of Louisa Stead's life she offered these words through her tears: "Tis so sweet to trust in Jesus." You see, she had lost her husband because he jumped in to save a drowning boy, but the boy took him down with him. Out of her tragic experience came a song that ministers to us today. Consider the faith that penned these words: "just to trust His cleansing blood, just in simple faith to plunge me 'neath the healing, cleansing flood."

You have a song as well. If some opportunity presents itself today to pass on your song to someone who needs to hear it, sing out.

Sara Terlecki is married to her husband, Bill. They moved to Knoxville from Ohio. Sara has worked in the church office since 2010. They have two grown children. Gerri married Michael Nath and blessed them with granddaughter, Ellie. Bill Jr. married Hope Whittington and blessed them with two grandsons, Allen and Evan.

God is Good All the Time

Over the years I have seen friends, family and acquaintances go through very difficult situations. So often when their prayers are answered in accordance with their request, the response goes out to all "Praise God!" It's interesting that when the outcome is not what they had hoped, I never seem to see anyone saying "Praise God!" I have a friend who ends all of her emails with the following phrase "God is so good, all of the time." I agree!

We need to give praise to God even when the answers to our prayers are not what we had hoped for. What better way to display our faith to others and to encourage our brothers and sisters in Christ? This kind of faith would certainly cause those that are lost to want to know the reason for the hope that is within us.

1 Thessalonians 5:16-18 says, "Rejoice always, pray without ceasing, in everything give thanks; for this is the will of God in Christ Jesus for you."

For this reason I have a sign in my house that reads "In everything, give thanks." It is by the door to our garage so we can see it every day, multiple times a day. Pictures of my daughter and my son (who lived only three short months) surround it. It reminds me to give thanks and praise to God...in all things.

Gerri Nath has been a member at Karns since 2009 and has been a Christian since 1977. Gerri is married to Michael and they have a daughter, Elliana Grace. She is the Vice President of Accounting Services at Marriott International, Inc. , and enjoys spending time with Ellie, watching her play softball, photography, traveling, scrapbooking, reading, and writing.

My Yoke is Easy

The only time my Lord ever used the word, "easy," it was attached to a yoke. We all want things to be easy. We want a life of ease, our tasks to be easy and our requirements simple. But, we all know that all good things in life come with a price and that price is not always so easy to pay.

Even though our Lord said that His yoke is easy, it is a yoke none the less. A yoke is not used as a decoration to be hung about our necks as we would wear a sign calling ourselves "Christian." Rather the yoke is a tool used to make sure that we have a firm grip on what we are pulling. We are pulling for the Lord.

We are the bride of Christ, and as such we need to be ready for the day He returns for us. We must get our house in order so that it is presentable to Him. We cannot do enough to merit our salvation, but we are expected to be busy about our Father's business. I often start my days wondering what opportunity the Lord has in store for me to do some good thing in His name.

If we have been looking for the "easy" way out in our service to the Lord, let's decide that it is time now to put on our yokes, start pulling and give the Lord His due.

The effort will be rewarding and the results will bring honor and glory to God.

Gregg Woodall is an elder of the Karns Church of Christ. Gregg is married to Sherrye and they have four children, Stephanie, Tiffany, Benjamin, and Jonathan. They also have four grandchildren, Wrigley, Walton, Adalynn, and Brooklynn. Gregg enjoys golfing, dirt bike riding, spending time with family, and is a fan of the Tennessee Volunteers.

My Favorite Bible

Through the years, I have owned quite a few Bibles. I have two shelves in my office containing nothing but Bibles. But of all the Bibles I own, the one that I treasure the most is a little Red Letter New Testament. It's the kind of Bible given to little children, and it is small enough for them to hold it in their little hands. The print in this Bible is just about too small for me to read. So what makes this Bible so special to me? Allow me to read the inscription on the first page:

"This New Testament is being presented to Steve Higginbotham for being the first in his Bible Study class to be able to say from memory all the 66 books of the Bible. Keep up the Good Work. God Bless you always.
Your Bible Class Teachers,
Mrs. Hester Shultz & Miss Sandy Wilson

Isn't it amazing the impact that a few words of encouragement can have? I was just 4 years-old when this Bible was presented to me, but I still have this little Bible in my possession. I'm sure Hester (who is now deceased) and Sandy had no idea that something done so long ago, and something that cost so little, and took only but a moment of their time, would be so treasured by the little boy to whom they presented it.

Friends, be an encourager! Take the time and the little extra effort to compliment, commend, and encourage another. Chances are, long after you've forgotten your words of kindness, they will be locked-up, and cherished as a prize possession in the store room of someone's mind.

Steve Higginbotham has been the pulpit minister for the Karns church of Christ since 2010. Steve is married to Kim and they have four children, Kelli, Michael, Matthew, and Anne Marie. Steve enjoys writing, playing golf, and is a fan of the Pittsburgh Steelers, the WVU Mountaineers, and the Andy Griffith Show.

Insurance and the Christian

The past few years have been very tough for me personally. The storm began about ten years ago with my father's decline due to lung damage from 50 years of smoking. He just could not stop. Finally his lungs were so damaged that he was on oxygen all the time. He would take the mask off and smoke then put the mask back on. At some point, his lungs could not function and filled with fluid and he died as the staff tried to put a tube into his lungs to help him breathe.

My mother died a horrible death with gangrene a few months later. Next, I stood at a hospital bed with my father-in-law with his family as he died from cancer. A few years later my wife was diagnosed with brain cancer, from which she died 23 months later. Five months after her diagnosis, I had a stroke during heart surgery and came very close to death.

Today I have a realistic knowledge that this life is temporary and we need to make preparation not only to pay for the storms of this life, but thank God for the transition to eternal life. Since that time I keep an updated Will, have a pre-planned and paid-in-full funeral in place. I seek to find reasons to thank God every day.

I have made preparation for the tent I will leave behind, but my main insurance was paid in full by the blood of Christ which has pre-paid for my new home prepared for me in Heaven. The Spirit serves as my confirmation of my paid-in-full reservation. We insure our items in this life, and need to insure our passage of our soul. Enjoy every day in this life; it is a gift from God, but make preparations for entry to your eternal home.

Rick Slagle came from a diverse religious background. He began attending Karns Church of Christ in 1981 with a woman soon to become his wife, Debbie Insell. They were married almost 30 years before her death from brain cancer. Rick and Debbie both taught Bible classes and worked with young people through their lives together.

Wheat or Tares

Will you be the wheat or the tares (Matthew 13:24-30)?

I was thinking of this as I was sorting through an accumulation of paper, magazines and things that need placing where they belong. Paper for the recycling bin, magazines to the hospital, personal papers to the shredder, things I've taken from other rooms and never taken back.

When I leave this earth, how will the Lord sort me out? Or you? Are we living so that we will be placed with the wheat or the tares?

Satan's best work is against us as Christians. Are we tares hiding in the wheat? Do we have sorting boxes for our spiritual lives? We can't assemble Wednesday evenings because that's soccer practice and that's the family box. Our prayer box is only when someone specifically asks us to, not a daily communication with the Father. If we miss communion Sunday morning because guests dropped in on us, well we can always take it on Sunday night. After all we don't see our guests that often. Of course, we could have invited them to go with us to worship.

Oh and how well do we know our fellow Christians? Are we visiting? Are we checking on our widows? If we can't physically do that, are we encouraging those who do? Can we pick up a phone and call? My widow friends tell me they are so lonely most of the time. We all grow together, let us all be wheat, that others may see our good works and glorify the Father.

June Agee was born and raised in the UK and came to the United States when she married Wendell and became a U. S. citizen in Santa Fe, NM. June and Wendell have four living children and five grandchildren. June is a member of the Karns Church of Christ.

Opportunities

Most of you have heard about the man possessed with a legion of demons in Mark 5: 1-20, but have you ever really looked into it?

The Bible says that there was a man who lived in a graveyard, ran around naked, cried out day and night as he cuts himself with stones, and who couldn't be bound, even with chains. Understandably, when people saw him, they saw his supernatural strength, wild behavior, and avoided him. I doubt that anyone, with the exception of possibly his immediate family if he had any, was even willing to try to look past his flaws to see who he truly was.

When Jesus met this man, he looked past all the demons and the wild behavior, and saw the man behind the demons. Jesus had pity on this man, cast out the demons, and the man was free! In fact, this man was so thrilled that he begged Jesus to let him go with him. However, Jesus told him to return to his home, and tell everyone what God had done for him. When he did, they were all amazed.

I think that far too often, we as Christians are too quick to judge others based solely upon the faults we initially see in them. We don't try to look past their faults and into who they really are and the potential they possess. Who knows what good can come from the ones you least expect good to come from? They could be like the man who, because someone saw through his flaws and cast out his demons, made everyone around him marvel at the power God displayed in him.

Matthew Higginbotham is the son of Steve and Kim Higginbotham. He's 15 years-old and a Sophomore at Karns High School. Matthew loves music. Matthew plays the trumpet and has marched in the Glasgow High School Band (as a seventh grader) and currently is the sophomore representative for the Karns High School Band.

A Certain Mechanic

My dad was an automobile mechanic—and a very good one at that. Religion, however, was not his thing. When I wrote him to explain why I was going to become a preacher, he told my cousin that he buried the letter under a rock.

Why was my dad like that? You don't just wake up one day hating religion. Eventually, I discovered some answers. First, he was raised in a hyper-strict religious environment; ignorance led to a very harsh, terrifying view of God. As a child my father saw God as an unloving tyrant, eager to send him to Hell!

In addition to this uninviting picture of God, my father grew to feel that Christians were a bunch of hypocrites—especially preachers! After learning this, I felt lucky he didn't bury me under a rock. Obviously, all people who claim to be Christians are not fakes. Nevertheless, we all know such "Christians" do exist. A hardened man close to the bottom of the social ladder tends to have a finely tuned hypocrite-detector.

As time went by, I sent my dad some books about the Bible. He actually read them and made some positive comments, but then he died. At his funeral, Mr. Shea, the only preacher my father ever respected, called me aside. I was shocked to learn that sometime before he died my dad asked Mr. Shea to immerse him for the remission of his sins!

My dad never "went public." Nobody but Mr. Shea knew about his most improbable moment. I wish Daddy had seen more of the real deal. Jesus was the kind of man even a certain mechanic could love.

Edwin Jones has been with Karns and the school of preaching for almost 27 years. Currently he is the Dean of Students with the school. Edwin and Sara have three children and four grandchildren as well as a variety of "adopted" family members they have incorporated into their mix over the years.

Monday Mornings

Why do Mondays follow Sundays? Shouldn't there be an "in between day" where you could mourn the loss of the weekend? Get psyched up for the battle that lies ahead?

Sometimes Monday doesn't even wait. It starts on Sunday evening. Church is over, supper is done. Then there's nothing to do except watch the clock tick. The ghost of "Monday future" creeps in and haunts what's left of your weekend.

But I've found a verse that helps me deal with Monday. Matthew 11:28 says, "Come unto me all ye that labor and are heavy laden and I will give you rest." I know that's talking about salvation, but I read it in my car, before walking into my office.

The NASV has a footnote that translates the word "labor" as "ye that work to exhaustion." I think Jesus wants me to work hard; with all my might, but he doesn't expect me to give more to my company, my school, or anything else than I give to him. His yoke is light.

If the yoke of work, with all its people and problems, feels heavier than even what the Lord expects me to bear, than that's too much. Only the Lord should get that part of me. I only have one master. I don't think he expects me to give more at work, than my reasonable service. Not to sacrifice my life and soul.

So then, I can take a breath and be thankful for my job, knowing that my heart belongs to the Lord.

Alan Goins is a 53 year-old Corporate Financial Analyst here in Knoxville. He is from the mountains of Eastern KY. He would rather sing for a living than count numbers, but he just can't figure out a way to get paid for his voice. At least not yet.

What I Learned from 4 Year-Olds

I have taught the Wednesday night Bible Class for 4 year-olds for 23 years. There is much to be learned from these precious children. Sometimes you teach the Bible lesson and think they were not even listening, but the next week, when reviewing the story, they are able to answer all of the questions about last week's lesson. I guess they really were listening!

I learned the books of the New Testament along with my 4 year-olds and some of the Old Testament books. Sometimes I will start telling a Bible story and they will start telling me all about the story, so I allow them to finish the story. Some of these children have Bible knowledge that could surpass some adults.

The love they have for each other is unconditional and sweet. As their teacher, many want to come and find me before or after services to get a hug. Little eyes are always watching and little ears are always listening. Sometimes, I even learn family secrets. More than one child has announced the family secret that they are getting a new baby at their house. These children have an excitement that cannot be contained, whether it is a family secret, or learning God's Word.

A special thank you is given to the parents who make an effort to bring their little children to Bible class and teach them God's Word at home.

Matthew 19:14 says, "But Jesus said, 'Let the little children come to me, and do not forbid them, for of such is the kingdom of heaven.'"

Marilyn Snyder has been a member of the Karns Church of Christ for 23 years. She has 4 children, Sherrye Woodall, Terrie Owens, Jim Snyder and Jeff Snyder. She has 12 grandchildren and 5 great-grand-children.

You Are Your Brother's Keeper

In Genesis 4, after Cain kills Abel, God asks Cain where Abel is. In his reply, I think he asks one of the most important questions in the world: "Am I my brother's keeper?" This question is essential to all of us, because the answer is: "Yes! We are our brothers' keepers."

God places us in our families and expects us to watch over and take care of them in every way, particularly spiritually. In fact, 1 Timothy 5:8 says, "But if anyone does not provide for his own, and especially for those of his household, he has denied the faith and is worse than an unbeliever." That's very serious! We also have our spiritual family to look after and encourage in the Lord. God says, "Therefore, as we have opportunity, let us do good to all, especially to those who are of the household of faith" (Galatians 6:10). And, "By this all will know that you are My disciples, if you have love for one another" (John 13:35).

Sometimes people get out of contact with, rebel against, or disown their family. God's calling us to love, provide for, and be ever closer to them. We're called as Christians to love everyone- would that not obviously include the families God has placed us in? What a shame it would be to preach the Gospel to many, but neglect to preach it to our families. Or give money to the poor, yet have our own family in need.

We see from Scripture that we are indeed our brother's keeper. Let's make sure we're loving and looking after them the way God would have us to.

Kimberly Powell lives in Karns, TN and attends Karns Church of Christ. She is the wife of Harrison Powell and mother to their daughter, Katherine. Kimberly started the adventure of a lifetime when she was saved as a teenager and now strives to lead as many as possible to Christ, grow ever deeper in Him, and learn about His vast love for us.

Enjoy the View

One morning I was hiking up a narrow mountain trail. It wound around rocks and trees with exposed roots and across dry streams, so I needed to watch my step, but I was making good time up the mountain and was enjoying the hike.

Then it hit me... here I am going up a mountain, and I'm watching my feet. My eyes were not on the mountaintop, the valley, or any of the other wonders around me. I was only paying attention to the task of plodding along.

After stopping to enjoy the view, I thought how much like life this is. It is so easy to get tied up with the mundane tasks of "making a living," instead of trusting Him who watches the sparrows. We strive after the wind instead of the whisper. Like the Pharisees, we focus on minutiae and miss the important.

Much like I had a goal of making it up the mountain, we all have the goal of reaching that city that is set on a hill. Yet we so often busy ourselves with life, instead of him who is the source of life. Just as reaching the top of the mountain requires placing one foot after the other, life requires many things of us. Yet these tasks, though necessary and good, are not what is truly important and worthy of our primary attention. If we let it, living this life can distract us from finding everlasting life. God, and God alone, is the preeminence. Everything else is secondary.

"Seek ye first the kingdom of God, and his righteousness; and all these things shall be added unto you" (Matthew 6:33).

Kyle Lindner is married to Mary and is the father of Kathryn. When not working in IT, he enjoys his family, travel and biking.

Priorities

I remember the first Thanksgiving dinner that was to be at our house. I tried to plan everything out perfectly. I washed the tablecloths, washed the china and crystal. I was very busy planning and preparing. The table had to be just perfect with a spot for everyone. The day came and I was ready. I went about the day making sure everything was right but I don't think I even stopped to think about the reason for the occasion.

I seem to always have many things I am involved in or planning, but I lose focus of why. In Luke 10:38-42, Jesus talks to us about Mary and Martha. This passage is written for me. I am a Martha. Verse 41 could easily say, "Leah, Leah, you are worried about many things." What is it I am doing or involved in today that is so important? My thoughts and actions are usually focused on day-to-day tasks and what I think needs to be done, what project or event is coming and how I can make it better than it really has to be. Jesus tells me in verse 42 that I only need to be focused on ONE thing. I need to be a Mary. I need to sit at Jesus' feet and hear His word.

My focus, while with good intent, is not always on what brings glory to God. Will it really matter if I get that extra turkey decoration on the kid's table? Someone might notice it, but wouldn't my time and effort be better spent sitting at Jesus' feet and focusing on him?

Leah Baldwin has been a member at Karns church of Christ since 1988, and is a teacher for the 2 year-old class. She is married to David and they have 3 children, Victoria, Eli and Charlotte. Leah is a stay at home mom and enjoys sewing, reading and spending time with her family.

10 Character Traits People Need Which We Can Become

Here is a list of ten things that we need to work at becoming. None of them are too hard. All of them are within our power to become.

1. Become a healer. We are all either healers or hurters. Some hurt with words and put downs. Some make things better, some make matters worse.

2. Become an encourager. Some people seem to have a knack of showing where you went wrong. It doesn't cost money to be an encourager. It's so needed and pays great dividends.

3. Be a listener. Communication, or lack of it, is behind most of the hurts of the world. How much time do you spend talking to your kids and family?

4. Be a hugger, an encourager with arms. Hugs say "I care. "

5. Be a lover. Love seeks the best interest of its object.

6. Be a forgiver. Grudge-bearing is harder on the grudger than the "grudgee." Forgive people because they need it. Forgive because you need it.

7. Be a helper. Volunteer to do works of service.

8. Be a believer. We all need people to believe in us and we need to believe in people.

9. Be a supporter. A supporter is one who stands by your side and cheers you on to victory.

10. Be a saver. You can save a lot of things but especially bring the lost to Jesus. This is the greatest work in the world.

Doris Finger was born in Knoxville and has lived in Knoxville all her life except for 3 years. She is currently retired and enjoys spending her time helping others. Doris has taught primary classes for 45 years with 42 of those years here at the Karns congregation!

Family Reunion

Have you ever been to a family reunion? How about having all of your family together for the holiday like Thanksgiving or Christmas? I love it when all of my family is together. Sadly, I don't always get to see my brother or sister as often as I would like. They usually are not able to make it for the holidays, but they are definitely missed.

Well, when we gather together with our Christian family, there are those that either can't make it for medical reasons or some that just choose not to come. We miss them all the same! God knew that we needed help in our Christian walk so he gave us a church family to help us day by day. When we sing the song "God's Family," I can't help but think about how much God loved us and wants us to love each other.

Some day there will be a great family reunion in Heaven! It will be great to be reunited with those who have gone on before us. Many from our own church family will be waiting for us, what a great and wonderful day that will be. But there will also be those that don't make it for whatever reason. Just like at family reunions, we want everyone in our family to be there. We also want all of our church family to be with us in Heaven!

Are you spending time with your church family now, so that you can make it to the family reunion later? "For this reason I bow my knees to the Father of our Lord Jesus Christ, from whom the whole family in heaven and earth is named" (Ephesians 3:14-15).

Sherrye Woodall is married to Gregg. They have 4 children: Stephanie Harder, Tiffany Dresser, Benjamin Woodall and Jonathan Woodall. They have 4 grand-children: Wrigley Harder, Walton Harder, Adalynn Dresser and Brooklynn Dresser. Sherrye has taught the 3 years old class at Karns for over 32 years.

Be Still and Know that I am God

Are you busy? Are you anxious? Do you have children, a busy job? Do you need the comfort of the soul?

God knew our lives would get busy and hectic. He knew we would be running around like chickens with our heads cut off. He knew we would need to be still to contemplate on His wonders, His creation, and His deep love for us.

Clearing our minds and making sure our thoughts are pure and godly may be a full-time job. In God, we can find a deep-settled peace in our souls.

One of my "calmers" is sitting by a mountain stream. The sounds and beauty that surround us lead us to an appreciation of God's creation and His awesomeness. The same could be said of a beautiful sunset or sunrise. For you, it may be being quiet in your own room, in your closet, at your job, or somewhere else that calms you. For busy mothers it may be the restroom! Anywhere you can go to be alone with God for a few moments - to clear your mind and turn your worries over to your Father, our Creator, the One who knows us best.

I encourage you to take a few minutes from whatever you do each day to go there, to be still and know that He is God!

"Be still, and know that I am God; I will be exalted among the nations, I will be exalted in the earth" (Psalm 46:10).

Kim Gill is a long time member of the Karns Church of Christ. Her parents were James & Mae Gill. Kim has taught the 2 & 3 year-olds as well as 2nd grade. Kim oversees care of her brother, Jim, who is bedfast with MS. Kim also is guardian to her great niece, Chloe Gill and great nephew Collin Baker. She enjoys Scrabble, genealogies, meeting people, and loves children.

The Name Above Every Name

There is a song I just cannot get out of my head. Has that ever happened to you? The song is a simple little tune composed in 1974 by Naida Hearn. Its words are, "Jesus, name above all names: beautiful Savior, glorious Lord, Emmanuel, God is with us, blessed Redeemer, Living Word." There are actually many more names for him in scripture.

Some additional ones are: Son of Man; Lion of the tribe of Judah; Chief Cornerstone; High Priest; Son of David; Holy and Righteous One; Messiah; Teacher; Lamb of God; the Good Shepherd; the Way; Lord of Lords; Anointed One; Counselor; Bread of Life; Mighty God; Heir of All Things; Lord of Glory; Alpha and Omega; Morning Star; Wonderful; King of Kings; Prince of Peace; the Most Holy; the Vine; the Door; Everlasting Father; the Truth; Almighty God; High Priest; the Life; the Light of the World; and the Christ.

Each name allows us to see another beautiful facet of Jesus' uniqueness. There is no other person's name that has impacted and continues to impact humankind more than His. It is undeniable. Paul conveyed this when he said, "Therefore God also has highly exalted Him and given Him the name which is above every name, that at the name of Jesus every knee should bow, of those in heaven, and of those on earth, and of those under the earth, and that every tongue should confess that Jesus Christ is Lord, to the glory of God the Father." (Philippians 2:9-11).

If there was ever a song one should not get out of the mind it is, "Jesus, Name above All Names."

Teresa Hampton, along with her husband, Gary, were members of the Karns congregation while he served as director of East Tennessee School of Preaching. Teresa has authored several ladies' books and currently writes a women's e-zine called Wellspring. Teresa and Gary recently moved to Jackson, MS where they labor with the Siwell Road church of Christ.

A Gloria Story

In high school, my friend Gloria was sewing a quilt which she carried from class to class. Science, French, anywhere but Gym, she'd be stitching. She asked everyone to bring bits of cloth. Pieces only two inches in size were framed in stitched squares to become a cathedral quilt.

God knows about putting pieces together. Somewhere during college, I began to need my understanding of the Old Testament in relation to the New Testament to be more cohesive. Reading a chronological Bible was useful. No breakthrough moment, but sorting and sifting brought me to a priceless word. The word interprets and integrates the Bible for me. It also frames great love and great steadiness on God's part. It is the word, "remnant." I read it in passages such as 2 Kings 19:4 and 30, Jeremiah 23:3, Isaiah 1, 10, and 11. God has always had a remnant. He always knew He would. He always knew His intentions for them. There always will be a remnant. The wonder of it is in every page of the Bible. When Jesus entered mankind, He walked among His remnant. He touched, healed and taught His remnant. Now we are His remnant and greatly loved. (Romans 11:5, Joel 2:32)

Gloria's quilt featured remnants singly and in unison. That's how we view the saints through the ages. When Gloria's quilt ended up in her family's yard sale, she snatched it back and gave it to me. I see snippets of cloth that speak of many friends' contributions and many a Science lab. In God's Word, remnant is a beautiful handmade portrayal of His people.

Melea Nash Smith is married to Steve. They have four children, Jordan, Melea Jean, Bryan, and Sarah. Melea is a non-seamstress. Sewing lessons in Girl Scouts, 4-H, and Mrs. Jackson's Home Ec. were all unsuccessful.

The Missing Piece

We are always wanting to find that missing piece whether it be to a simple childhood puzzle or to our lives. Have you ever thought that you are the missing piece?

When we are in our Christian walk, there are times when we are looking for a piece to the puzzle that seems to elude us when that piece could be looking at you in the mirror.

As Christians, we are called to be above the world and be transformed by the word of God. As part of Christ's body, we are a piece of the puzzle for the cause of Christ.

The world is always looking for the missing piece of their lives. Whether it is a teenager who wants to find the right group to hang out with or a single person who wants to find the right person to spend their life with, they want to find it as quick as possible and move on to what they believe is the next missing piece. Many times, they find the wrong pieces that they think will fit, then have to put that piece back and start again. I know, I have been there.

As Christians, we are to trust in God to find those pieces for us in the time he says is right for us whether we agree with it or not.

So, go out into the world and be the missing piece that the world needs to find Jesus Christ.

Wayne Begarly has been a member of the Karns Church of Christ since 2011. Wayne graduated from UT in 2007 with a Bachelors in Communications. Wayne is involved with the local United Way and American Cancer Society. He enjoys sports and the outdoors in his free time.

Honoring Your Mate

Marriage has little to do with getting your own needs met and everything to do with meeting the needs of your mate. When you transition from single life into marriage, your God-given purpose changes. 1 Corinthians 7:32-33 tells us, "But I want you to be without care. He who is unmarried cares for the things of the Lord --- how he may please the Lord. But he who is married cares about the things of the world --- how he may please his wife."

Many people quit on their marriages when they become sick and tired of being sick and tired. Marriage involves hard work and a devotion to each other's well-being. Over our 25 years together, Adrian and I tried to focus on meeting each other's emotional and physical needs. We made it a point to make our spiritual walk a priority. We learned that you must commit yourself to meeting these needs daily.

Today, many marriages lack a vital component: Honor. We become so familiar with our spouses that saying things like good-bye before leaving; "thank you,' "you're welcome" and "please" have vanished from our conversations.

I remember Adrian would call me at various times during the work day just to check on me and that made me feel like I was always on his mind. Keeping honor in marriage helps us hold on to the feeling we had at the time we said, "I do."

Lisa Marsh has been a federal employee since 1991. She is married to her high school sweetheart and they have one son together. Lisa enjoys traveling, family time, meeting new people, entertaining, reading and watching movies.

Jesus Music

A few years ago I was searching for the radio station that played Christmas music 24/7. I was surprised that my favorite station had switched from easy listening to Christian music. Not a big deal since I was listening to Christmas music.

I continued to listen after the holidays. At first I thought the songs all said pretty much the same thing: God is love, praise Jesus, Jesus is Lord. There were times I thought about going back to my favorite country station but decided to really give the Christian station a chance.

Then I attended a Karns Ladies' Retreat that focused on Philippians 4:8. This verse talks about keeping your mind on things that are true, noble, just, pure, lovely, and of good report. It reminded me of the Christian music that I had started listening to. It also reminded me that the music I had been listening to previously was pretty much the opposite: not noble, just or lovely at all. So I made a decision to only listen to music or watch movies or read books that are reflective of Philippians 4:8. I thought it would be difficult to change these bad habits but it really wasn't hard at all. In fact, I keep this verse posted at my desk as a reminder of what I decided to do.

I only listen to the Christian station and now I find I have a better frame of mind when my "Jesus music" constantly flows into my ears. I no longer worry that the things I am putting into my brain are inappropriate. After all, there is enough bad stuff in the world that gets into my head without purposely putting more stuff in there.

 Jill Cheatham is a graduate of the University of Tennessee. She is married to Daniel and they have two sons, Jonah and Conner. Jill is an avid couponer, reader, and proud supporter of Powell High School Marching Band.

Mood Rings

I'm sure you heard the one about the husband who bought his wife one of those "mood rings?" When she's in a good mood, it turns green, and when she's in a bad mood it leaves a red mark on his forehead.

While we may get a chuckle from this joke, failing to control one's anger is a serious spiritual problem. I've sometimes heard people brag about how they lost their temper and really "let someone have it." But such attitudes stand in stark opposition to one who has a Christ-like spirit.

Please don't lose sight of the fact that gentleness, longsuffering, kindness, and self-control are fruits of the Spirit.

You may say, "But you don't know my spouse," or "You don't know what my in-laws are like," or "You don't know just how frustrating my children or co-workers can be." Well, you're right. I don't know to what extent one's patience is tried. But I do know that the spiritual disciplines of gentleness, longsuffering, kindness, and self-control, when put into practice, allow Christ to be reflected in one's life.

The next time someone threatens to ruin your mood, instead of leaving a red mark on their forehead, allow Jesus to leave his mark on your life.

"And be kind to one another, tenderhearted, forgiving one another, even as God in Christ forgave you" (Ephesians 4:32).

Steve Higginbotham has been the pulpit minister for the Karns church of Christ since 2010. Steve is married to Kim and they have four children, Kelli, Michael, Matthew, and Anne Marie. Steve enjoys writing, playing golf, and is a fan of the Pittsburgh Steelers, the WVU Mountaineers, and the Andy Griffith Show.

Eleven Cents

I don't question God, but I often have questions for God. We recently left our two dogs at the kennel. The dogs ended up staying an additional night, so we had to pay an additional $25.00. Not an outrageous amount at this time, but there have been times when I would have loved to have an extra $25.00.

After picking up the dogs, I took them to the groomer. While waiting for the business to open, I walked my dogs around the parking lot. I thought about the extra $25 I had just spent and wondered if I really needed to come up with twenty bucks one day, would I be happy if I stumbled on just a couple of dollars somewhere? Would I be excited about finding a quarter on the street or in the washing machine?

A few steps later, I found my answer. A tarnished dime laid at my feet. Not just a penny, but big money as far as finding coins goes. It struck me that I had just received my answer. A few more steps, and the answer was made even more clear. I found an old penny. With just as much excitement, I bent down to pick it up and explained to the dogs how I was even luckier because now I had eleven cents!

That day I walked into the groomer's with a grin on my face, knowing that I had just received exactly what I needed. No, not the dime or the penny. I think my question was really deeper than anything to do with money. From time to time, I think we all need a reminder that God is there and looking out for us. He knows what we need and He will provide. He knows better than we do. I didn't need twenty bucks or eleven cents, I needed an answer to my question, and that's what He gave me.

Jill Green is used to seeing things differently. She grew up with brothers and is the only girl in her house with her husband, Craig, and two sons, Jake and Duncan. Her life is filled with blessings in her family, job and even in trials. She has an English/History degree from UT, buFt says she has yet to figure out what she wants to do with her life.

I'm In

A local high school football team had signs made that read "I'm In" and hung them above the locker room door that led out to the football stadium.

As they would leave the locker room to go on to the field they would slap the sign with their hand. This signified to themselves and to their teammates that they were ready to play and be part of the game. Whether they stood on the sidelines or played on the field, the players were going to give it their all.

These two words not only have meaning in the sports arena, but also have meaning in a spiritual way. We must ask ourselves the question, "Am I in or out when it comes to living like Christ?"

Paul was a man who was in the game. He was zealous about teaching others about Christ. No matter what obstacles were in his way, he always proclaimed the word of God. What a perfect example of someone who was in the game!

In 2 Timothy 4:1-8, Paul talks about us being ready in season and out to proclaim God's word. We must be willing to stand up for what we believe in no matter what happens to us or what others think about what we believe. In verse 7, Paul goes on to say that he had fought the good fight, had finished the race and had kept the faith.

Ultimately, by being in the game we will have a crown of righteousness that will be awarded to us on the day of judgment (2 Timothy 4:8).

Lee Toothman has been a member of the Karns congregation since 2006. He was born and raised in San Antonio, TX and has been married to Lynlee Robinson since July 2007. Lee enjoys golf, hunting, fishing, Dallas Cowboys football, and NASCAR racing.

I've Been Working Toward that Day

Brother Gholson, a faithful Christian, developed a serious illness. The doctor examined him and told him he had three to six weeks to live. The doctor was shaken by brother Gholson's response and how calmly he took it. He said, "I have been working toward this day the better part of my life."

Brother Art Gibbs, a former elder at Karns, was very sick in the hospital. His wife died while he was in the hospital. Some of our students visited Art to comfort and console him. They were surprised when Art said, "We have been working toward this time the better part of our lives."

We are encouraged to set our affections on things above (Colossians 3:1-2). Abraham looked for a city (Hebrews 11:10). We must lay up treasures in heaven (Matthew 6:20-21). After a faithful life Paul believed there was a crown of righteousness laid up for him in heaven (2 Timothy 4:7-8). If we continue to walk in the light we too can peacefully face the time appointed to all men (Hebrews 9:27).

James Meadows was born March 10, 1930. He graduated from High School in 1949, and Freed-Hardeman College in 1955. He later attended Union University and Harding Graduate School. He has done local work in Tennessee, Kentucky, and South Carolina. He served as Director of ETSPM from 1996 to 2006, and presently serves as Dean of Students.

Grow an Inch, Grace Gives a Mile

Remember when you were little and you were obsessed with measuring yourself? If you were really lucky your parents let you mark on the wall each time you grew. I believe the measuring obsession never really goes away; it just appears in less literal forms. We constantly measure our progress by comparing our skills, social adeptness, spiritual healthiness, life accomplishments, etc. against an array of impossible standards.

If you're like me, you're constantly striving to meet the most un-attainable standard of all—your own. Turns out, God has a different standard in mind for us: "For I determined not to know anything among you except Jesus Christ and Him crucified." (1 Corinthians 2:2).

Now there's one of two ways you can take this:
- Fall into despair and dwell on the impossibility of you, yourself being able to attain such a height.
- Allow yourself to really embrace the freedom of such an incredible standard! Realize that God doesn't ask you to do the impossible, but only what's within your reach.

With Christ as your standard you're freed from all aspects of life that truly don't matter; which, if you really meditate on this, eliminates a great many sources of worry. This means that all the things deemed "little" by worldly standards, suddenly become great things—treasures in Heaven!

So, just for today, cut yourself some slack. All the "little things" you've been doing, God sees, and magnifies those efforts. So pull out a crayon and mark your progress. You're growing!

Melea J. Smith is a graduate of Freed-Hardeman University and holds a Bachelor's in Social Work. She enjoys walking barefoot, Happy Hour at Sonic, and collecting jokes and stories from small children. If she could be any holiday affiliated figure for a day she would be the Tooth Fairy and discover once and for all what is done with those millions of teeth.

"Oh No, She's Up!"

"**B**e the kind of woman who, when your feet hit the floor in the morning the devil says, 'Oh no, she's up!'" I really like this saying; it applies to women and men alike.

Start your day with a prayer before you even get out of bed, and your day is off to a great start. This is our way of talking to God. Now allow God to speak to you through His Word. Make time in your day for Bible study. Our lives should be filled with doing so much good for the cause of Christ. Each day make the decision to be involved in some task or activity that would be helpful or encouraging to others.

Ladies, attend Ladies' Bible class, help with showers, teach a children's Bible class, prepare communion, or make bread or cookies for someone who needs encouragement. Guys, volunteer to speak at Wednesday night devotional or youth devotionals, teach a Bible class for teens or adults, make hospital visits, or help shut-ins with yard work. The list could go on and on.

I am a list maker, if I make a list of things I plan to do the next day then I tend to get most everything done. Put some of these things on your to-do list. If we spend our time in service to God, studying His Word and in prayer that will leave very little time for an idle mind. Remember, we want the devil to be saying of us, "Oh no, they're up!"

"And do not give the devil an opportunity" (Ephesians 4:27).

Sherrye Woodall is married to Gregg. They have 4 children: Stephanie Harder, Tiffany Dresser, Benjamin Woodall and Jonathan Woodall. They have 4 grandchildren: Wrigley Harder, Walton Harder, Adalynn Dresser and Brooklynn Dresser. Sherrye has taught the 3 years old class at Karns for over 32 years.

The Greatest of These is Love

Love suffers long and is kind; love does not envy; love does not parade itself, is not puffed up; does not behave rudely, does not seek its own, is not provoked, thinks no evil; does not rejoice in iniquity, but rejoices in the truth; bears all things, believes all things, hopes all things, endures all things. Love never fails. . ." (1 Corinthians 13:4-8a).

Jesus is patient, Jesus is kind. He does not envy, He does not boast, He is not proud. He does not dishonor others, He is not self-seeking, He is not easily angered, He keeps no record of wrongs. Jesus does not delight in evil but rejoices with the truth. He always protects, always trusts, always hopes, always perseveres. Jesus never fails.

(Your name here) is patient, (your name here) is kind. He/She does not envy, he/she does not boast, he/she is not proud. He/She does not dishonor others, he/she is not self-seeking, he/she is not easily angered, he/she keeps no record of wrongs. (Your name here) does not delight in evil but rejoices with the truth. He/She always protects, always trusts, always hopes, always perseveres. (Your name here) never fails.

Jesus is love, are you? Would others fill your name in the blanks? Can you fill your name in the blanks? Loving others is not easy. Accepting one another even at our worst is even harder, yet God does this every day. Because God knows who we have the potential to be, He loved us so much He sent us His greatest love to save us.

Deanna Hudson became a member of the Karns church family in the Spring of 2011. She is the mother of two children, Zoe and Patrick.

The Depression Era

I was born during Calvin Coolidge's administration and reared in the Great American Depression. My father, a soldier in the army in World War I, was afflicted by the great flu epidemic and told that he had 6 more months to live. Yet, he died at age 70. In spite of his short life expectancy, he worked diligently and taught all of us, his children, to follow his example. Following his example, I earned money the following ways:

- At age 7 sold Liberty magazine
- Cut grass with a hand-pushed reel mower and a sickle
- Trimmed shrubs with a pruning shear
- Delivered daily newspapers
- Washed windows
- Delivered repaired shoes to customers
- Worked as a warper-creeler in a textile mill
- Worked as an apprentice butcher in a meat market.
- Then, I entered the U. S. Navy in World War II

By being obedient to our parents we believed that we were being prepared to face whatever issues life might present. How mistaken we were! The booming economy during and after World War II and the attendant descent of decent moral values led to an America being increasingly separated from a righteous and loving Heavenly Father. We became increasingly aware that the admonition Jesus gave to the "Rich Young Ruler" also applied to us. The most important issue of life required that we also respond to God with all our heart, soul, mind and strength.

G. C. (Grover Cleveland) Robinson, Jr. has been married to Mattie Lou Geer since June 27, 1954. They have four children: Timothy, Amy, Andy, and Penny; and three grandchildren: Victoria, Quintin and Ransom. G. C. is a retired mechanical engineer. He turned 86 December 1st, 2012.

A Snake or a Stick

As a girl who grew up in the city of Miami, a summer visit to the country in Middle Tennessee was always exciting. It was a very different way of life, and I soaked up as much as I could about farm life.

I always looked forward to visiting one of my relatives who had a milking business. One day after milking the cows, my cousin and I went down to the creek behind the milk barn. All of a sudden, she yells, "Water Moccasin, run!" No thought was needed; I was out of there like a jackrabbit.

To this day I don't know if there really was a snake or just a stick, and she got a huge laugh out of scaring me to death. From the way she was laughing and acting I believed it was the latter.

If we could develop the same fear about immorality as we have about snakes, we could avoid the deadly bite of it from our lives. We would run with everything in us to stay away from temptation. We are warned about avoiding temptations, but there is one we need to constantly heed.

"Flee sexual immorality. Every sin that a man does is outside the body, but he who commits sexual immorality sins against his own body" (1 Corinthians. 6:18).

May we be diligent in running with all our might from this sin.

Barbara Tanner is married to Dale Tanner and has 3 children: Brenda, Sarah and Daniel. She has one son-in-law, Clint Patterson and a daughter-in-law Jessie. She likes reading, hiking, and history.

Focused Living

When Anne Marie was just a one-year-old baby girl, I once came home and found her in a very fussy mood. Kim was exhausted, so I took Anne Marie in her bedroom, got down in the floor with her, and we began to play blocks. And you know how that game goes with a child. You get a few blocks stacked, and the child knocks them down. Well, that's okay for a little while, but I was working on a really neat castle! So whenever Anne Marie got close to the blocks, I'd push her back so she couldn't knock over my masterpiece. It didn't take very long for her to begin crying again. There she sat on the floor crying, while I was playing with the blocks. (It would have made a good picture). But then it dawned on me that something in this picture wasn't right. I had lost focus. I had taken Anne Marie into her room to play with her in an effort to stop her from crying, but somewhere along the way I lost sight of that goal.

One of the most amazing traits in the life of Jesus is that he never got off track. He never got distracted from his goals. He never lost focus. From the time he entered the world until the time when he left it, he never lost sight of his goal, not even for a moment. His life was such a focused life from beginning to end, that his very last words on the cross reveal his focus as he said, "It is finished."

Me? Well, as I have revealed, I struggle with staying focused. I dare say I'm not alone either. Maybe it would be good for all of us to just take a step back and look at our lives objectively. Where are we headed? What are we doing? What are our goals? Could it be that we have we lost our focus? Give it some thought.

Steve Higginbotham has been the pulpit minister for the Karns church of Christ since 2010. Steve is married to Kim and they have four children, Kelli, Michael, Matthew, and Anne Marie. Steve enjoys writing, playing golf, and is a fan of the Pittsburgh Steelers, the WVU Mountaineers, and the Andy Griffith Show.

Kicking Against the Goads

When Evan was less than a year old, we were fighting a case of "the crud." This battle involved everything a first-time mom could throw at an infant's respiratory distress.

At one point, I had him on his changing table, attempting to clean out his nose, when he decided he was done with being suctioned! He thrashed, screamed, turned bright red, pushed, kicked my hands, and when I had his hands, legs and body pinned down, he did all there was left to do and flailed his head from side to side to avoid my advances at all cost! As I tried to calm him and assure him that I was trying to help him breathe, he was screaming; fighting me with all he had, and producing more snot in the process. He was certain I was aiming to harm him, though he was the one making his situation worse. The momentary discomfort of that blue suction bulb would bring him relief from his struggle for oxygen.

It was by that changing table (almost in tears, myself), that I was struck by God's patience with us when we kick against the goads (Acts 26:14). We can be so short-sighted, blinded by what we think is best for us, that we forget He is the one who lovingly knit us together and is able and willing to help us in ways greater than we could even think to ask of Him (Ephesians 3:20; Romans 8:26-28). He created us, knows and is eager to meet our needs, but we have to walk with Him, in faith, even when His path is not the painless way to go.

Jennifer Alsup has been a member of the Karns family for 19 years. She met, got engaged to and married her husband, Brad, at the Karns church building. They have been happily married for 8 years and have two children, Evan and Allie, whom she teaches at home. Jennifer enjoys sewing, baking, gardening, reading with her kids, and sipping coffee with friends.

Keep on Climbing

"I have fought the good fight, I have finished the race, I have kept the faith" (2 Timothy 4:7).

Several years back, Sherrye and I often watched our son, Jonathan, at the rock climbing center as he climbed the various courses on the wall, which were chosen for the competitors. He did very well and worked hard. The courses selected were progressively harder and eventually became too hard for some to complete. In watching him and thinking about spiritual applications, I thought of the apostle Paul and his struggle to succeed in living the Christian life.

As Jonathan climbed there was a belayer who always had a firm grip on the other end of his rope as he climbed the wall. There was also a monitor to watch him and there were many who had already climbed the wall giving him guidance of where to grab and hold. In addition to all of this there was a host of others there including ourselves encouraging him in his ascent to the top.

In many ways, this is similar to us as we climb through our Christian life. There are many who have been through various difficult courses in life and are willing to offer help to us. There are those who keep a firm grip on our rope to protect us if and when we fall. And assuredly there are a host of fellow Christians always ready to encourage us in our efforts to live faithfully.

Let's all strive to be as helpful to others as we can, and let's resolve to keep on climbing.

Gregg Woodall is an elder of the Karns Church of Christ. Gregg is married to Sherrye and they have four children, Stephanie, Tiffany, Benjamin, and Jonathan. They also have four grandchildren, Wrigley, Walton, Adalynn, and Brooklynn. Gregg enjoys golfing, dirt bike riding, spending time with family, and is a fan of the Tennessee Volunteers.

Using Our Talents

Please read the Parable of the Talents in Matthew 25: 14-30. This parable has a strong relationship to our lives. In this parable, talents are a monetary coin. God is our master and he has entrusted us with many "talents." How we choose to use them is up to us.

The servant with 5 talents is what we would call the "Seeking Servant." He took what his master gave him and put it to work and increased his reward. His master entrusted him with a bigger task. The servant with 2 talents, we will call the "Selfless Servant." He wanted to increase his Master's wealth but was more cautious and not willing to take as big a risk. The servant with 1 talent is the "Satisfied Servant." He felt his Master had enough wealth and was unsure if he deserved it. He was more comfortable burying the talent and then returning it to his master safe and sound.

In our lives we can become like the Satisfied Servant. We have our cozy lives with a schedule and plan and are content in keeping it that way. We go to Bible Study on Wednesday and worship on Sunday. We help when someone asks us but never seek opportunities to do more. We become paralyzed, unable to move.

God has given us many "talents" to put to use. Some of us can sing, others are wonderful teachers, some are leaders, some are preachers. There are plenty of jobs in God's kingdom to go around. We should examine ourselves and put our talents to use to grow God's kingdom. God has commanded us to do so.

Carla Tooley is a mother, nurse, and preacher's wife. She is the wife of Doug Tooley, SEIBS student. They have two children- Logan and Aubrey.

Train Up a Child

"Train up a child in the way he should go, And when he is old he will not depart from it" (Proverbs 22:6).

These words have been a source of both comfort and grief through the annals of parenthood. Why is this so? Why do some children, even within the same family, follow the Biblical teaching they have received and others turn away from it?

Let us remember the Proverbs are general principles, not absolute truths. Nevertheless, for the benefit to be received, "when he is old he will not depart from it," there must first be the action, "train up a child in the way he should go." The parental role requires us to know the way a child should go and second, to train the child in that way. Parents must also know the natural tendency of their child, lest we "provoke your children to wrath" (Ephesians 6:4). It is the combination of knowing God's will for our children and their natural inclinations that allow us to train them in the way they should go.

Notice, scripture does not tell us to ask the child which way they want to go. If we relinquish the choice of training to the children, heartaches are sure to come. Fathers, you cannot have Joshua 24:15, "But as for me and my house, we will serve the Lord," hanging on your wall and the children be in charge! You may be dad of the year, but I wouldn't wear the medal on judgment day. To end right, you have to start right, and starting right is doing it God's way!

Jeff Smith is married to Sherry and they have two children, Lauren and Hannah. Jeff and his family have been members at Karns since 2001. Jeff has served the congregation as an elder and is often referred to as "The Bible Bowl Man." He enjoys reading, writing, congregational singing, and passionate gospel preaching.

Home is Where the Heart Is

When we go on vacation we are always glad to get back home. If you have ever been in the hospital, you know how eager you are to get home. When our children were away at college, they looked forward to coming home for a weekend or breaks. Sometimes we ask, "When are you coming home?" Why is it that we long for home? Maybe it is Mom, Dad, brothers, sisters, unconditional love, acceptance, comfort, forgiveness and security. It is not our actual houses that we miss, but the feelings that home generates in us.

The church is like home because it is a family. When I am away on vacation or sick, I miss my church family. If I am at home sick, I always want to know what happened at services and if anyone missed me. I feel love, acceptance, comfort, forgiveness and security when I am with my brothers and sisters. We are family and we should treat each other the same way we would treat our own brothers and sisters or parents. How about our brothers and sisters who have fallen away? Do we ask them when they are coming home?

We have an even greater home waiting for us in Heaven. As family, we need to encourage each other to long and strive for that home in Heaven. As a mom, I want all of my family to make it to Heaven. As a part of the Karns Family, I want us all to be in Heaven together. Are we longing for our Great Home in Heaven?

Sherrye Woodall is married to Gregg. They have 4 children: Stephanie Harder, Tiffany Dresser, Benjamin Woodall and Jonathan Woodall. They have 4 grandchildren: Wrigley Harder, Walton Harder, Adalynn Dresser and Brooklynn Dresser. Sherrye has taught the 3 years old class at Karns for over 32 years.

Memorials

Recently we visited a Civil War battlefield and observed several memorials to men who died in battle (gave their last full measure of devotion, as Lincoln famously said). These memorials were erected on the spot where these soldiers died. With a little research, you will find many of these sites are controversial since they were usually designated about 20 years after the battle. Therefore, you cannot be absolutely sure of the accuracy of the memorial location.

What a contrast to the memorials established by our Lord and our God. Paul tells us in 1 Corinthians 11 that Christ established the Lord's Supper on the night he was betrayed. This was days before his death. Further this memorial was to be observed until his return (1 Corinthians 11:16). Remember that God did the same, directing the observance of the Passover even before the exodus from Egypt (Exodus 12:17). Only the Lord or God can establish a memorial before an event happens!

Both of these memorials emphasize vitally important Bible truths. First, God keeps his promises and his predictions are accurate. The events portrayed in the memorials came to pass precisely as God and Jesus stated. The Passover occurred with the death of first-born, both man and animal, if they were not protected by the blood of the lamb. Jesus' death on the cross occurred as he predicted. Second, God and Jesus established laws and ordinances we are expected to observe. If we believe in God we must seriously consider these truths and dedicate ourselves to obedience to an all-knowing, all-powerful God.

Dave Benner is married to Sue and they have three children. Dave retired after 40 years with USDA. He and his wife, Sue moved back to TN in 2012. He enjoys hunting, fishing, and is a fan of the Pittsburgh Steelers.

There is No Fear in Love

The year was 1987 and I was a guard at Y-12. It was lunchtime, and we were all eating together; African-Americans, every one of us. Mr. Carlos said that he was prejudiced once. What changed him was that he was drowning in a swimming pool and this white boy pulled him to safety. This one selfless act ended his prejudice. In response to Mr. Carlos' statement, Mr. Clark said that his grandfather always said, "Whatever you fear most will come to claim you." I will never forget that statement. 1 John 4:18 says, "There is no fear in love, but perfect love casts out fear..."

The conversion of Cornelius and his household in Acts 10 spoke to Jewish prejudice. We Gentiles are recipients of the death of our dear Lord the same as the Jews (Acts 10:34, Hebrews 2:9, 2 Corinthians 5:14).

The Good Samaritan in Luke 10 embodied relationships with two of the greatest scriptures in the entire Bible, and on these two hang Moses and the prophets (Deuteronomy 6:5 and Leviticus 19:18). These Scriptures let us know that our neighbor may be someone of a different race. Jesus came to earth to end prejudice and to bring us back together to love one another (John 17:21, John 13:34).

After the flood the Ark landed at Mt. Ararat. We had to separate to populate the earth. I bet they waved at each other as far as they could see. Their footprints were eroded by time, the wind and the rain. We were separated by oceans, mountains and language. It was Jesus who came down to earth and set up His Church, to bring us back together.

Bennie Williams has been a member at Karns since he was 13 years-old. He is employed at B&W at Y-12 for over 30 years. Bennie loves discussing the Bible, history, exercising, playing the guitar, and restoring old cars. He is married to Jacquie and has one son, Jerrell Williams and two grandchildren, Levi and Avani. My favorite bible verse is: Psalm 139.

You Are Valuable

Due to our keen awareness of our own imperfections, we are often made to wonder, as did the psalmist, "Who is man that you are mindful of him?" (Psalm 8:4).

We sometimes wonder how God could possibly still love us after all our sins. Maybe the answer to that question can be best understood by way of illustration.

Suppose I were to offer you a crisp, new $100 dollar bill, would you want it? Of course you would. But suppose I crumpled the money up in my fist before giving it to you. Would you still want it even though it's crumpled and wrinkled? That wouldn't change your mind, would it? Well, suppose I then threw the crumpled $100 dollar bill on the ground and twisted it into the dirt with my shoe. Would you still want it? Well, of course you would. You see, whether crumpled or crisp, clean or dirty, the $100 dollar bill retains its value.

Likewise, it matters not to God how dirty we get from wallowing in sin, God still sees our value and wants to possess us.

Friends, don't ever sell yourself short. Do you feel guilty for all your sins? Good! You should. But don't let your sins cause you to think that God no longer wants you. You are his creation, his offspring, and consequently he will never stop loving you. Don't allow his love to go unrequited.

"For God so loved the world that He gave His only begotten Son, that whoever believes in Him should not perish but have everlasting life" (John 3:16).

Steve Higginbotham has been the pulpit minister for the Karns church of Christ since 2010. Steve is married to Kim and they have four children, Kelli, Michael, Matthew, and Anne Marie. Steve enjoys writing, playing golf, and is a fan of the Pittsburgh Steelers, the WVU Mountaineers, and the Andy Griffith Show.

It is Finished

"So when Jesus had received the sour wine, He said, "It is finished!" And bowing His head, He gave up His spirit" (John 19:30).

"It is finished!" What an amazing statement. Jesus had accomplished His purpose. He had come to earth, lived as a man, suffered as a criminal, and endured pain beyond comprehension. He did it all without sin. He did it despite the nagging temptations of the devil. When all was accomplished, He could truthfully say that his mission was completed successfully. Jesus won and Satan lost. There was no longer anything that could thwart God's plan to redeem man from sin.

When Jesus uttered those words from the cross and commended His Spirit to God, He paved the way for each of us to go to heaven. He accomplished all that God could accomplish with regards to the salvation of man and still be in keeping with His perfect and holy nature. From that point on, it has been up to man to complete his work so that he could say, "It is finished" at the end of his life.

No matter how difficult your life is, Jesus had it harder. He was beaten, mocked, and hung from a cross, none of which He deserved. He did it all and then declared the finality of His work. How about you? Will you be able to say it is finished when your life nears its end? Will you be able to peacefully send your spirit to God, knowing that all has been accomplished in your life? Jesus has shown us how. Are you willing to follow His lead?

Brad Alsup serves as a deacon at the Karns church of Christ. He is married to Jennifer, and they have two children, Evan and Allie. Brad is a hunter, a cyclist, and an avid reader.

Look a Little Deeper

Have you ever stood in line at WalMart and witnessed a child having a major tantrum while the parent appears to be doing nothing about it? Have you ever thought to yourself, "If that was my child, I'd..." I too, have seen the tantrums and had the same thoughts, however having experience working with children who have autism and other disabilities, I have learned not to be so quick to judge. A child who may look totally normal on the surface, may have some severe disabilities that affect their behavior.

In the past, I have worked with children who lived in foster homes. The reason was because their biological homes were something you couldn't even imagine in your worst nightmares. The foster parent did all they could to create a loving home for a child who knew nothing but dysfunction and aggression.

Next time we see a child acting out, instead of being quick to judge maybe we should look past the obvious. Unless you walk in their shoes, you cannot imagine the difficulty and despair faced by parents of children with disabilities. Unless you have had a difficult upbringing, you may have no idea what kind of abuse some children are growing up in that leads to their excessive aggression and difficult behaviors.

Rather than being quick to judge one who is having a problem, could we not just stop and pray for them? "Be of one mind, having compassion for one another" (1 Peter 3:8).

Kim Higginbotham grew up in Poplar Bluff, MO. She is married to Steve and has four children: Kelli, Michael, Matthew, and Anne Marie. Kim teaches children with multiple disabilities for Knox County, a ladies' class at SEIBS, conducts teacher training seminars, and maintains two blogs, "Teaching Help," and "Relative Taste." She enjoys teaching and cooking.

The End of Our Driveway, Our Mission Field

I went to a basketball game at our local high school and parked in the church parking lot across the street. After the game ended I went to my car and pulled out to leave. As I left the parking lot I saw a sign that read, "You are now entering your mission field."

That sign resonated with me, but I would add a slight revision. I think we should all have a sign in our yard that reads, "Your mission field starts at the end of the driveway." Too often we fail to see our neighborhood, state or country as a mission field.

I have been to Honduras twice on mission trips and have no problems viewing this as a mission to plant the word of God. I often forget, though, that our country is in dire need of God's word and grace. I go about my daily business without thinking that my neighbors, co-workers and friends need to hear about how Jesus came to Earth and died for our sins, and that they can be saved through his blood shed on the cross.

In Mark 16:15 Jesus said, "Go into all the world and preach the gospel to every creature." He did not say, "Only go into foreign lands." He said go into ALL the world. Our country needs Christians who view the nation as a mission field, willing to go and preach the gospel to our neighbors, coworkers, and friends. We should resolve to remember that "all the world" includes the part of it closest to our homes.

Tony Turner is a retired Army officer who has been a member of the Karns Church of Christ since May 2011. He works at the Oak Ridge National Laboratory. He is married to Kathy and has three children: Richard, age 17; Joel, age 15; and Brigitte, age 9. He enjoys watching high school and college football, playing golf, and officiating soccer.

A Breed Within Ourselves

I own miniature horses. My horses have been to numerous farm days, visited schools and been in skits. People often exclaim, "What cute little ponies." I always cringe when I hear this because, although similar, minis are not ponies. I was excited when I came across an article and read: "Miniature horses are not ponies; they are a breed within themselves." This got me thinking about Christians. We, too, are a breed within ourselves.

We look like people of the world, we have jobs and attend school like people of the world and we have common interests such as sports, music, and hanging out with friends. Christians, at first glance may seem like any other person, but we are actually set apart from others. We pay close attention to what comes out of our mouth, what images we look at and put into our heads, and how we act around others and in various situations. We have put on Christ in baptism.

Christians get up every Sunday to worship God. We participate in as many church activities as possible to be with other Christians. Our ultimate goal is to get to Heaven and bring as many other people with us as possible. In 1 Peter 2:9, Paul calls us a "peculiar" people. This means that we are supposed to be different. We are to be in the world but not of the world.

Miniature horses will never become ponies, but all people can become Christians. We are told in Romans 12:2, "Do not be conformed to this world, but be ye transformed...and discern what is the will of God." Begin your transformation today.

Catherine Albert is a home-schooled senior who trains and shows miniature horses. Her hobbies include playing the flute, piccolo, piano, and guitar, singing, reading, and caring for her menagerie of animals. She is active in 4-H and coaches the Horse Bowl/Hippology teams. She plans to attend college and major in Animal Science and Music.

Are We Like Stephen?

In May 2012, North Carolina held a primary election where an amendment that pertained to the issue of "same-sex marriage" was on the ballot. A high school student at my congregation got to vote for the first time in her life on that day. She was proudly wearing her "I Voted" sticker when some of the other students asked her how she voted on the amendment. She told them that God specified marriage between a man and a woman. Some of her classmates began to call her a bigot and other awful names, but she continued to hold strong to her beliefs even in the face of ridicule from her classmates.

When I heard this story, I began to think of the Biblical account of Stephen that starts in Acts 6:8. Some men rose up and argued with Stephen. "And they were not able to resist the wisdom and the Spirit by which he spoke" (Acts 6:10). These men accused Stephen of blaspheming against Moses and against God (Acts 6:11).

We have this same problem today. Many people will accuse us of blaspheming or misrepresenting God when we share with them the truth about the one true God. They are not convicted enough to learn who God truly is.

Stephen showed his conviction to our Lord through his commitment to teach the truth regardless of the consequences. Do we have that same conviction? Do we stand firm, like the high school student, when we are ridiculed? We should see everyone as souls, and remember that our God wants them all to repent and serve Him (2 Peter 3:9).

Matthew Waters is originally from Easley, SC. , but moved to Durham, N. C. He is presently a student here at SEIBS. Matthew has worked as an Accountant, a Computer Support and Technical Support Specialist. Matthew enjoys sports (he's a huge fan of the UNC Tarheels), watching TV and movies, and playing video games.

Be Still, Watch, and Listen

This summer my sister and her children visited me for a week. Every day the kids wanted to eat outside on my back porch. After we ate, we would sit and listen to all the wonderful sounds God gives us. We heard three baby cardinals in a nest crying for food. We saw the mother feed the babies and take care of them. We saw squirrels, other birds and heard insects. I am amazed how much God takes care of the animals and loves us and takes care of us too. He tells us we are more important than the animals. That is an awesome feeling. Whenever you get down, take time to stop and listen to the great sounds outside. Watch how the animals are provided for by God.

I know it is hard for us to stop very long or for a long time, but just try a few times a day, then a few days a week. Maybe it will become a habit. God wants us to appreciate His world. He has created it for us to enjoy. That is a wonderful love for us. Take time to thank Him for it.

Reflect on these scriptures that will help you to know God loves you very much. He created us to be His children, to take care of us, and to have an everlasting relationship with Him. You get a renewed spirit when you are still, watching and listening.

"Be still and know that I am God" (Psalm 46:10). "Look at the birds of the air; they do not sow or reap or store away in barns, and yet your heavenly Father feeds them. Are you not much more valuable than they" (Matthew 6:26)?

Yvette Guthrie is married to Todd and they have two children, Ethan and Daniel. She enjoys reading, spending time with friends and family, traveling and helping others. They have been members at Karns since 2002.

God's Time

"My brethren, count it all joy when you fall into various trials, knowing that the testing of your faith produces patience" (James 1: 2-3).

I often wonder why things happen the way they do, curiosity I guess. Sometimes, though, it stems from the way things are in my own life and the order in which they happen. At times I become very discouraged with the arrangement in my life. I only took over a decade to get through college. I married when I was 30, and had a child at the age of 36; long after all my best friends had accomplished the same things. Those years were exactly the way they were meant to be.

After miscarrying my first child at 33, I began to wonder if being a mom was for me. Then a few more years went by, and I assumed it wasn't so. What I soon realized, was that it's all about the timing: God's timing. We would be blessed with a child when God wanted us to have one.

We now have a baby girl, perfect in every way. God's gifts come on His clock, not ours. As most people know, I lost my mother seven years ago, and I often wonder how I am supposed to be a mom, without my mom. Sad as it may be that she is not here to hold my baby girl, I know she is very much a part of my daughter's life, in many ways. My mother's blood runs through my daughter's veins—and, in many ways, life has come full circle.

Heatherly Stiles was born and raised here in Knoxville. She is married to Jeremy Stiles and is the mother to baby Avery. She is also a fan of the Tennessee Volunteers.

When Did the Magic End?

Do you remember the first time you saw Mickey Mouse come on TV, or went to Disney World when you were little? You were so excited the first time you saw him in person. Why was that? It was because you believed he was real. The theme parks and TV brought to life this amazing character. Now, years later, when you come back to Disney World, you would rather go on the rides than to see your favorite childhood character. That's because somewhere in your life, you've lost your child-like belief in him.

Now, let me ask you this question: where in our lives, have we lost the innocence we had as small children? Somewhere, along the path of life, we lost our childhood innocence to the ever-changing world around us. Matthew 18:2-4 states, "Then Jesus called a little child to Him, set him in the midst of them, and said, 'Assuredly I say to you, unless you are converted and become as little children, you will by no means enter the kingdom of heaven. Therefore whoever humbles himself as this little child is the greatest in the kingdom of heaven.'"

As the verse states, we must humble ourselves to please God as much as we can. When we do fall short, we need to work harder next time to honor God who was to us (and still is) bigger than life.

If we find ourselves going through hard times, hold fast to God's word. He can help us if we are willing to become innocent once more. Unlike Mickey Mouse, God is real and alive. We must always believe that and never out-grow or lose our faith in Him.

Austin Hoffarth has lived in Tennessee all his life. He attends high school at Webb School of Knoxville. He likes to draw, play tennis, go camping and hiking. He became a Christian in 2011 and enjoys the activities within the youth group at Karns and area-wide churches.

Running the Good Race

I've been a Christian for nearly six years now and in my very short life I've seen a few things. I'm only 15 and I have already been through the struggles of being a Christian. Whether it be temptation, trials, or circumstances, being a Christian is hard work; but the hardships of this life are worth going through because our everlasting reward is just one lifetime away.

Many new Christians or non-Christians are intimidated by older more mature Christians. They think that we're unreachable or are too holy for them. We are not, and I'm here to tell you that we are all runners in this good race.

In 2 Timothy 4:7 Paul says, "I have fought the good fight, I have finished the race, and I have kept the faith." We as people are in a constant battle with sin whether we know it or not. We have morals for a reason and we must fight the good fight. We have not finished the race but we must continue running and loving God and keeping his commandments until the end of our lives. To be a true Christian you must believe the word of God and follow his commandments like being baptized and living faithfully.

In 2 Timothy 4:8 Paul says, "Finally, there is laid up for me the crown of righteousness, which the Lord, the righteous Judge, will give to me on that Day, and not to me only but also to all who have loved His appearing." We will be in heaven one day if we just love God and keep on running.

Ethan Guthrie is 15 years-old and has been at Karns for nine years. He loves writing, drawing, reading, and soccer. He's a sophomore at Hardin Valley Academy. Ethan is the son of Todd and Yvette, and the older brother of Daniel.

Travis' Toothbrush

Whenever I catch myself being materialistic I remind myself of Travis' toothbrush. Travis cuts my hair. Several years ago, he took six months off and hiked the Appalachian Trail. Whenever he talks about his experiences on the trail, it is obvious that this hike changed his life.

He started his journey with all the things one would need. After carrying certain items for several miles and several days he found he really didn't need everything he had. He began to unload his pack. When he had pared down his pack to essentials, he began to assess the excessiveness of his essentials.

He determined he didn't need the maps in his trail book that covered parts of the trail he had already hiked, so he used them to start his campfire. As he got closer to the end of the trail he knew how to survive with less and less. Then one day he got to the point where he was looking at his toothbrush, he decided that the handle was excessively long, so he broke it off!

In less than six months a toothbrush handle had become a luxury item in his life! Whenever I find myself struggling with the decision to keep something or throw it out, or having a talk with myself about whether the thing I have my eye on is a want or a need, then I think about Travis's toothbrush handle.

". . . for I have learned in whatever state I am, to be content: I know how to be abased, and I know how to abound. Everywhere and in all things I have learned both to be full and to be hungry, both to abound and to suffer need" (Philippians 4:11-12).

Pam McCoy and her husband, Darren, have worshipped at Karns since 1997. Pam was the church secretary from 98-2001. She is now working part-time for an architecture and design firm doing interior design for commercial projects. She enjoys her full time job as a homemaker, traveling, and spending time with family and friends.

Is God Exhausted?

Our children have all gone to church camp from the time they were two years old. One of the advantages of camp is all the devotional songs one can learn.

My son, Michael loved to sing at camp. One year, when Michael was still very young, we had just finished a week of camp and as the camp began to disappear in my rearview mirror, Michael began singing one of the new songs he had learned that week at camp. You know the song. It's entitled, "I Will Call Upon the Lord." But I doubt if you know the words to Michael's version of it. Here's what he sang. . .

". . . The Lord liveth, and blessed be the Rock, and may the God of my salvation be exhausted. . ." Well, needless to say, I got a good laugh from that one.

But as we drove home that day, his confusion over the lyrics of that song did set me to thinking. From a human standpoint, we sometimes must feel that we do indeed exhaust God. The foolishness of our sins. . . the frequency of our sins. . . and the general failure from time to time to imitate Jesus makes us wonder if God's patience and forgiveness isn't exhausted.

Fortunately for us, we serve a God who delights in mercy (Micah 7:18) and is rich in it (Ephesians 2:4)! Be assured though, God does not look lightly upon sin. After all, it cost him his precious Son. However, be comforted in the fact that he is a God who will not be exhausted by our sins if we will humble ourselves and seek his forgiveness (1 John 1:9).

Steve Higginbotham has been the pulpit minister for the Karns church of Christ since 2010. Steve is married to Kim and they have four children, Kelli, Michael, Matthew, and Anne Marie. Steve enjoys writing, playing golf, and is a fan of the Pittsburgh Steelers, the WVU Mountaineers, and the Andy Griffith Show.

Have You Looked in the Mirror?

I bet before you started reading this that you got up and looked in the mirror. Mirrors can be a great insight into who we are and who we become in many different areas.

We usually get dressed, comb the hair and do other things to make us look good, so when we look in the mirror again, it isn't as bad. To most, that also gives us the confidence we need to get through the day.

There is one mirror that you can't hide from and that is the mirror with which you look at yourself spiritually. Do you like what you see? Sure, you can look once, go clean up on the outside and look again, but have you changed anything, or just covered it up?

We have all done things in our lives that we have tried to hide or put away, hoping nobody finds out.

No matter how we look on the outside, it is what is on the inside that counts. Our souls will reveal our true identity in the end. Our sins will eventually reveal our true self to everyone.

God wants us to be pure and free from sin. We know that we fall and by His grace, He forgives us when we ask. But if we think we can hold onto sin, just until the right before we pass on, then our true identity will be revealed.

So as you get ready to head out to represent God, make sure that you are seen like God wants you to be and not how you try to be when hiding sin.

Wayne Begarly has been a member of the Karns Church of Christ since 2011. Wayne graduated from UT in 2007 with a Bachelors in Communications. Wayne is involved with the local United Way and American Cancer Society. He enjoys sports and the outdoors in his free time.

Escape

"God is faithful, who will not allow you to be tempted beyond what you are able, but with the temptation will also make the way of escape, that you may be able to bear it" (1 Corinthians 10:13).

Family trips to my mother's home place gave us some West Texas memories. My grandparents' land bordered ranches which stretched out flat with distant windmills and cattle. In the other direction, a few miles would bring us to the breaks (which are small canyons of deepest red), cliffs, and rugged growth. Then the road leads to the town of Dickens, the Cap Rock, and Blanco Canyon, which is white in contrast to the red of the breaks.

One summer Uncle Stan, a deputy, came by telling of a local jailbreak. The search was on for two men who had escaped. We were able to see and hear the helicopters searching the breaks. Long about the second day, the men were seen. They were running and waving to flag the helicopters! After two days and nights, they wanted to be found and rescued! They probably wished they had never removed the air conditioner to escape.

Now here's the lay of the land. If God has provided a way of escape and we by faith and foresight have chosen it, we will not find ourselves in the mesquite with the scorching sun. On the other hand, if we have chosen some oddball way of our own to solve some fix we don't like, we may find ourselves waving, stumbling and chasing down some help to get us out of the rattlesnakes.

Melea Nash Smith is married to Steve. They have four children, Jordan, Melea Jean, Bryan, and Sarah. Melea was raised in East Tennessee by a mother who collected rainwater before it was the environmental thing to do.

Through It All

Andre Crouch wrote a song that I love - maybe you've heard it. It's called "Through It All." I think I could have written it, mostly because I think I've lived it. The song speaks of how that we need to learn to trust God through all of life's circumstances.

I have a request for my funeral: I want someone to sing "Through It All."

You know, that's how God taught me to trust him. He stayed with me through it all. He didn't take "it all" away. He went through "it all" with me. The tougher it got, the closer we got, God and me.

It is through it all that I had opportunity to receive the "peace of God, which surpasses all understanding" (Philippians 4:7). Each late night prayer, each petition as I washed dishes or drove to pick up the kids from school became a sacred time for us to spend together – God and me.

It is through it all that I learned to trust. I learned to wait upon the Lord. I learned to depend on the promise made, not just to all of Israel, but also to me in Leviticus 31:8, "He will not leave you nor forsake you."

When we learn to trust God "through it all," our struggles, fears, and obstacles can actually strengthen our faith instead of weakening us. For it's in our struggles, we learn that God is big enough to overcome our greatest fears and struggles.

Sara Terlecki is married to her husband Bill. They moved to Knoxville from Ohio. Sara has worked in the church office since 2010. They have two grown children. Gerri married Michael Nath and blessed them with granddaughter, Ellie. Bill Jr. married Hope Whittington and blessed them with two grandsons, Allen and Evan.

Outlive Your Life

Being fans of the Andy Griffith Show, Kim and I decided to visit Mt. Airy, NC, the hometown of Andy Griffith, and the model town for the fictional town of Mayberry. We went through the Andy Griffith Museum, took a few pictures, and headed home. Within hours of returning home from our trip, we learned that Andy Griffith had passed away.

After hearing the news of his passing, I listened to an interview he gave a couple years earlier. The interviewer asked him if he could remember all the episodes of the Andy Griffith Show. Surprisingly to me, he said, "No." Oh, he remembered many of them, had some favorites, but just didn't remember all of them. I found that amazing because there are thousands of people across the country who remember every episode, can tell you what's going to happen next, and even quote lines. But Andy, himself, couldn't.

That caused me to reflect on how our influence can long outlive our lives. Some of the episodes that Andy Griffith actually participated in were not remembered by him, but thousands of people who simply "looked on" remember every detail. What that tells me is that I had better be cautious about my words, attitudes, and actions. What I might say or do today, and forget about tomorrow, may never be forgotten by an "onlooker," even long after I am dead and gone.

The passing of Andy Griffith reminded me of a truth spoken by the apostle Paul, "For none of us lives to himself, and no one dies to himself" (Romans 14:7). Make sure that the influence you have on others is the kind that you want to outlive you.

Steve Higginbotham has been the pulpit minister for the Karns church of Christ since 2010. Steve is married to Kim and they have four children, Kelli, Michael, Matthew, and Anne Marie. Steve enjoys writing, playing golf, and is a fan of the Pittsburgh Steelers, the WVU Mountaineers, and the Andy Griffith Show.

Let There Be Honor

The United States is one of the most powerful countries in the world, yet we will kill each other over a pair of shoes or just because someone makes us angry. We hear in the news daily of husbands killing their wives or wives killing their husbands. Children are killing their parents and parents are even killing their children. Where does it stop? Even in history when we were "less civilized," men respected women, children showed respect for their parents even if they did not agree with them or even like them. Men who were enemies showed respect for each other. Fights had to be "fair" and you didn't shoot an unarmed man or shoot a man in the back and you never hit a woman. Now we are killing people over things. The "things" have become more important than the man.

Romans 12:10 states: "Be kindly affectionate to one another with brotherly love, in honor giving preference to one another."

Webster's definition of honor: a good name; nobility of mind; an act that shows great respect or regard. What would our country be like if we were trying to "outdo" each other in showing honor to our fellow man? We would be so busy trying to do good to each other that there would be no room for killing, dishonesty, hateful words, scams or anything that shows dishonor. We would be back to trusting each other on a "word and a handshake."

Do this by starting with ourselves. Let us make it a priority to be noble of mind and show great respect to all. Let us . ...outdo one another in showing honor.

Terry Albert is a home-school mom of two teenagers and a 4-H volunteer leader with a BS in Animal Science and MS in Rehabilitation Counseling. Her hobbies include reading and sharing the family's many animals through a variety of 4-H, school, and community activities.

As You Are Going About

In Matthew 28:18-20, we are given what is considered to be the great commission. The beginning of verse 19 says "Go therefore and make disciples of all nations..." While at the Freed-Hardeman University Bible Lectureship a few years ago, a speaker made the point that another way of looking at this would be, "As you are going about..." I believe this to mean, that as I go about my daily routine that I should be glorifying God.

Are you kind to the cashier at the grocery store? Have you thought to invite them to church? How about when you go out to eat, take tracts and leave them with your tip? We have a couple of favorite restaurants and have gotten to know some of the waiters and waitresses very well. We have Bible discussions with them and have invited them to services. They have yet to come but we will keep asking.

Make opportunities to bring up things that are going on in our congregation with your neighbors, such as Friendship Day, Vacation Bible School, Bible Lectureship and our regular Bible studies and worship. At the last Friendship Day, a lady from the community came because over 20 people invited her. Go the extra mile for Christ! Have you ever been given back too much money at a store? Did you think to correct the cashier or did you keep it? What about paying for someone's meal without them knowing who did it, but leaving a church business card or tract? It's the little things that we do that can make all the difference in the world. Remember, "As you are going about..."

Sherrye Woodall is married to Gregg. They have 4 children: Stephanie Harder, Tiffany Dresser, Benjamin Woodall and Jonathan Woodall. They have 4 grandchildren: Wrigley Harder, Walton Harder, Adalynn Dresser and Brooklynn Dresser. Sherrye has taught the 3 years old class at Karns for over 32 years.

Raised in the Church

Sometimes I will hear a brother or sister say how grateful they are to come to know Christ on their own versus having been "raised in the church." I do have a great appreciation for this as my wife came to know Jesus Christ through her own searching.

I am equally thankful that my grandparents and parents were Christians whom through their love for the Lord, I came to know Christ. While each Christian's path is different, we are all to work out our own salvation (Philippians 2:12). It may be thought that the latter path is easier, but in many ways it can be more difficult. A child that is "brought up" in the church, so to speak, will come to know God's expectations sooner in life than perhaps others. That child will mature and will likewise be exposed to the same temptations as the unchurched.

The world may not have a problem with sin (drinking, profanity, immodesty, etc.), however the pressure can be great on the Christian to resist the lures of the world. If a child of God succumbs, the consequences are great (2 Peter 2:20-21) and it would have been better for them to not have known the Lord at all.

Perhaps we resolve that the erring Christian should have known better since they were after all "raised in the church." Let us always pray for one another regardless of when or how one became a Christian. The ways of the world have a tremendous pull on us. How great when we do restore a brother or sister (Galatians 6:1-2 and James 5:19-20).

Terry Clark serves as a deacon at the Karns church of Christ. Terry is married to Teresa and they have two sons, Spencer and Seaver. Terry is a graduate of Tennessee Technological University, which is where Terry met Teresa. Terry enjoys hiking, camping and watching a good western movie with John Wayne or Clint Eastwood.

Getting to Know Jesus

Jesus asked a key question during his ministry: "Who do you say that I am?" Jesus knew that it was crucial for his followers to truly know and understand who he was.

Many people in the religious world today make statements like:"I have come to know Jesus," "I have accepted the Savior," or "I have invited Jesus into my heart."

Howver, do you think most of those making these statements have any real knowledge or understanding of who Jesus really is? Many making these claims have never even read through the Bible, and know very little about the teachings of the scriptures.

How good of an understanding do you think most Christians have of who Jesus is? Many have never really studied the man or His life. Can we really be effective at following Jesus and modeling ourselves after Him if we don't have a thorough understanding of who He is?

Scripture tells us that it was through Jesus and for Him that all things were created (Col 1:15-17). He is the crux and hub of all Christianity. It is not possible to serve Jesus effectively without a clear understanding of who He is.

Jesus came to fulfill God's plan for eternity and to save us from our sins. It is imperative that we understand and know Him if we are to be effective in our Christian walk with Him. We can begin getting to know Jesus today by starting a thorough and systematic study of the four gospels in which much of His life is portrayed.

Sara Jones was born in Camden, AL and became a Christian in 1969. She received her education at Alabama Christian College where she met and married Edwin S. Jones. They have three children and four grandchildren. Sara is the manager of Evangelist Bookstore and teaches women's classes at SEIBS. Her hobbies are interior decorating and gardening.

Who's Your Hero?

Right now, we're in the middle of football season. When it finishes, basketball will continue on for another month. Then at the end of basketball season, baseball will be in full swing. And then it starts all over again.

We all have our favorite teams and players. Everyone has their champion and tends to idolize such individuals. Our world is "hero oriented." We will vehemently deny any wrong-doing on the part of one of our heroes. In our minds, at least, they can do no wrong.

In the religious world, it is much the same. Most everyone has their favorite preacher, their favorite TV evangelist who can do no wrong. If they become involved in some controversy and/or begin to preach something new, we tend to defend the personality without considering the substance of their doctrine. I pray that God will give us wisdom to realize that only one can truly be our champion and that is Christ Jesus. He is the only one we need to defend. Our words are important and defendable only as much as they are in agreement with His Word, for it is by these that we will be judged (John 12:48). We will not be judged on personality or charisma, but rather on agreement with God's revealed truth.

May we have the spiritual maturity to "search the Scriptures" like those of Berea (Acts 17:11) "to see whether these things are so," and to heed Paul's admonition to the young preacher Titus "speak the things which are proper for sound doctrine" (Titus 2:1).

Wendell Agee was born and raised in Pikeville, TN. He served 20 years in the USAF and was a successful business man for over 30 years. Wendell has served the Lord as a missionary to Cuba, Jamaica, Honduras and other countries. He's a member of the Karns Church of Christ.